D1565926

LAW ON THE LAST FRONTIER

Law on the Last Frontier

TEXAS RANGER ARTHUR HILL

S. E. Spinks

TEXAS TECH UNIVERSITY PRESS

This book is typeset in Melior.
The paper used in this book meets the minimum requirements
of ANSI/NISO Z39.48-1992 (R1997). ∞

Book design and composition by Mark McGarry
Texas Type & Book Works

Library of Congress Cataloging-in-Publication Data
Spinks, S. E.
Law on the last frontier : Texas Ranger Arthur Hill / S.E. Spinks.
        p. cm.
Includes bibliographical references and index.
ISBN-13: 978-0-89672-619-2 (hardcover : alk. paper)
ISBN-10: 0-89672-619-3 (hardcover : alk. paper) 1. Hill, Arthur, 1909–1987.
2. Texas Rangers—Biography. 3. Peace officers—Texas—Big Bend
Region—Biography. 4. Frontier and pioneer life—Texas—Big Bend Region.
5. Law enforcement—Texas—Big Bend Region—History—20th century.
6. Crime—Texas—Big Bend Region—History—20th century.
7. Big Bend Region (Tex.)—History—20th century.
8. Big Bend Region (Tex.)—Biography.
9. Texas. Dept. of Public Safety—Biography. I. Title.
    F391.4.H55S65 2007   363.2092—dc22
    [B]   2007025003

Printed in the United States of America
07 08 09 10 11 12 13 14 15 / 9 8 7 6 5 4 3 2 1

Texas Tech University Press
Box 41037
Lubbock, Texas 79409-1037 USA
800.832.4042
ttup@ttu.edu
www.ttup.ttu.edu

To Arthur and Ruby Hill,
whose lives were an example and an inspiration.
To all Rangers past and present
who have dedicated their lives to the service of Texas
and the pursuit of justice.

Contents

Illustrations

Foreword

TEXAS RANGER Arthur Hill served twenty-seven years, 1947 to 1974, as a "Garrison Ranger." Colonel Homer Garrison directed the Texas Department of Public Safety (DPS), organized in 1935, for thirty years, 1938 to 1968. Garrison knew that his background in the Highway Patrol would discomfit Rangers who worried that the new department foreshadowed their ultimate extinction. Instantly, he issued orders that all Ranger captains report directly to him, bypassing all other levels of command. Thus began a rapport between the director and the Rangers that ripened over three decades as Garrison shaped them into an elite crime-fighting unit known and admired around the world. Every Ranger commissioned by Garrison loved the colonel, and for the rest of his life they gloried in the distinction of "Garrison Ranger." Arthur Hill proved no exception.

Legend, myth, and public perception depict Texas Rangers on horseback, and virtually all media portrayals deal with these Old West Rangers of the nineteenth century. Less celebrated are the twentieth-century Rangers, especially the "motorized" Rangers that emerged after the creation of the DPS in 1935. Their adventures and achievements rival, and perhaps surpass, the record of their predecessors. Yet once the Rangers dismounted, public interest flagged.

Working from Hill's official and personal records and countless interviews with her grandfather-in-law, Sharon Spinks helps remedy this imbalance. Her rendering of his service is uncommon in two ways. First, here is the detailed story of a twentieth-century Ranger. Second, although a "motorized" Ranger, Hill recalled an earlier time. Virtually all of his service took place in the rugged Big Bend country of West Texas. He drove a state-issued vehicle wherever possible, but more often than not he had to travel on horseback.

As Garrison Rangers took shape, they fell into two distinct groups: the "concrete Rangers" of rapidly urbanizing East Texas and the more traditional Rangers of old who policed West Texas. The former operated much like city detectives. The latter, although modernized by twentieth-century technology and skills, relied heavily on the same techniques that guided their predecessors of the nineteenth century. Arthur Hill, as Spinks notes, was unique as a modern old-timer.

The two groups specialized in such different crimes and such different methods that individual Rangers rarely transferred between East and West Texas. Sometimes natural disasters or especially demanding cases required Rangers from all over the state to converge for the duration of the need. But permanent reassignments occurred infrequently. Arthur Hill served for a little more than a year in Dallas-based Company B in 1957–1958. During this time he played a significant part in the chase and shootout that ended the career of two notorious gangsters, Gene Paul Norris and William Carl Humphrey. As the company's sergeant, he also led the Rangers who were brought into Daingerfield, in northeastern Texas, for the violent Lone Star Steel strike.

Yet, Hill yearned for his beloved Big Bend and the kind of service he performed there. Although slated for a captaincy, he persuaded Colonel Garrison to let him return to West Texas as a Ranger private. Based in Alpine, he remained for the rest of his career a modern old-time Ranger.

The six Ranger companies maintained headquarters in selected cities; Hill's Company E was based in Midland. But the Rangers themselves were scattered around the company's huge jurisdiction and given almost sole responsibility for a number of assigned counties. Hill alone covered Presidio, Brewster, Pecos, Terrell, and Jeff Davis Counties.

Duty of such magnitude reinforced three precepts of Colonel Garrison's vision of what Texas Rangers should be, indeed had to be. First, they had to be endowed with superior individual initiative. Captains instructed their men not to ask for help unless essential. Rangers were expected to apply their own judgment to problems. Second, they had to cultivate and work closely with local lawmen, mainly county sheriffs and their deputies, but also border patrolmen, customs officers, and even national park rangers. Third, they had to possess the total dedication to their jobs that kept them instantly responsive to calls for help day and night and to devote whatever time and effort their cases required. Arthur Hill exemplified the Garrison vision.

Spinks's narrative describes many of the cases Hill worked. His counties were mainly devoted to stock raising, so stock theft dominated the caseload. Thieves worked both sides of the Rio Grande, running their animals across the river to sell to buyers on the other side. Smuggling, largely liquor and drugs but also the prized wax of the candelilla plant and almost anything else that required customs charges, also demanded constant vigilance. Burglary, an occasional murder, assault, gambling, extortion, forgery, and other crimes varied the mix.

Spinks focuses on the special conditions that made the investigation of such crimes in the Big Bend unusual in police annals.

The tortured landscape of the Big Bend alone made travel and especially the tracking of fugitives a daunting challenge. Vast distances, sandy soil, rocky outcrops and sheer cliffs, plunging canyons, cactus and a host of other thorny vegetation, scarce water, heat, and cold all hindered the easy movement characteristic of East Texas.

The Rio Grande border afforded refuge to criminals. An offender could usually be across the border (into Mexican or U.S. haven as the case might be) before lawmen even reached the crime scene. Extradition from Mexico bogged down in the technicalities of Mexican law and practice. In response, a special bond developed between American and Mexican lawmen. Usually they worked well together, and a case fraught with potential complications could be vastly simplified if lawmen—Mexican or U.S.—quietly escorted the wanted person across the river and into the custody of waiting officers. Finally, a sparse population supported few local lawmen, throwing an extra burden on Ranger Hill.

The international border meant a multicultural population. Balancing the mostly Anglo ranchers, Mexicans—legal or illegal—worked on ranches and accounted for most of the inhabitants of the border communities. Presidio and Ojinaga were the largest border towns—the one in Texas, the other across the Rio Grande in Mexico. Hill had to steep himself in the culture and language of northern Mexico. He came to respect Hispanic culture and gained much information and insights from his Mexican friends and informants. A robust mutual respect proved both a personal satisfaction and a professional asset.

The last years of Hill's career, the late 1960s and early 1970s, brought a formidable new challenge to him and his fellow lawmen. The rise of Mexican drug lords, awash in cash garnered from running hard narcotics into the United States, corrupted Mexican officialdom and produced a violent culture worse than any Hill had known. Rival gangs, equipped with the most modern weaponry, warred for dominance and instantly killed any who impeded them. The Big Bend became a major corridor for drug-running, straining the minimal law enforcement establishment and placing officers at greater peril than ever before. The scourge would only worsen after Hill's retirement in 1974.

In that year Arthur Hill reached the mandatory retirement age of sixty-five. He stepped down and settled into a quiet life in Alpine. Rightly proud of his service, aware of its significance in Ranger and regional history, he freely shared his papers and memories with his family. Sharon Spinks has made certain that her grandfather-in-law's service to his state and his adventurous life would not sink into obscurity.

The result, *Law on the Last Frontier,* is an important contribution not only to the history of the Texas Rangers but to the Big Bend region as well. Through Hill's eyes we see the twentieth-century evolution of the Rangers and the evolution of this corner of Texas. The book offers a rare view of the services of often-overlooked Texas Rangers, plying their profession in traditional ways in a forbidding country. Their fellow officers in urbanized East Texas usually command the spotlight, but the West Texas Rangers deserve the attention that Spinks has brought to them.

In every way, Arthur Hill lived up to the vision of Homer Garrison. In his dedication, in his performance, in his professionalism, in his tireless effort to uphold the laws of Texas, he fully merited the distinction of "Garrison Ranger."

ROBERT M. UTLEY
Georgetown, Texas, 2007

Preface

COLD AIR blasted from the air-conditioning vents of the 1982 Grand Marquis. Through the windshield, convection currents were visible above the sticky asphalt of the Lajitas Highway. Arthur Hill sat in the passenger seat with booted ankles crossed, surveying the passing landscape from under his ever-present gray Resistol cowboy hat. A cane rested against his leg. In his lap, his fingers intertwined with thumbs slowly circling one another—a habit that I came to understand indicated deep thought.

He spoke when he was ready, or when a mountain peak, ranch gate, or road sign spurred his memory. For every turn of the highway threading through the Big Bend, Texas Ranger Hill had a story. At times the effort of remembering evoked strong emotion, leaving him with clenched fists and undoubtedly elevated blood pressure. Other recollections brought laughter and fond memories of the people of the border country.

*

In the course of that day, as well as many others, I rode along with my husband and his grandfather through the Texas Big Bend region. We covered only a portion of the territory that Arthur Hill patrolled during three decades as a Texas Ranger, but with each trip and each remote vista, he provided insight into the history of the region, the Ranger Service, and the heart of the man who was so much a part of both.

Armed with Hill's taped conversations and interviews, as well as his comprehensive records including case reports, communications, and memoranda, I set about piecing together his life and career. My research into the mid-twentieth-century Texas Rangers soon met an impasse. The Texas Department of Public Safety (DPS) had destroyed most Ranger records dating from 1935 until the early 1960s due to difficulties in storing the enormous quantity of paperwork generated in a precomputerized society.

At the time of this writing, few works exist that examine the experiences of mid-twentieth-century Rangers. Only limited personal archives and a handful of autobiographical accounts document their contributions. This work strives to chronicle Ranger Hill's life and career but, more important, to illuminate through his experiences the trials, methods, and services of the Texas Rangers and of law enforcement in the Big Bend during his era. I hope to give the reader the chance to ride through the Big Bend with Hill and hear of the Texas that once was and the Texas that emerged on his watch.

A torrent of heat rushed in when we reached Santa Elena Canyon and opened the car doors. With assistance, and relying more on his cane than he liked, Hill made his way to the bank of the Rio Grande. He stood quietly examining the canyon walls and the banks along both sides of the fluid border. The canyon had not changed in forty years, but he had, the Rangers had, Texas had. He smiled.

Acknowledgments

This work would not have been possible without the help and contributions of many people. My thanks go out to Jim Coffey of San Angelo, who originally encouraged me and showed enthusiasm for the project.

I appreciate the contributions of Rangers and other law enforcement officers including Ranger Lieutenant Bob Bullock of Midland and retired Ranger Joe Davis of Kerrville, who provided important information and insight into the Ranger Service and brotherhood. Thanks also to Ranger Sergeant Dave Duncan, who currently holds the post at Alpine, for sharing his experiences and thoughts on law enforcement in the Big Bend. I am grateful for the contributions of Jim Heim, of the U.S. State Department, and Joe Thompson, retired U.S. Customs Service agent, that helped shed light on Hill's later years as a Ranger. They explained the changes the border underwent and continues to undergo in terms of the federal law enforcement presence. Thank you for your time and service.

Special thanks also to Professor Saúl Armendáriz Olivar and the Villalobos family of Ojinaga for your hospitality, patience, and willingness to share your insights. You made me feel at home in Ojinaga, introducing me to everyone on the plaza and helping me to better understand perspectives from south of the border.

My thanks also go to Edmundo Nieto, Arturo Ochoa, and Richard Morrow for sharing memories of Presidio County through firsthand accounts of people and events, and to Lee Bennet for exemplary commitment to the preservation of Presidio County history and dedication to the education of area youth.

The Texas Department of Public Safety was the original source of many of the photographs in the Hill Family Collection. Thank you for your generous contribution of these images to the collective history of the Rangers and the DPS. Delia Herrera and Charley Lacy translated materials from Spanish to English, and Alice Geron and Edith Bahner Kelley helped immeasurably in proofing early versions of the manuscript. Thank you, all.

I would especially like to recognize the Hill family—Ruby Hill; Marjorie Hill King; Martha Hill Spinks; and George, Stanley, and Andy Spinks—for sharing your memories and realizing the importance of Arthur's contribution to the Ranger Service and the Big Bend. I am honored to tell his story.

LAW ON THE LAST FRONTIER

Introduction

IN 1947, Arthur Hill accepted the post of Texas Ranger at Alpine, Texas, in the heart of Big Bend country. This title defined not only his duties but also the man.

To appreciate the Ranger character, understanding the basics of Ranger Service history is useful. Ranger history parallels that of Texas itself. Stephen F. Austin, the "father of Texas," inaugurated the forerunner of the Ranger Service in 1823 with his decree to "employ ten men . . . to act as rangers for the common defense."[1] Although specific duties have changed through the years, Texas Rangers still heed Austin's call to protect the citizens of Texas.

Early Rangers scouted the frontier of colonial Texas, protecting settlers from marauding Indian tribes.[2] During the Revolution of 1836, Texas Rangers—then more formally established through legislation—continued in this capacity. Revolution-era Rangers focused their efforts on the frontier established from the Trinity

River to the Colorado River.[3] In the Republic of Texas era, 1836 to 1845, the Rangers' attention was often focused on the border and the threat of Mexican invasion.[4]

After statehood, federal troops assumed the responsibility of border and frontier patrolling. However, the soldiers' previous experience and training did not prepare them for the terrain and Indian warfare in Texas. The Rangers quickly returned to service, as their skills in scouting, horsemanship, and marksmanship made them experts in the particular brand of frontier justice desired at that time.[5]

The Civil War and secession of Texas from the Union marked a period of comparative inactivity and neglect as many Rangers joined the Confederate army.[6] By the early 1870s, the effects of the war and of Reconstruction had taken their toll on Texas. Native Americans continued to resist settlers' encroachment on the western frontier. Mexican bandits raided relentlessly along the Rio Grande. Lawlessness was rampant.[7]

In 1874, the Texas legislature authorized the formation of two groups to deal with these issues. One, a Special Force of Rangers under the command of Captain Leander H. McNelly, took on the challenge of taming the famed "Nueces Strip," the region of South Texas that lay between the Nueces River and the Mexican border. The second group, dubbed the Frontier Battalion, comprised six companies of seventy-five rangers each, led by Major John B. Jones. Their area of responsibility was the western frontier and border.[8]

The Frontier Battalion worked to eliminate the threat posed by the Comanches and Kiowas.[9] The last Indian attack on Texas soil occurred in the Diablo Mountains in 1881. A small Apache party fled to Sierra Diablo after their raid on a stagecoach in Quitman Canyon. Captain George Baylor's Frontier Battalion, Company A, trailed them to their camp and engaged them.[10]

Although some of the methods of the Special Force Rangers

and Frontier Battalion Rangers are disreputable by today's standards, their ruthless efficiency moved the Texas frontier westward. The same efficiency ultimately ensured their obsolescence. From the earliest Anglo settlement, through Texas's fight for independence, during sovereignty as a republic, and through statehood and secession, the Texas Rangers protected Texas citizens, secured their frontier, and ensured their future. Texas would not be Texas if it were not for Rangers.[11]

The new century necessitated the emergence of a modern Ranger force. The reincarnated version of their frontier counterparts faced lawlessness as usual, but along with it came the new problems and situations of a changing society. The Mexican Revolution, which raged from 1910 until 1920, led to increased border tensions, as political unrest in Mexico spilled across the Texas border.[12]

World war brought the threat of insurgency and espionage across the border region. In 1918, the Eighteenth Amendment to the Constitution legalized Prohibition, which resulted in increased smuggling.[13]

Early twentieth-century Rangers still patrolled the border on horseback, but the automobile quickly became the primary mode of transportation where possible. Increased nationwide demand for oil and gasoline contributed to another challenge for the twentieth-century Ranger: the almost overnight development of oil boomtowns. The towns of Borger, Ranger, Desdemona, and Wink, among others, called on this new breed of Ranger to tame the unbridled chaos.[14]

Politics also plagued the Ranger Service. Governor Miriam "Ma" Ferguson fired forty-four Rangers for partisanship after winning the gubernatorial election of 1932. Another forty Rangers quit the force in protest of political corruption. Ultimately, the force dwindled to a skeleton crew of thirty-two men.[15]

Crime was on the rise because of the economic difficulties of the times. With the Ranger force now depleted, Texas became a haven for lawless characters. Clyde Barrow and Bonnie Parker, George "Machine Gun" Kelly, and Raymond Hamilton gained fame and temporary fortune in crime raids across the state.[16] Former Texas Ranger Frank Hamer ended the crime spree of Bonnie and Clyde after doggedly trailing them for months.[17]

Public outcry demanded improved law enforcement. In 1935, the Forty-fourth Legislature established the Texas Department of Public Safety (DPS). All state-level law enforcement personnel and resources, including the Ranger force, were now grouped under a single organization.[18]

No longer under the Adjutant General's Office, the Ranger Service underwent drastic changes. Formal training now included fingerprinting, ballistics, and investigative techniques. This transition laid the groundwork for development of the Rangers into the modern investigative law enforcement body that it remains today.

In twenty years the working Ranger transitioned from horseback patrol, with little formal training, to patrol cars, using fingerprint kits, centralized criminal records, and early two-way radio communication with the establishment of KTXA at Camp Mabry in Austin.[19] The world of the Rangers changed rapidly and irreversibly.

As technological advances altered the equipment available and thereby the procedures of law enforcement, certain factors remained constant—the character qualities of the Rangers who enforced the laws, the nature of those who chose to break the laws, and the desolate border country of the Big Bend. Flexibility and ability to take action as needed to ensure public safety are hallmarks of the organization and of individual Rangers, as well as an essential part of the Ranger tradition passed down from one generation to the next.

"Every Ranger who has ever worked," Ranger Lewis Rigler explained, "leaves his mark on the Ranger Service." Each has a commitment to honor the past and a responsibility to safeguard the future. Ranger Rigler added, "Arthur Hill leaves a mark that is one of the most outstanding marks that has ever been put down. . . . Of all the Rangers I have known, [he] exemplif[ies] what a Ranger should be."[20]

Arthur Hill did not seek the spotlight or recognition for his accomplishments. He strove to "do right because it was right" and to make a difference in his corner of the world: the country he loved, the rugged Big Bend region, Texas's "Last Frontier."

1

In the Shadow of Santa Anna Mountain

I have a vivid recollection of standing guard near the base of the
mountain. At that time instead of hearing the shrill whistle of a
locomotive through the night, we heard the lonesome howl of
the prairie wolf. . . . Near the mountain that evening we chased
four cougars and succeeded in killing one of them.

Ranger Andrew Jackson Sowell (1886),
in Cox, *Texas Ranger Tales II*, 242

ARMED with a mesquite-branch rifle, young Arthur crouched to
examine footprints in the parched soil of the cow pasture. He
moved slowly, evading prickly pear and watching for snakes as
he crept up behind the barn. If his tracking was accurate, his
brothers (the "bad guys") were hiding out in the chicken coop.

With his back against the barn, he felt his shirt pick up wood
splinters as he tipped his hat back to peek around the side. The
bad guys were squatted on the ground, peering away from Arthur.
With surprise in his favor, he rounded the side of the barn and
opened fire. Chickens scattered and the chase was on. The band
of boys ran and dodged across the pasture, shooting, laughing,
and squealing.

Hill's earliest memories included playing Rangers and bad
guys or Rangers and Indians on the family farm at the base of
Santa Anna Mountain, near the Texas town of the same name in
Coleman County. The mountain stands two thousand feet above

sea level, three hundred feet above the surrounding countryside.[1] From this peak, Lipan Apaches and Comanches signaled the location of water and buffalo.[2] Settlers and surveyors used the point as a landmark. U.S. Cavalry soldiers viewed the movements of Indian parties on the western plateau.

At the onset of the Civil War, the observation post on Santa Anna Mountain was abandoned by federal troops.

After the war, Texas Rangers adopted the post for the same purpose as the Cavalry.[3] The Frontier Battalion Rangers of Company E maintained twenty-four-hour scout duty atop the mountain. Rangers rode out daily from Camp Colorado for patrol rotation at daylight and dusk.[4] These Rangers deterred the Indian threat, thus allowing development of the town known as Gap, later renamed Santa Anna.

The Santa Anna of Hill's childhood was steeped in Ranger history, its very existence owing to the Ranger presence. Like many

Moving a building on the Hill farm in Santa Anna (1915). *Left to right:* Arthur, J. S., and Frank Hill.

West Texas counties, Coleman County bears the name of a Ranger, Robert M. Coleman.[5] Every child heard the stories passed from one generation to the next, and the community's reverence for Ranger heroism contributed to Hill's early interest in law enforcement.

The Hills were relative newcomers to the region. In January 1913, Frank and Susan Hill and their ten children made the 150-mile trek from Belton, Texas, in a horse-drawn wagon and on horseback.

Arthur Watts Hill was born July 24, 1909, in Bell County, Texas.[6] Friends and family called young Arthur "Doc," as his middle name was that of the doctor who delivered him.[7]

Arthur Hill atop Santa Anna Mountain (1933).

Frank and Susan left behind extended family and deep roots in East Texas to take their chances in a new land between the Edwards Plateau and the rolling hills of the west-central part of the state.[8] Hill's family was part of the ongoing westward settlement of Texas. With the large cattle ranges of the previous century being fenced and divided, small farms and ranches flourished, the Hill family farm among them.

The Hill children walked around Santa Anna Mountain to school, or rode in the hack (horse-drawn carriage) during inclement weather. Arthur carried his lunch—a "latchit," or sandwich—in a small metal pail with a kitchen towel or flour sack as a lid.[9]

Hill grew up working the soil as well as cattle. He helped cultivate the fields with a horse-drawn plow and later seeded and harvested. He learned to anticipate the movements of cattle, to rope and ride. Most important, he learned to work until the job was finished and to take pride in work well done.

Each of the Hill children assumed certain responsibilities. Arthur and his brothers performed most of the farm work, while his sisters helped with domestic tasks inside and around the home. Arthur's father oversaw the farming and ranching enterprises and trained the boys, but his increasingly fragile health prohibited more active physical involvement. Frank Hill was a child during the Civil War and fifty years old when Arthur was born.

Between farm work and school, there was time for little else. Nevertheless, the Hill children, particularly the boys, managed to entertain themselves, often with practical jokes and subsequent fights.[10] By the time the older sons were teenagers, the Hill boys had established a local reputation for their rowdiness and quick tempers.

Susan Hill, a strong-willed religious woman, stood less than five feet tall. Arthur recalled a day when she tried a different approach to taming her wild sons. In the kitchen, a fight broke out between Arthur and his brother F. B. (Frank Bean). Later, Arthur could not remember who or what instigated the brawl, but soon the boys tumbled out of the house and into the front yard. Susan, worried that they would hurt themselves, followed the pair outside.

Unable to separate the boys physically, she did the next thing that came to mind. While her sons continued their full-blown assault on one another, Susan dropped to her knees and began to pray loudly. Her exaggerated wails to the Almighty drew the boys' surprised attention.[11]

Arthur remembered that he and his brother hovered over their mother as she cried, staring up at the heavens, pleading with God for their deliverance. Dumbfounded, Arthur looked to his brother for an answer. F. B. was equally perplexed, with mouth agape. Unsure of what they should do, the boys stood rooted to the spot. Susan then stood, dusted off her apron, and went back inside; she had achieved her goal.

Arthur shared many of his mother's characteristics, including her adventurous and indomitable spirit. For instance, it was Susan's urging that precipitated the family's move west.[12]

Despite a rambunctious nature around other boys, Arthur, in the Southern tradition, practiced formal etiquette in interacting with women. He always removed his hat when greeting a lady or upon entering a building. He always stood when a woman entered the room and never used improper language in the presence of a woman.

Each of the Hill children assumed responsibility for the next youngest sibling. Arthur was responsible for his younger brother, J. S. (Jewell Smith). His job involved keeping J. S. out of trouble and helping him perform chores and other daily routines.

Both boys were in high school when the family received word that J. S. had found serious trouble. The message indicated that the principal was going to "beat the tar" out of him. This news immediately upset Susan. Arthur, taking responsibility for his younger brother, tore out of the house and drove the family car the few miles into town at high speed.

Arriving in town, Hill made the turn toward school off the main road. His excess speed caused the car to slide and throw dust onto several old men playing checkers on the corner. They hollered and shook their fists, but Hill did not slow his pace.

Arthur somehow managed to get his younger brother "off the hook," and the boys returned home. In later years, Hill could no longer remember the cause of the trouble. He believed J. S. probably was guilty of wrongdoing and deserved some punishment but not a beating.

Weeks later, the Hills received a ticket for reckless driving on the date of Arthur's trip to the school. The ticket noted the driver as J. S. Hill, not Arthur. A strong resemblance marked all of the Hill brothers, so such a mistake was easy to make.

Both sons accompanied Frank Hill to the courthouse. The senior Hill stood before the judge and contended that J. S. did not have to pay the fine. Confused, Arthur looked slowly to his father—he had admitted his part in the incident and his responsibility for the fine.

The judge snapped back emphatically that J. S. certainly did have to pay the fine. Arthur was getting nervous. His first fine and his first time in a courtroom, and his father was lying to the judge.

Frank Hill held firm, restating that the fine was invalid. The judge, now angry, asked if he was calling the men on the corner liars, implying that they had not seen what they claimed. Frank's broad smile did little to diffuse the situation. Frank then conceded that the fine was correct but they had the wrong perpetrator. Arthur let out a relieved breath. Frank motioned for Arthur to pay the fine. He had made his point about unconfirmed facts and mistaken identity.[13]

Always enthusiastic about sports, Arthur was a running back on his high school football team and a pitcher for the baseball team, and he ran sprints and sprint relays in track. He was described in his high school annual as "the best kind of all around sport, with the courage to do and to dare."[14]

Hill's interest in sports continued all of his life. He trained tirelessly as a student athlete. As an adult, Hill continued to exercise, lifting weights, swimming across large lakes, wrestling, and building gymnastics equipment in the yard for use in strength training.[15] Although small in stature, he made up for it in effort and heart.

Hill relished competition, the pitting of physical ability and mental strategy against an opponent. The desire for similar challenges drew him into law enforcement.

**Arthur Hill in Santa Anna
football uniform (1927).**

The community atmosphere and folklore of Santa Anna influenced Hill's interest in law enforcement, as previously noted. Certain individuals also made an impression on Hill at a young age and encouraged this interest. Ranger Hill noted on many occasions that his interest in law enforcement stemmed from two sources: interaction with local law enforcement officers in Santa Anna and a theme paper written as a senior in high school. Hill explained, "I was interested in the Ranger Service from the time I was a small boy. As a senior, I wrote a theme on the Texas Rangers."[16]

Hill never liked writing in any form or fashion. In the Ranger tradition, his case reports were brief and to the point. Therefore, the fact that he mentions writing a term paper as a turning point in his young life is a testament to the men he discovered as he researched his topic and interviewed local Rangers. Hill admired the virtues of individual Rangers, intrigued by the challenges they faced in their work.

Hill noted Frank Mills, Bob Massengale, and Martin Koonsman as instrumental in his decision to pursue law enforcement. Ranger Frank Mills rode the Mexican border in the 1920s. He served as sheriff of Coleman County from 1928 until 1938 when he returned to the Ranger Service.[17]

"I knew several of them [Rangers] from my hometown," Hill explained. "I admired Frank Mills very much when I was a boy. It gave me a desire to enter law enforcement as soon as I was able to."[18]

A career in law enforcement, however, would have to wait. Hill graduated high school in 1930, less than a year after Black Tuesday. Although located south of the Dust Bowl, west-central Texas agriculture suffered due to drought as well as the depressed economy. Markets bottomed out and many farms failed.

With little prospect of employment in Santa Anna, Hill and a high school friend, Elan Cheatham, set off on motorcycles to tour the Southwest.[19] The pair found work outside a small southeastern New Mexico town, building steps in a cave, Carlsbad Caverns.

Carlsbad Caverns became a national park in 1930. Hill and Cheatham's work in the new park involved the construction of a trail and steps from the lower cave to the Top of the Cross—a decided improvement from the bat-guano mining buckets previously used for touring the caverns.[20]

Preparing for work one day, Arthur looked down into the cave and saw complete darkness broken only by the weak beam of light emitted from his helmet. He glanced above where natural light from the opening quickly dissipated into the darkness that surrounded him. For one used to open spaces, the closeness of the cave was unnerving.

He secured his harness and connected to a rope-and-pulley system designed to direct workers and as a safety measure. Arthur heaved a load of lumber onto his shoulder and started down the narrow path. Although he had made the trek many times, it was no less treacherous.

He arrived at his workplace, unloaded the lumber, and began the difficult task of erecting a wooden staircase on a steep ledge in veritable darkness. His footing continually slipped where moisture landed in drips from the surface above. Each blow of his hammer sent an eerie echo resonating throughout the unknown depths of the cave.

A crash and screams for help abruptly stopped his hammering. He recognized the voice as Elan's. "I heard him call out," Arthur remembered, "and it scared me because I knew he had a heavy load of lumber with him."[21]

Elan had slipped on the trail and dropped a load of lumber, narrowly missing a man below him. The lumber fell quietly into the darkness.

Hearing calmed voices from below, Arthur knew that Elan was unharmed. He returned to his work, where only moments later

Elan was seen "sprinting" past him headed toward the surface. Arthur laughed. "He hollered he was never going down there again." He followed Elan outside the cave. The event marked the end of their work in Carlsbad Caverns.

Traveling back to West Texas, Hill and Cheatham landed cowboy jobs on the Joe B. Eden Ranch, a cattle and sheep operation in Schleicher County, Texas.[22] Cattle ranching would continue to be an interest and part-time endeavor throughout Hill's life.

Hill moved around from job to job as a young man during the Depression. Eventually, he landed in Midland, Texas, operating a filling station for Humble Oil & Refining Company (which later became Exxon).[23]

At the Humble station on West Wall Street, Hill pumped gas and performed minor repairs. But the sight of a petite young woman walking primly by the station interrupted these mundane tasks on a daily basis.[24] Arthur watched her through the large plate glass windows at the front of the station. He instinctively knew she would be part of his future. His instincts were seldom wrong.

Ruby Kerby passed the station on her way from home to her job as a babysitter. The oldest of six children, she certainly had experience in this area. Her love of children drew her ultimately to a career as an elementary school teacher.

Ruby's father, Jesse James Kerby, owned the successful Andrews Water Company.[25] The Kerby family was comfortable and influential in the community, although not affluent.

A quiet and reserved young woman, Ruby enjoyed classical music and literature. She enjoyed participating in church activities, helping her mother in their home, and cultivating close friendships. Her genteel upbringing produced her china-doll appearance, but great inner strength and faith lay beneath the delicate surface.

The pair met through an introduction by Ruby's more outgoing sister, Leola, and a courtship began. Despite vast differences

Arthur Hill and Ruby Kerby at her home in Midland, Texas (1933).

in personality and upbringing, Hill's instincts were indeed accurate. The couple married on April 25, 1933.

Hill notified his family of the marriage in typical understated fashion. He sent a telegram mentioning an upcoming visit and added, "There will be two of us."[26]

The couple moved into a house on the family farm in Santa Anna and began to raise cotton and grain crops.[46] Unfamiliar with farm life and struck by the contrast of her new family's boisterous ways, Ruby had adjustments to make. Life on the farm was not much different from that of the previous century. Although they had a car, they lacked electricity, telephone service, and indoor plumbing. Ruby cooked on a wood-burning stove.[27] Determined to adapt, Ruby planted a garden and learned to can the produce. She maintained a flock of chickens and a milk cow and even helped in the cotton harvest.

From 1933 to 1935, Arthur spent long days in the field behind a horse-drawn plow. He worked nights at the Magnolia Petroleum Company gas station in Santa Anna in an attempt to make ends meet in the midst of a sagging cotton market.[28] Hill joined the National Guard as a private in the Howitzer Company, 142nd Infantry. He served part-time in that capacity until his honorable discharge in 1936.[29]

Toiling through sixteen-hour workdays, Hill was determined to make a life for his young family. Faced with the poor agricultural economy of the time, drought, and hail damage, the couple, now with a baby girl, Marjorie Ann, decided to secure a more stable future.

In January 1935, Arthur entered John Tarleton State University and began pursuing a degree in agricultural education. He enjoyed farming and ranching. A degree afforded the opportunity to work within the field of agriculture in a manner less subject to the whims of markets and nature. The family sold their last cotton crop and Ruby's saxophone, canned as much meat and vegetables as they could, and moved to Stephenville.[30]

Hill lasted only one semester at Tarleton, with Ruby writing most of his papers. His heart was not in it. He realized that his future was, as he had known early on, in law enforcement. Hill returned to Santa Anna, this time obtaining a commission and part-time work as a deputy constable. Although he continued to farm and ranch, he set his sights on a career as a peace officer.[31]

Hill first applied to the U.S. Border Patrol.[32] But with the family now including a second daughter, Martha Louise, Ruby was not enthusiastic about raising young children directly on the U.S.-Mexico border.

Hill applied for a position with the Department of Public Safety (DPS) as a Highway Patrol officer. He was accepted, and on September 1, 1941, Hill reported to Camp Mabry in Austin,

Texas, as part of the Seventh DPS Highway Patrol School. It was the first step in a long history of service to the department.[33]

Hill's early life in the shadow of Santa Anna Mountain influenced the man he became both personally and professionally, for there was little distinction. The frontier ethos, which lingered in the small community, remained forever embedded in Hill's thinking.

Yet, Hill's generation witnessed changes in American society and lifestyle more pronounced than those experienced by any previous generation. His experiences ranged from everyday transport by horse and wagon, to seeing the safe return of *Apollo 11* to Earth on his sixtieth birthday, July 24, 1969.[34] The two worlds intersected in Arthur Hill, preparing him for a future as a Ranger.

2

"Five Hundred Dollars Is Too Damn Much for a Highway Patrolman"

No man in the wrong can stand up against a fellow that's in the right and keeps on a-comin'.

Captain Bill McDonald, TSHA,
s.v. "William Jesse McDonald"

SEEKING a career in law enforcement, Arthur Hill anxiously responded to the following ad in the July 20, 1941, Santa Anna newspaper: "Written examinations for men seeking the 110 new jobs in the State Highway Patrol will be given August 15 at district headquarters, Captain E. M. Wells announced Friday." The ad went on to note that more than three thousand had already applied for the positions and at least two thousand more were expected. Those making the highest grades on the written test would then advance to training school.[1]

Employment remained difficult to obtain toward the end of the Great Depression. The appeal of steady work and a paycheck drew many recruits of Arthur's generation. Arthur took the test and quickly received notification from Hill Foreman, then chief of the Highway Patrol, of his acceptance into the Seventh DPS Highway Patrol School.[2]

He rushed home from the post office to inform Ruby and the

girls of his acceptance. With only two days before Hill was to report for training, the family hastily set about packing up their belongings, boarding up the farmhouse, and assembling all necessary items listed in the correspondence.

Trainees were required to bring "gym trunks" for calisthenics and to purchase two sets of "work clothes" needed for the training. These consisted of "two khaki shirts and two pair of khaki breeches." The uniform with "fore-and-aft" cap, black tie, and canvas belt closely resembled that of the army.

Chief Foreman advised appointees not to bring a "motor vehicle of any description." After the period of training, all "patrolmen" would travel to their respective stations in state-owned equipment.

The form letter warned would-be patrolmen that "if you do not believe that your past record is such that you and this department would not be embarrassed by your being employed and dealing with the public, please do not accept this tentative appointment." Hill had no such concerns.

Furthermore, new appointees received a challenge and encouragement from the DPS director, Colonel Homer Garrison: "We expect to build this organization into one that, not only the Department of Public Safety and the present members of the Patrol will be proud, but the people of Texas will sanction. . . . It might be interesting to know that you have been selected out of more than two thousand applicants."[3] Ultimately, five thousand applied, two thousand took the examination, one hundred were accepted to enter the Seventh DPS Highway Patrol School, and ninety-two completed the schooling. Arthur Hill was in exclusive company.

Hill wired his acceptance of the position and reported to the office of the chief at Camp Mabry in Austin on the morning of September 1, 1941.[4] Thus began his association with the DPS that would span thirty-three years.

Most Texas Rangers commissioned after World War II typically received their earliest law enforcement training in the Highway Patrol. Yet, little documentation exists regarding early DPS
training schools or activities.

The Highway Patrol was established in 1927 when the Texas
legislature authorized the Highway Department to hire license
and weight inspectors and a chief inspector to enforce traffic
safety laws. Of the utmost concern at the time was the prevention
of damage to highways and bridges by trucks.[5]

The increased use of trucks, many of which were homemade
contraptions with inadequate brakes, steering, and tires to support the loads they carried, had created a hazard to public safety.
This increase was due primarily to growing oil exploration and
pumping activities and the transportation of baled cotton from
central, northern, and eastern Texas to coastal ports for export.[6]

The early years of the Highway Patrol saw slow growth and
limited funding. Retired patrolman Bill Harris recalled the first
patrol training school. "When the Highway Patrol first began, we
were just hanging out there at Camp Mabry. We didn't have uni-
forms, no transportation yet."

As appropriations became available, the fledgling Highway
Patrol received funding for transportation. The Patrol first used
motorcycles for their cost efficiency. Later, automobiles were
added to the fleet. But, as Harris explained, "We still used the
motorcycles though because we didn't have the money to operate
the cars."[7]

At the outset, Highway Patrol officers had limited police powers and were only able to deal with misdemeanor traffic violations. By 1931, however, their policing powers had been increased and the force expanded to 120 men with their first chief,
Louis G. Phares, at the helm.[8]

In 1935, at the recommendation of Chicago-based Griffen-
hagen and Associates, hired to research the need for statewide
law enforcement, the Forty-fourth Legislature created the Depart-

ment of Public Safety.[9] The new entity included three divisions: the Texas Highway Patrol, the Headquarters Division, and the Texas Rangers.[10] This move gave the Highway Patrol full policing powers. The Ranger Service became part of a more accountable system and was also subject to less political upheaval than it had endured under the authority of the Adjutant General's Office. The new DPS developed a centralized information and education system that ultimately allowed Texas law enforcement officers access to the most advanced law enforcement information and training, crime-scene analysis, and communications technology available at the time.[11]

Louis Phares, first chief of the Highway Patrol, assumed the position of first acting director of DPS.[12] A young Highway Patrol captain, Homer Garrison, aided Phares in organizing the new department, assuming the position of assistant director. Garrison's initial responsibility was development of an officer training program.[13]

Colonel Horace H. Carmichael replaced Phares as director in 1936, although Phares retained his position as chief of the Highway Patrol.[14] Personnel changes continued to alter the face of the DPS command structure. In 1938, Carmichael suffered a fatal heart attack while sitting in his car in Zilker Park in Austin. Homer Garrison succeeded him as the third director of the Department of Public Safety.[15]

In Garrison, the department acquired leadership and vision that guided and defined it for four decades. Under Garrison's tutelage, the DPS gained national prominence and respect. Garrison focused on the selection of quality personnel, thorough training of and trust in the abilities of officers, and his own example of integrity and service. Hill had numerous opportunities to interact with Garrison on a personal and professional level. He listed Garrison among the most admired and respected associates of his career.

Every Texas Highway Patrol trooper or Ranger who ascended

the ranks through DPS has a story or two about the DPS training school. The high standard set for Highway Patrol officers, historically and at present, originates in the vigorous training regimen.

From 1935 until 1953, the DPS training school was based at Camp Mabry in Austin, aptly referred to as the "West Point of Texas Police" by the *Dallas Morning News*.[16] Hill arrived at Camp Mabry before nine o'clock on the September morning as instructed. He carried his duffel through stone gates and up to the long, two-story brick building bearing the Department of Public Safety name. Broad, white-railed verandas spanned the length of the building on both stories. Camp Mabry retained the appearance of its first incarnation as a military post during the Spanish-American War and World War I.[17] Hill checked in and waited with the other recruits.

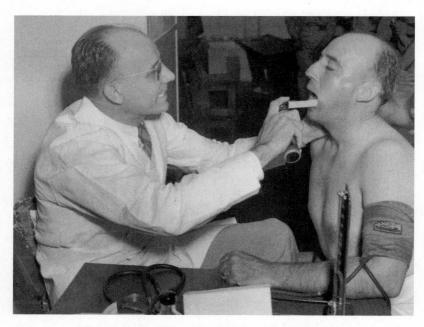

Hill undergoing cadet medical exam at Camp Mabry (1941).
Courtesy *Dallas Morning News*.

Instructors assembled the group of anxious cadets on the parade field. Here, they assigned each recruit to one of four platoons. Separate military barracks housed each group.[18] Hill joined the fourth platoon along with future Ranger captain, and friend, Frank Probst.[19]

Of the ninety-two cadets in the Seventh DPS Highway Patrol School, five later served as Texas Rangers: Hill, Probst, Jim Riddles, Lewis Rigler, and Gene Graves.[20] They remained close friends throughout their careers, sharing a bond that began at Camp Mabry.

The training program simulated military training in many ways. The cadets' schedule began well before sunrise and continued until eight or nine at night. Platoons marched in formation to meals, classes, and other activities.

Instruction was comprehensive and steeped in modern crime-fighting techniques. Hill's classes included fingerprinting, ballistics, scientific crime detection, interrogation, marksmanship, geography, public speaking, law, first aid, narcotics education, crime scene photography, and crime lab methods.

Training also addressed the physical aspects of police work. Trainees participated in extensive calisthenics, wrestling, and boxing. They learned techniques to disarm suspects as well as the mechanics of motorcycle operation.[21]

Originally, Ruby and their daughters had rented a small apartment in Austin for the duration of the seven-week training. She believed that Arthur might visit his family on some evenings and weekends, perhaps on Sunday at least. That hope soon faded.

Because of the rigorous schedule and demands of Arthur's training, Ruby and the girls rarely saw him. On one occasion, he was so "tired and beat up" that he fell asleep in the chair with one girl playing quietly on each knee, Ruby recalled in later years. She and the girls moved in with her family in Midland for the remainder of Arthur's training. The expense of rent and cost of living in Austin certainly did not seem worth it.[22]

**Motorcycle training at Seventh DPS Highway
Patrol School, Camp Mabry (1941).**

Hill described the morning routine as much like that of an army training camp. Cadets lined up in platoon groupings for the morning address by commanders. At this time—before extensive prebreakfast calisthenics—cadets had the opportunity to request medical attention if they were sick or injured. While severe cases received immediate care, this morning routine chiefly served to "wash out" those who lacked dedication.

Arthur recounted this daily occurrence: "When anyone got hurt they'd say, 'All right, any of you "sick, lame, or lazy" get over here in line.' Then they'd take them to the doctor."[23]

At one such assembly, Hill stood at attention. A wrestling injury the previous evening left him with a deeply cut and swollen lip. He could hardly talk. Unable to eat dinner the night before, he was not looking forward to the prospect of breakfast.

The cut reopened and began to bleed. Hill stood frozen at attention while the blood dripped down to dot his khaki uniform shirt.

An instructor ambled through the group and posed the question, as he had every morning, whether anyone needed medical attention. Arthur kept his gaze fixed forward, his arms at his side. He explained, "I didn't say anything. I didn't want to be put with the sick, lame, or lazy."[24]

With experience in motorcycle operation from his excursions around West Texas and New Mexico, Arthur had no trouble with this part of the training. He had some on-the-job law enforcement experience and a keen interest in the topics covered. He was intelligent and physically fit. Therefore, the remainder of the training, though difficult, was within his grasp.

The one area that challenged him was his height. The minimum requirement for a Texas Highway Patrol officer was 5 feet 8 inches. While wearing riding boots, Hill may have attained this height. He was not about to work this hard only to be drummed out of training school because of an inch or less.

Hill questioned an instructor after class about the height requirement. The man responded that the department identification card records official height along with each cadet's weight, hair color, eye color, and fingerprints. With graduation fast approaching, Hill knew that time was running out. He asked when the measurement was scheduled. The instructor said that it would occur the following morning during calisthenics. Before leaving the classroom, the instructor turned and eyed Hill up and down, adding, "No shoes."

Hill's platoon buddies devised a plan. He was hesitant at first but gave in, realizing it was his only hope. Hill lay on his bunk in the austere barracks, gazing in disbelief at the activity that bustled around him. His friends, using rope procured from the supply hut, rigged a hoist mechanism in which they cradled his chin. They attached the other end to the bed's head posts and secured his ankles to the foot posts. With the contraption in place, Hill's mates applied tension, much like the rack of a medieval torture chamber. Hill stretched out like a dressed deer.

Surely, by increasing tension throughout the night, they could stretch Hill for the inch or so he lacked. Hill spent a sleepless night, hooked up to the hoist. Every hour one of his friends awoke to tighten the tension. Dawn could not come too soon.

Hill's cohorts also knew that a person is at his tallest when first awakening in the morning, before gravity begins to take its toll. At reveille, his friends picked up his bed and started toward the drill field. After lying in the same position all night with pressure on his neck and ankles, each jostle of the bed shot through him. They finally arrived at the field and stood the bed up on end directly in front of the person performing the official measurement.[25]

It had never happened before, and never since, but on that day Arthur Hill measured 5 feet 8¹/₂ inches tall. He made the required

Upon graduation, Hill received Highway Patrol badge #337 and was assigned to Seymour, Texas, for his first duty station (1941).

5 feet 8 inches, as recorded on his official department ID card, with a half inch to spare.[26]

On October 25, after seven weeks of grueling training, Arthur Hill and the other cadets of the Seventh Highway Patrol School graduated. Governor Coke Stevenson handed each his commission in a ceremony on the parade field at Camp Mabry.[27] Arthur Hill was now Texas Highway Patrolman #337.[28]

Hill wore his Highway Patrol uniform for the first time during the ceremony; it was composed of a blue shirt with tan epaulets, tan riding pants with a blue and red stripe down the side, a black bow tie, and black riding boots. Troopers wore tight-legged riding pants and high black boots, as these were most practical for riding motorcycles. Silver buttons ran down the shirt front and at the points of the shoulder epaulets. Each button bore the letters T-E-X-A-S between the points of a star located in the center of each button. This symbol was identical to the one on the ceiling the state capitol rotunda, simulating a flag used when Texans fought for independence from Mexico in 1835.[29]

In a letter from the chief of the Highway Patrol, Hill received his duty assignment: "This is to advise you that effective November 1, 1941, you are being stationed at Seymour, in the Wichita Falls District, and Captain Jim Line will be your commanding officer."[30]

The seat of Baylor County, Seymour was located at the junction of four heavily traveled U.S. highways.[31] Highway Patrolman Hill and his first partner, T. R. Dobbs, dealt with a high volume of speeders, drunk drivers, and traffic accidents, among other problems.

During his first months in Seymour, Hill and Dobbs became familiar with the community and the realities of doing their jobs astride DPS-issue, 1941 Indian Sport Scout motorcycles.[32] One event that made an impact on Hill early in his tenure at Seymour occurred during a high-speed chase. Observing a speeding car in

Arthur, *right,* and his first partner, T. R. Dobbs, astride their 1941
DPS-issue Indian Sport Scouts in Knox City, Texas (1942).

oncoming traffic, Hill and Dobbs turned on their sirens. The car
accelerated, and it soon became clear that the driver did not in-
tend to pull over.

After making a U-turn, Hill and Dobbs, in slightly staggered
position with Hill in the rear, accelerated in an effort to reach the
fleeing car. The two men had attained a speed of one hundred
miles per hour when Dobbs's motorcycle slipped slightly on the
pavement. Hill watched helplessly as his partner began to lose
control. The motorcycle wobbled only briefly before Dobbs skill-
fully laid it over on the highway.[33]

Hill quickly outdistanced his fallen partner. He watched behind him as the friction of the highway brutally slowed Dobbs's
progress. Dobbs slid out of control, sparks flying out. Hill slowed
his motorcycle as quickly as possible and turned around, rushing
back to the wreck to see if Dobbs was dead—at that speed, afraid
it was inevitable.

Hill arrived at the scene as Dobbs attempted to stand. Scraped
from head to toe, his uniform torn from him by the abrasion of the
pavement, Dobbs still managed to get to his feet with Hill's help.

Dobbs's leather holster had worn through, as had the side of his riding boot. The metal cylinder and a portion of the barrel of his revolver were ground down. Evidently, Dobbs slid primarily on his side, balanced atop his firearm, which saved him from greater injury. Upon investigation, Hill determined that Dobbs slid 124 yards. Although not badly injured, Dobbs was not enamored of motorcycles after that incident.

One month and six days after Hill arrived at Seymour, an event occurred that would drastically transform the Highway Patrol's responsibilities. On Sunday, December 7, 1941—the "date which will live in infamy"—the Hill family first heard of the bombing of Pearl Harbor from the radio of a car parked in front of the church as they exited after Sunday services.[34]

Because many patrolmen immediately enlisted or soon received draft notification, fewer were available to carry out the already difficult tasks assigned to the Highway Patrol. Hill struggled with the decision of whether to enlist, and in the end, he remained at home.

Dobbs remained at Seymour until 1942. After that, Hill's few partners were young and single and soon joined the military. As a result, Hill tirelessly worked the thirteen counties on his own. "That kept me working almost day and night," Hill remembered. "We didn't think of having an eight-hour day then. We just worked as long as was necessary."[35]

During the war, a patrolman's responsibilities expanded to include the escort of military convoys and the training of air wardens. The Highway Patrol now also enforced a lower speed limit of thirty-five miles per hour, instituted to conserve gasoline and tires during wartime.[36]

The workload of the DPS Headquarters Division also increased. The DPS, which maintained a fingerprint database rivaled only by that of the Federal Bureau of Investigation, processed classified fingerprints of people employed in vital or strategic industries. Headquarters Division also investigated signs of sabotage on items concerned with the war effort.[37]

In war and in peace, law enforcement officers confront human behavior at its worst. The most abhorrent, Hill attested, were domestic in nature, particularly those involving children.

While in Seymour, Hill investigated a double murder and suicide involving a soldier. Although the case was not within the purview of a Highway Patrol trooper, the lack of local officers prompted officials to seek Hill's assistance. Called to the crime scene by the justice of the peace (JP), he began to investigate.

The JP removed the three bodies prior to Hill's arrival at the apartment. Witnesses were so distraught that they were incapable of answering any questions. Hill began in the living room where three pools of blood, an opened suitcase, and a .380 Colt automatic pistol provided the only evidence of the incident. Hill collected the evidence and left for the funeral home to question the mortician regarding his findings and to obtain bullets if possible.

He returned the next morning to interview the only eyewitness. Through tears, she revealed the details of a tragic story. The woman's daughter and grandson lived with her in the apartment. Her son-in-law, Corporal Raymond Lewis, had served in the army overseas. He was injured in combat and sent home for treatment at Ashburn Hospital in McKinney, Texas.

Corporal Lewis learned of his wife's plans for divorce and took a furlough from the hospital. Upon arriving at the witness's home, he insisted on seeing his wife and stepson. He walked into the living room, opened his suitcase, and pulled out the pistol. Corporal Lewis fired across the room, first hitting his wife in the head. He then fired another shot into the head of the boy, before turning the weapon on himself, firing twice in rapid succession to his temple.[38]

The murdered boy was the best friend of Hill's youngest daughter. In her first-grade class, the two held hands across the aisle of desks.[39] Hill investigated the murders, and then had to go home and try to explain the unexplainable to his six-year-old daughter.

In another incident, Zack Gray, the night watchman in Munday, Texas, about twenty miles southwest of Seymour, asked Hill to accompany him on a domestic disturbance call. When they arrived, they found the home's front steps and sidewalk covered in blood. Witnesses explained that Bill Mitchell had attacked his wife with a knife. She escaped out the front door and ran screaming down the steps to the street. Neighbors took her to the local pharmacy for emergency treatment, as there was no doctor in the small town.

Hill and Gray made their way up the bloody sidewalk toward the now quiet house. Hill motioned Gray around the back while he climbed the steps and entered the front door. He moved quietly through the house, listening for any sound.

Turning down a hall toward the bedrooms, he listened at the closed bathroom door. He carefully tried to turn the knob and discovered that it was locked. Hill called to Mitchell, who did not answer. Then he decided to confront the suspect in the most expedient way he knew, by breaking down the door.

Hill spotted Mitchell at the end of the long rectangular bathroom. Blood was splattered over the white tub and tile. Mitchell had slit his own wrist. "He stood with his knife in one hand and a whiskey bottle in the other, challenging me to try to take him," Hill said.[40]

Without immediate attention, Mitchell would die. Hill rushed in, overcoming Mitchell by force, but not without sustaining cuts to his own left wrist and arm in the process of disarming the suicidal man. Once he had Mitchell secured, Hill quickly applied pressure to the man's injured wrist. The bleeding slowed, and medical assistance soon arrived. Mitchell survived to be convicted for the attempted murder of his wife.

The duties of the Highway Patrol included rendering assistance in the event of natural disaster. In April 1942, Crowell, Texas, suffered a devastating tornado, which left 94 percent of the population homeless. Nine of ten businesses in the small community were destroyed.[41]

Hill worked in the town to prevent looting and provide assistance to emergency services. The destruction was overwhelming—families displaced, homes and churches destroyed, lives lost. This was the first natural disaster in which Hill assisted, but it would not be the last.

Of the most significance to Hill's experience as a young officer in Seymour, Texas, was the prevalence of illegal production, transportation, and distribution of "moonshine" alcohol—"bootlegging" or "whiskey running." In 1935, the Twenty-first Amendment was ratified, which repealed nationwide prohibition. Section 2 of the amendment effectively gave state governments control over grain alcohol; Texas delegated this authority to counties, many of which remained "dry" or partially dry. Despite lowered speed limits during wartime, moving alcohol contraband at high speed over the highways thrived.

Hill frequently pulled over cars for speeding or other violations, only to find the vehicle loaded with contraband whiskey. Much of the confiscated evidence, however, which was kept at the county courthouse, disappeared before the cases came to trial.

Hill began hiding evidence at his home, at one time amid the children's Christmas presents. He then waited until trial to produce the evidence.[42] This practice resulted in a higher conviction rate, but the nucleus of the criminal ring remained beyond prosecution. The whiskey-running operation was well organized and apparently involved people in positions of power.

In an attempt to identify a pattern and determine relationships among those involved, Hill began an investigation. He focused on Cotton Houston, who had recently moved into the area from Fort Worth. Hill knew, from fellow officers in Fort Worth, that Houston had experience in the illegal production and distribution of alcohol. Apparently he had expanded his territory of operations, and Hill's aim was to discover the others in Seymour and surrounding areas who were involved with the Houston operation.

With search warrant in hand, Hill approached Houston's home. He knocked, but no one answered. The house appeared empty. He entered and walked carefully throughout the house seeking evidence. The wooden floor of the frame house creaked with each step. After searching everywhere, Hill found nothing. He was forced to concede failure.

On his way out the kitchen door, however, Hill noticed a slight inconsistency in the pattern of the linoleum flooring. He squatted down and pulled back the linoleum to reveal a trapdoor. Opening the door, he discovered hundreds of bottles of "liquor and whiskey" within the crawlspace under the house. "I just left it be for then to see if I could find out who all was in on it," Hill explained.[43]

Deciding to stake out the scene, Hill obtained the keys to the local water tower from the night watchman and used it as an observation post. Using binoculars, he scrutinized the people who came and went from Houston's house, although he was not at all sanguine. Hill was afraid of heights, and the old water tower swayed and shook with the wind.[44] But his efforts paid off. From this surveillance, Hill established a connection between Houston and a prominent merchant in town by the name of McMillan.

While investigating the whiskey-running ring, Hill continued to observe the effects of the illicit alcohol trade in the form of DWI arrests and related accidents. Driving with his youngest daughter, Martha, Hill came upon an accident. He sternly instructed Martha to stay in the car as he ran up to the scene to render aid. She knew not to budge.

After assisting emergency services and officers on the scene, Hill returned to the car. He sat silently looking out the rain-dotted front window for a long time before he looked over to his daughter. Finally, he told her of the three small children killed by a drunk driver. He asked her to think about those parents who would never see their children alive again. Then he drew Martha to him, his arm around her shoulder as they pulled away.

She watched out the window where the remnants of disaster for one family lay strewn along the highway. "That is what alcohol is good for," he told her.[45]

Hill devoted himself to ridding his counties of whiskey runners. Although he lacked enough evidence for arrest warrants for the key players, the pressure he applied to their operation cut

Daughters, *left to right,* Marjorie Ann and Martha Louise on Hill's 1941 Indian at Seymour, Texas (1942).

into their profit. As a result, Hill received threats against his life and his family members.

During this period Hill saw on the main street sidewalk a group of men, composed of business owners, farmers, and others whom he did not recognize. He suspected that some in this group were involved in the whiskey trade.

Hill could not hear the men's conversation. Their eyes darted back and forth, watching him as he crossed the street and then returning to each other. When Hill got closer, one man spoke up. He informed Hill that Cotton Houston had been to Fort Worth and had met with some "friends." He shared a private exchange and smirk with the other men gathered around to bolster his importance. Hill waited for his performance to end. The man looked back to Hill and added, "He says he can get you killed for five hundred dollars." The man smiled, satisfied with himself.

Hill moved directly in front of the man, into the middle of the group. His steely gaze fixed the man where he stood. "Five hundred dollars!" Hill exclaimed, glaring at the man, who quickly lost his earlier confidence. "That's too damned much for a Highway Patrolman. I think we can get it done for less than that. You tell him I said that."

Hill turned to leave the stunned group, his suspicions confirmed. Hill later revealed, "You know, that just made me more determined."[46]

The time had come to pay a visit to McMillan. Hill arrived at McMillan's warehouse office unexpectedly. The feed and seed store provided the perfect cover for loading and warehousing contraband. He began to question McMillan about his involvement in whiskey running.

McMillan denied Hill's assertions, fidgeting with items on his desk as they talked. He turned his chair with his back to Hill, continuing his rambling account of innocence out of Hill's view. In midsentence, McMillan jumped up and ran down the hall. Hill quickly followed and saw the fleeing man duck into a doorway at the end of the short hall. Hill followed closely behind, but slowed and cautiously entered the doorway.

McMillan waited there, poised to strike Hill as he rounded the corner. Seeing this, Hill drew his .38 revolver and used the butt to strike McMillan across the head. McMillan slumped, unconscious, to the floor. When he hit, Hill watched the man's handgun fall to the floor beside him. Armed with a pistol, McMillan had posed more of a threat than Hill realized. Nevertheless, McMillan had chosen to try to hit Hill with his fist rather than shoot him.

In the warehouse, there was enough evidence to link McMillan to the whiskey ring. When he was convicted, he was surrounded by, as Hill noted, his "dirty lawyers and a bunch of those other bootleggers."[47]

McMillan's political influence, which had masked his involvement in the whiskey trade, caused other problems as well. For instance, he attempted to bring charges against Hill. At the time, permission was required from the legislature to sue an officer, and McMillan secured a lawyer who traveled to Austin to obtain it. The legislature denied permission based on the facts of the case.[48] McMillan's efforts did not end there, however.

A short time later, Hill returned from a rare day off—which he spent fishing—to discover that the chief of the Highway Patrol, W. J. Elliot, had traveled to Seymour to investigate him. The chief spent the day in town, observing and questioning other officers and citizens. Hill anxiously awaited an opportunity to learn details of the investigation and to explain his side of the story.

A few days later, the chief called Hill to meet with him in Abilene. Chief Elliot first questioned Hill regarding the McMillan arrest. Hill explained his actions, "Well, Chief, there were three things I could have done. I could have shot him and killed him, I could have done what I did, or I could have run. . . . I just did what I thought was best."[49]

Satisfied at Hill's explanation, the chief considered his next statement. His investigations in Seymour had made him aware of the extent of the whiskey trade, as well as the threats made against Hill and his family.

The chief finally addressed the heart of his concern. Elliot told Hill that he had driven by his house in Seymour. He could see Hill's family through the windows as they prepared supper. "Arthur, they could lay in wait for you to get out of your car when you are working at night," the chief explained. "They could kill you and there wouldn't be anything anyone could do about it."

Hill let the statement sink in before responding. "Maybe so, but I would surely try to take some of them with me."[50]

The chief offered to move Hill's duty station to "any town in the state." Hill informed Elliot that he had no desire to move. He was determined to clean up the whiskey running and bring to justice those who threatened his family. To Hill, a move represented a silent defeat, the coward's way out.

An exasperated Elliot allowed Hill to remain at his duty station at Seymour. But he advised Hill to decrease the intensity of his investigation. "I'm afraid you're not going to live until we can get you away from the trouble."

In the formal letter notifying Hill of the findings of his investigation, Chief Elliot emphasized that the primary duty of the Highway Patrol is the "handling of traffic." He chided Hill, "I do not want you to make any more whiskey cases than are necessary and they must be in connection with patrol work."[51]

Despite the warnings, Hill's nature would not allow him to shrug his duty or to let a criminal think he had gotten the best of him. It seemed only natural to pursue those who broke the law. Whiskey runners drove recklessly and created a safety hazard, and the alcohol they provided led to many DWIs and accidents.

The investigation soon took an unexpected turn. While working traffic on the road to a bi-district football game at Anson, Hill spotted Cotton Houston speeding. Hill flipped on the lights and pulled him over. With no outstanding warrant, Hill could only issue a ticket for the current infraction.

He handed Houston the ticket and notified him of his need to appear before the judge regarding the charge. Houston grabbed the ticket and took off. His tires spun out and sent dirt flying all over Hill, still standing on the side of the road. Hill got back in his patrol car and initiated pursuit.

Houston's vehicle sideswiped cars on both sides before he ran headlong into a bridge railing. The impact caused his car to rebound into oncoming traffic where he crashed into two other cars. He ended up in the ditch on the far side of the road. Hill pulled Houston from the car, handcuffed him, placed him in the patrol car, and brought him into Anson to appear before the judge.

Houston quickly posted bail and confronted Hill on the steps of the courthouse. He stormed up to Hill and informed him that he wanted to "have it out."

Hill glared back, his dark brown eyes boring a hole through the man. "Anytime, anywhere. You name it."

After brief thought, and consideration of the intensity of Hill's response and chilling glare, Houston judiciously began to backtrack. The Highway Patrolman's efforts had thwarted his whiskey-running endeavor. "I've fought you ever since I've been here," Houston told Hill, "and one way or the other, I haven't won one yet." Rather than fight Hill, Houston decided he had "had enough of Seymour" and went back to Fort Worth.[52]

Although Houston had provided the expertise and supplies for the whiskey ring, Hill discovered that the financial backing and transport were local. Even with Houston's return to Fort Worth, the established trade continued.

Hill received information from a former Highway Patrol officer of whiskey-running routes and names of participants. Hill arrested the Blackburn brothers for transporting liquor. The arrest provided a big break in exposing the workings of the organization, which slowly began to crumble.

The former patrolman sent a letter of praise to the chief of the Highway Patrol, applauding Hill's efforts and skill in cleaning up the illegal alcohol trade. He did not realize that the chief had warned Hill to limit his involvement in the whiskey cases or transfer out of the area for his safety. Upon hearing of this letter, Hill laughed. "Oh Lord, here is where we get sent to China."[53]

Hill's six years of experience as a patrolman in Seymour both challenged and enlightened him. He was promoted sergeant after four years of service. During this time, he learned several things, including the fact that, although he enjoyed the work of a Highway Patrolman, he had a natural inclination toward criminal investigation. His sense of justice, together with his tenacity and powers of observation, made it difficult for him to limit himself to the job description of a trooper and halt the trail of investigation at the highway.

Understanding that this type of activity was typically outside the bounds of the Highway Patrol, Hill took the next logical step: application to the Ranger Service. In a letter to Homer Garrison, dated August 14, 1947, Hill listed his qualifications and expressed his desire for Garrison to consider him for the position of Ranger. He also included, "Due to the fact that I was raised in the ranch country, I feel that I would be best qualified for the western part of the state."[54] Before hearing any response from Garrison, Hill was transferred to Alpine, Texas, as a patrolman.[55]

Hill was unaware as he wrote his letter that Garrison and Company E Ranger Captain Gully Cowsert had already made similar plans for him. Garrison had closely followed Hill's work at Seymour. He believed that Hill's skills and experience qualified him for the position of Ranger, and that his personality and background best suited him for Captain Cowsert's company of West Texas Rangers.

Captain Cowsert informed Hill of his appointment to the Ranger Service. "I don't know just where I will make your station but I thought you would like to know about your job," Cowsert wrote in his casual manner. He added, "Don't tell anyone at this time that you are going into the Ranger Service for I will possibly want you to do some undercover work after you get in."[56]

In his resignation from the Highway Patrol, Hill wrote to the chief, "For six years as a Highway Patrolman I have lived it and loved it. I am not going to say that I am leaving the patrol, because it will always be a part of me."[57]

Hill received his appointment as a Texas Ranger and started work at his duty station, Alpine, Texas, on September 1, 1947. Seventeen years after writing his high school theme paper, and nearly thirty years after playing Texas Rangers and "bad guys" in the pastures of his family farm in Santa Anna, Hill's dream had become reality.

3
The Last Frontier

The Big Bend is a world unto itself, a ruggedly forbidding penin-
sula of land left remote and isolated by the irresponsible antics of
the Rio Grande. This geologic fantasyland is the perverse creation
of that mighty river as it plunges deep into Mexico and then, as if
changing its mind, partially reverses its course in its search for
the distant waters of the Gulf of Mexico. The land held in its em-
brace—the Big Bend of Texas—is one of our last frontiers.

Kenneth Ragsdale, foreword to W. D. Smithers,
Chronicles of the Big Bend

TO SEE the Big Bend region of West Texas is to come as close as
is possible to a view of the Texas frontier that once existed and
that, in many ways, remained in 1947. Although a twentieth-
century Ranger, Arthur Hill assumed his post in a setting essentially unchanged from the previous century. The people, terrain,
history, and culture of this remote region made Hill's Ranger experience a unique one for his time.

With Hill's arrival in Alpine, he began his assimilation into
the vastly different environment of his new station. The diver-
sity and sheer scale of terrain dwarfed his previous duty posts.
The family moved into the only available rental housing, the
decommissioned Marfa Army Air Field. Located between Alpine
and Marfa, the base, referred to as "Mar-pine" during wartime
use, provided temporary, albeit rough, housing.[1] The coal stove
and minimal insulation in the living quarters made for a difficult winter.

Ranger Arthur Hill, *left,* and Ranger Joe Bridge in Alpine, Texas (1947).

Hill succeeded Ranger Joe Bridge, who then transferred to Kingsville under the command of Captain Alfred Allee. Born in San Angelo, Bridge was the son of H. J. M. Bridge, a Ranger in Frontier Battalion, Company D.

Prior to his Ranger service, Joe Bridge had worked as the ranch manager for the Hogg-Dixon Ranch in Coahuila, Mexico, for fourteen years. Soft-spoken and courteous, Bridge was fluent in Spanish, and his understanding of Mexican culture and of ranching served him well in his twenty years as a Ranger in the Big Bend and South Texas. Bridge was a compassionate man who often helped the families of those he sent to prison. He died unexpectedly in 1956 while still in the Ranger Service in Falfurrias, Texas.[2]

Hill quickly discovered that when a new law officer came to town, there were those who would attempt to "try him out." One morning, Hill drove into Alpine from "Mar-pine." He arrived at the Brewster County Courthouse, which housed his office, ready to begin the day.

The previous night, Hill had arrested a ranch foreman at the Gilmer Ranch on an outstanding warrant carried over from an investigation conducted by Ranger Bridge. The foreman's boss, rancher Gilmer Morris, met Hill on the courthouse lawn that morning. Morris established the rules for people on his ranch, and he proposed to do the same with Hill.

Morris approached the new Ranger, halting his staggering gait too close for Hill's liking. He began his tirade, pointing his finger at Hill. Morris informed Hill that the Texas Rangers could not enter his place unless he wanted them to and demanded that Hill release his foreman. Hill let him finish his rant. Morris was drunk, and "that didn't set so good."

Everyone on the busy courthouse square stopped to witness the interaction. Hill calmly informed Morris that he was under arrest for public intoxication. A shocked Morris jumped back and immediately took a swing at Hill. "After that," Hill explained, "he didn't fare too well."[3]

Before long, Morris found himself in the cell with his foreman. Word quickly spread of the new Ranger's public and proficient handling of Morris to any who would attempt to "try him out."

Hill believed that all people should receive the same treatment under the law. He regarded everyone equally and fairly and, as a result, gained the respect of the community. This incident marked the first step in building a relationship of trust in the small community and the region that would last throughout his tenure.

One of Hill's early assignments demonstrates the frontier methods still used in the mid-twentieth century, at least in the Big Bend area. Hill spent many nights on "camp and horseback scout duty" along the border. From these camps, the Rangers of Company E performed mounted patrols up and down the Rio

Grande in attempts to deter smuggling and livestock theft. For Hill, the practice brought firsthand knowledge of the terrain and of his fellow Rangers.

When Hill arrived in Alpine, he brought with him his saddle, tack, and a stock trailer, all necessary equipment for Rangers of the time. However, he did not own nor have access to a horse, also mandatory for Rangers. Captain Cowsert loaned Hill a horse until he could find one.[4]

Hill's first Ranger captain, Gully Cowsert, was a third-generation Ranger. He previously ranched in Kimble County and worked as an investigator for the Texas Sheep and Goat Raisers Association prior to entering the Ranger Service.

Cowsert began his tenure as a Ranger captain in 1933. At the time of his retirement in 1958, Captain Cowsert boasted the longest tenure as a Ranger captain. Cowsert carried an old .45-caliber Colt single-action revolver, trusting the tried-and-true weapon over newer models.[5] He also preferred tried-and-true Ranger methods.

Cowsert's loaner horse, named Vick, was a bit headstrong. At Hill's first scout camp, he provided the source of morning entertainment for the other Rangers as they watched to see if the "rookie's" horse was going to buck. Vick untied his reins, chewed hats, pulled hair, bit, and aggravated the other horses. Hill appreciated Cowsert's supposed generosity, but always suspected that the horse served as an unofficial initiation, kept in the corral at Junction for just such occasions. He took it all in good humor, but quickly acquired his own mount.

Hill spent three months performing his first scout duty, except for a brief return to Alpine to testify in a murder trial. The tradition of Ranger scout duty dated back to the nineteenth century. But after three months with few arrests to show for the time and trouble, Hill questioned the effectiveness of this approach. "I think 'ol Cap [Cowsert] just liked to camp," Hill laughed.[6]

Would-be lawbreakers learned about the camps and avoided these areas. Flashes of light seen on patrol, Hill learned, were made by *avisadores*. In a practice that dated back centuries in Mexican culture, *avisadores* sent messages by reflecting the sun or campfire light from a polished stone or mirror. Long before fiber optics, Mexican *avisadores* conveyed messages along the Rio Grande at the "speed of light." Without radio or telephone communications along the border, the Rangers were at a decided disadvantage.[7]

In March 1949, Hill, along with Ranger Earl Stewart, pulled a horse trailer with his patrol car as far as they could maneuver the vehicles on the cow trails of a ranch along the border. Captain Cowsert and Ranger Houston White towed a converted pickup bed trailer, which served as a chuck wagon. At the end of the drivable trail, they set up a scout camp along Alamito Creek.[8]

With a tarpaulin windbreak stretched between the two trailers, the camp took form. Logs and metal folding chairs circled a

Ranger camp on the Rio Grande at Alamito Creek (1949).
Left to right: Ranger Houston White, Captain Gully Cowsert, Ranger Arthur Hill.

central campfire, which served as heater and stove, and a large tent housed the men from the elements. Typically, one Ranger stayed in camp while others broke trail along the river.

Hill rode out at daybreak with a full stomach of Ranger Stewart's Dutch oven bread and coffee. He watched his breath plumes and those of his horse in the freezing air. During the night, he rolled himself in all of his blankets plus an extra tarp but still did not manage to warm up. He slept with his boots on, owing to the cold but also to extremely tender feet. He would be of no use in an emergency during the night if caught barefooted.[9]

Leather leggings covered his jeans and protected his legs from brush and ocotillo cactus. With boots, western hat, and a rope secured to the leather ties on the swell of his saddle, his appearance was much like that of any cowboy in the region. Only the badge pinned above the left pocket of his denim shirt and the tooled-leather holster, holding his service revolver, distinguished him as a Ranger. Without formal uniform, Hill's Ranger attire suited the duty assignment.

Hill followed Alamito Creek to its confluence with the Rio Grande and started patrolling eastward. Soon the valley gave way to the canyons, where ancient volcanic mountains towered above the river, which, depending on season and rainfall, alternated between calm and raging. The creaking of his saddle and the knock of his horse's hooves against stone provided the perfect background for the scene he took in. He was not the first Ranger to ride this trail, and he probably would not be the last. But the times had changed.

Hill's trail took him through what is now Big Bend Ranch State Park.[10] He rode all day without encountering another person or sign of civilization. The Big Bend is a land of contrasts—from killing heat to freezing cold, drought to flash flood, arid lowlands to humid mountain woodlands.[11] Yet, with all these seeming barriers to human habitation, there is a rugged appeal to the Big Bend.

Hill admired the power of nature and the wildness of the frontier that endured.

Former Texas Ranger Everett Townsend shared Hill's appreciation for the beauty of the region. He lobbied the Texas legislature to develop Texas Canyons State Park to protect the wild canyons forged by the Big Bend in the Rio Grande. In 1944, Townsend convinced President Franklin Roosevelt to designate the area at the southernmost tip of the river as Big Bend National Park.[12]

Hill returned from patrol, riding up to camp at twilight. The smell of beans and Dutch oven cornbread greeted him a mile downriver. He listened to the men's voices and laughter as he fed and brushed down his horse and put away his tack. He soon pulled up a stump with a bowl of beans in hand and joined in the camaraderie of the Ranger camp.

In the coming years, Hill worked countless hours along the border, but the practice of "camp and horseback scout duty" soon

Company E at Ranger camp on Rio Grande (1948). On horseback, *left to right:* Houston White, Arthur Hill, Forrest Goulde Hardin. Sitting, *left to right:* Earl Stewart, Captain Gully Cowsert.

faded away for the Rangers of Company E. For Hill, however, the memories, skills learned, and the Ranger bond forged on the banks of the Rio Grande remained.

Company E boasted a long history in the region. Founded in 1874 as part of the Major John B. Jones Frontier Battalion, the Rangers of Company E continued the tradition.[13] In 1947, the company included Captain Gully Cowsert (Junction), Bob Coffey (Sierra Blanca), Ralph Rohatsch (San Angelo), Houston White (Sonora), Clarence Nordyke (Brownwood), Earl Stewart (Pecos), and Arthur Hill (Alpine). In 1948, Ranger Forrest Goulde Hardin joined the company stationed at Sanderson.[14]

The *Texas Sheep and Goat Raisers' Magazine* described Company E Rangers as follows: "Captain Cowsert's company is composed of ex-cowpunchers reared in the livestock country, not the

Texas Rangers Company E (1948). Sitting, *left to right:* Forrest Hardin, Arthur Hill, Houston White, Clarence Nordyke. Standing, *left to right:* Bob Coffey, (unknown), Lt. Colonel Joe Fletcher, Captain Gully Cowsert, Chaplain Pierre Bernard Hill.

drug store cowboy type with fancy Palomino horses and lots of silver buckles, but regular ducking jacket cowhands who know how to sleep on the ground and eat around the chuck wagon."[15] While an accurate assessment, it was not complete. The Rangers of Company E were also accomplished and shrewd investigators.

"They were all good officers and good men, every one of them," Hill said of his first company of Rangers.[16] Hill considered himself privileged to have worked with Rangers who received their commissions from the Adjutant General's Office and made the transition to the modern era.

In addition to his humorous initiation with Vick, the cantankerous horse, Hill underwent an informal Ranger mentor program during his first months in the service. Men invested as Rangers already had proven law enforcement experience, but Captain Cowsert used "old salts" to train in the "new hands." For Hill, this "salt" was Ranger Sam Houston White.

"Any time I'd get in a little trouble down here," Hill explained, "Cap would send Houston down." Captain Cowsert sent White to Alpine to oversee Hill's methods and provide insight as needed. At one point, White accompanied Hill for an interrogation of a murder suspect as part of an ongoing investigation. Afterward, White told Hill, "I don't know what good I'm doing you, Arthur. I just sit around here and stare at somebody." The comment indicated that Hill performed his job well and marked the end of White's mentorship.[17]

Born in Bell County in 1888, Ranger White served as sheriff of Hamilton County prior to joining the Rangers. White wore double pearl-handled Colt revolvers throughout his tenure. The weapons served as a reminder of and memorial to his brother, Ranger Homer White. Homer, who was gunned down in Weatherford in 1908, had worn the Colts during his Ranger service.[18]

Hill's primary Ranger duties consisted of executing criminal and special investigations, apprehending felons, suppressing major disturbances, protecting life and property, and rendering assistance to local law enforcement officials.[19] Although Hill investigated major crimes that occurred in his region, he also worked other areas of the state as directed by the governor.[20]

The Texas Rangers, the oldest law enforcement agency in America with statewide jurisdiction,[21] numbered fifty-one men in 1947.[22] They were organized into five companies (A through E), each headed by a captain who reported directly to DPS director Homer Garrison. With the majority of Rangers stationed in small towns, Garrison shaped the service into a type of rural constabulary in support of understaffed law enforcement departments and elected officials who often lacked training. Garrison led the Rangers into the modern era.

The DPS made great advances in communications, thanks in part to the technologies developed by the military during World War II. In 1948, with the installation in Pecos of KTXP, a radio transmission station, the DPS provided minimal two-way coverage in the northern reaches of Hill's service area.

By the following year, two-way radios were installed in DPS and Ranger vehicles around the state; however, the radio was largely ineffective for Hill except as a coffee holder. Radio communications in this region of vast distances interrupted by mountainous terrain were limited. In 1950, with the installation of automatic relay stations at Guadalupe Pass and McDonald Observatory, additional rural locations gained access to two-way communications, but the signals still did not reach the more remote areas of Big Bend country.[23]

When Arthur Hill requested a duty station in the "ranch country," he certainly got what he asked for. The region's Anglo settlement owes greatly to ranchers. Central Texas ranchers, seeking expanded rangeland, spearheaded white settlement of the Alpine Valley.[24] Soon cattlemen from around the state came to graze their herds, eventually establishing ranches and towns.

Texas Rangers played a vital role in developing the region that Hill now served. In the late 1800s, the Rangers, along with U.S. Army forces stationed in West Texas, minimized the Comanche and Apache threat, and that of Mexican raids, to newly established settlements and ranches. Rangers also provided protection for surveying crews and railroad employees whose work was essential to the economic growth of the region.

After their service, many chose to stay. Former Rangers who settled in the area included Captain C. L. Nevill, E. C. Sheffield, Julias C. Bird, J. D. Jackson, Doc Gourley, J. B. Irving, L. B. Caruthers, J. M. Sedberry, P. H. Pruitt, W. C. Nations, James Dawson, Alfred Gage, James B. Gillett, and J. T. Gillespie, who became the first sheriff of Brewster County.[25]

The "ranch country" that attracted many of the Frontier Battalion of Texas Rangers drew Arthur Hill to this remote and intriguing region of the state where he continued the Ranger tradition. Hill's assignment area included Brewster, Jeff Davis, and Presidio Counties and parts of Pecos and Terrell Counties, located along more than three hundred miles of the Rio Grande border between Del Rio and El Paso—the Big Bend in the river.[26] In total, Hill's area of responsibility encompassed approximately twenty thousand square miles (roughly the size of West Virginia), the vast majority of it desolate wildlands.[27]

Within this region, the strong influence of Mexican border culture created a varied experience for law enforcement. Through changes in government, economy, and language over the centuries, the settlers of Mexican origin endured. Their descendants, on both sides of the river border, maintained a culture that emphasized the importance of family, loyalty, and hard work.[28]

Although not as fluent in Spanish as he would have liked, Hill had informants and maintained friendships on both sides of the border. He gained the respect of the Mexican and Mexican American communities with his impartial enforcement of the law. Hill

explained, "Not everyone is qualified to work the Mexican border. You've got to have connections on the other side. . . . You
have to understand the people and the life."[29]

Ranger Hill received his education in border culture from one
of the region's most respected officers, Jim Nance. When Hill arrived in the Big Bend, Nance served as sheriff of Terrell County,
as his father had before him. Nance received a commission to the
Ranger Service in 1953, stationed at Sierra Blanca in Hudspeth
County. Fluent in Spanish, Nance had an outgoing, friendly personality that drew people to him.[30] As Sheriff Dogie Wright, son
of famed Texas Ranger Will Wright, said of Nance, "Jim has an
outstanding image as a Ranger and has built the image of the
Texas Rangers. He gets out among the people and makes
friends."[31]

Nance's friends consisted of people from all walks of life on
both sides of the border, including charismatic and colorful Mexican army general Jayme Quinonez, with whom he worked
closely on many border matters.[32] Nance helped Hill to develop
friends, informants, and important official contacts in Mexico.
The two forged a close relationship, with Nance and his family
visiting the Hill home frequently.

Nance had a special attachment to the Hills' two girls, as he
and his wife had raised daughters as well. At his retirement,
Nance gave Martha Hill the 1881 "good luck" silver dollar he carried in his pocket throughout his service as a Ranger.[33]

Hill took Nance's advice and began to develop an understanding of and respect for Mexican culture. He made friends within
the Mexican community and patronized Mexican-owned stores
as much as possible. In summary, Hill took the initiative, offering
friendship and respect, and in return received the same.

Hill made a point of selecting a barber in the Mexican section
of Alpine. At the time, the Southern Pacific Railroad formed a di-
viding line between Anglo and Hispanic parts of town. The barrio

was literally on the "other side of the tracks." By putting himself in a vulnerable position, reclined in a barber chair with a razor at his neck, in broad view of the street through large plate glass windows, Hill made a statement of trust to the Hispanic community. Hill later added, "You'd be surprised how much you find out about what is going on sitting in a barber shop."[34]

Due to the terrain, history, and culture of the region, Ranger Hill employed methods in the performance of his duties different from Rangers in urban areas, or even those in more accessible and developed rural areas. Many methods harked back to the Rangers who first brought law to the borderland, while some utilized the emerging technologies of the time. In Hill's service, he stood positioned between two centuries, utilizing the best of both.

4

Rio Grande Rendezvous

From Brownsville, Texas, to a point just west of El Paso, the Rio
Grande forms approximately 800 miles of the United States-
Mexico border. Nowhere else in the Western Hemisphere—and
probably in the world—does one international boundary separate two nations of greater economic disparity. For more than a
century, citizens of both nations have, without governmental
sanction, attempted to exploit this economic imbalance for personal gain. The process is called smuggling.

Kenneth Ragsdale, *Big Bend Country:*
Land of the Unexpected, 78

HILL worked for twenty-seven years as a Ranger, twenty-six
years spent in the Big Bend. During this time he investigated far
too many cases to recount individually; however, certain types of
cases predominated. Smuggling, livestock theft, burglary, gambling, and murder made up the primary categories of cases
worked in the Big Bend during Hill's early career.[1] The following
four chapters examine typical cases Hill investigated within each
category for the years 1947 to 1957.

For as long as there has existed a border, smuggling has posed
problems for law enforcement on the Rio Grande. Whether contraband is in the form of sotol liquor, livestock, candelilla wax,
automatic weapons, electronics, or drugs, a smuggler's game is
one of profit and risk margins.

The Volstead Act, passed in 1919 to enable the enforcement of the Prohibition Amendment, added a new dynamic to law on the border. With this immense opportunity came the conversion of many bandits to the life of a smuggler.[2]

Texas Rangers, the U.S. Border Patrol, U.S. Customs agents, and Mexican *fiscals* quickly shifted their focus to the problem of smuggling. Pack trains of burros loaded with liquor, protected by heavily armed smugglers, forded the Rio Grande. The further inland they traversed, undetected, the higher the price they could command. With stiff fines and imprisonment facing captured smugglers, many did not think twice about going down shooting if intercepted by American officers.

With the repeal of Prohibition in 1933, smugglers turned to other goods to fund their trade.[3] The candelilla plant grows prolifically along the border. Wax from the plant was used in cosmetics and floor polish, even as a sealant for munitions shipped overseas during World Wars I and II.[4] Soon wax production enterprises sprang up along the border.

In a typical operation, local landowners leased land for the candelilla harvest. Mexican laborers harvested the plants by hand on both sides of the Rio Grande. They then boiled down the plant at mobile wax camps to extract the raw wax for delivery to refineries in the United States.[5]

In 1935 the Mexican government imposed a heavy tax on the candelilla plant and wax exported to the United States. The export tariff served to bolster the domestic Mexican wax market and keep profits at home.[6]

Subsequently, the practice of smuggling the plant or wax out of Mexico increased. Imports of the plant or wax from Mexico, when declared through U.S. Customs, remained legal in the United States. Smugglers bringing wax shipments out of Mexico did not cross the border, however, at official U.S.-Mexico customs facilities. By evading Mexican authorities, they also bypassed their U.S. counterparts. American wax buyers positioned themselves at locations convenient to the border. These buyers required only a means to weigh and inspect the delivered goods and large quantities of ready cash on hand. Most of the transactions took place at night, effectively dodging customs. Unfortunately, the business of buying smuggled wax could be a hazardous occupation.

An example of such hazards was Joseph Kalamore, who owned the Kalamore Variety and Hardware Store in the border town of Presidio, Texas. For several years, Kalamore had purchased candelilla. Smugglers brought wax across the Rio Grande at all hours of the night.

Kalamore slept in his store. Typically, he woke to a knock at his door. He went with the smugglers across the street to his warehouse to weigh the product, and then returned to the store, opened his safe, and paid cash for the wax.[7] The practice ultimately proved fatal.

On the morning of July 24, 1952, a Kalamore employee arrived for work and found the store's back door ajar. She immediately left the building and notified Presidio County Sheriff Ernest Barnett. Hill, who was already in the area on another investigation, joined Sheriff Barnett behind the store.

After searching the store, the officers descended the stairs into the basement. Hill pulled the chain attached to a single lightbulb dangling from the ceiling, revealing Joseph Kalamore's lifeless body bound and gagged in a chair. Blood dotted the new furniture and appliances that surrounded him, which were warehoused in the basement for later display in his store. Hill looked cautiously around at the scene and found two long, heavy bolts covered in blood. "His brains had been beaten out," Hill revealed.

Back upstairs, Hill saw that Kalamore's safe door stood open and the safe was empty. Watches and pen sets were missing from glass jewelry cases. Theft was clearly the motive of the murder.

Hill called Colonel Garrison, who instructed forensic technicians to fly in from Austin to collect evidence and perform evaluations at the scene. With technicians en route, Hill shifted his attention to locating eyewitnesses or others with information that could lead to the identity of the murderer or murderers.[8]

After following several leads, Hill discovered that three teenaged boys witnessed some of the events of the previous night. Hill met with the boys, and they revealed what they had seen. The boys had watched an older-model blue Ford cross the International Bridge into Presidio from Ojinaga, Chihuahua, Mexico, that evening. They recognized the car as that of Francisco Martinez of Ojinaga. The driver they recognized as Alma Rico, Martinez's sister; however, they did not know the two men riding in the backseat. The car came to a stop in front of the Kalamore store.

Joseph Kalamore stood on the steps of the store talking with another man. When the blue car pulled up, Kalamore got in his car and drove around to the warehouse. The blue Ford followed.

Both cars soon returned to the front of the store. Alma Rico remained in the Ford while the four men entered Kalamore's store. Kalamore never left the store again.[9]

Hill contacted the Ojinaga police chief, who issued a warrant for Francisco Martinez. Hill then drove down the dirt streets of Presidio and crossed the rickety wooden bridge into Ojinaga. Along with the Ranger, Mexican officers quickly located and arrested Martinez and placed him in the Ojinaga jail.

Hill leaned against the adobe wall and watched as Mexican officials interrogated Martinez. He disagreed with their, at times, harsh methods, but could not argue with their effectiveness.

He understood only part of the Spanish dialogue, which Mexican officers translated. The suspect's body language and expressions, he understood. Martinez had been involved and knew the identity of the others.

Ultimately, Francisco Martinez admitted taking part in the

murder and robbery of Joseph Kalamore. He also implicated two other Mexican nationals, Manuel Sonora, and a man he claimed to know only as *La Cochina,* The Pig.

Hill listened intently as Martinez related the series of events that night. The group of men crossed the Río Bravo (Rio Grande) just north of the U.S. customhouse. Alma Rico drove the Ford across the International Bridge alone. Once on the American side, they met Rico along the river.

Inside the store with Kalamore, Martinez stood guard by the door. Sonora sold two sacks of candelilla to Kalamore. He asked for some gloves, stating that the river current was swift and he needed them to pull a raft across the river to transport additional wax.

Sonora then requested that Kalamore advance him six hundred dollars to acquire a truck to transport candelilla to the river on the Mexican side. Kalamore seemed to agree to the proposition, whether of free will or coercion. Sonora, *La Cochina,* and Kalamore then proceeded to the safe to retrieve the money.

At this juncture, Martinez said he could no longer see the men, and he claimed that he did not see or hear subsequent events. When Sonora finally emerged from the store's rear door, however, he carried a white canvas sack and his shirt was stained with blood.

The group crossed the river on foot and returned to Ojinaga. Once back at Sonora's house in Mexico, Martinez received three hundred dollars and a threat: if he spoke of the night's events, he could "rest assured they would come back and kill him."[10]

Early efforts to locate Sonora and *La Cochina* proved unsuccessful. Questioning in Ojinaga revealed a rumor that the pair, along with Alma Rico, had traveled to Mexico City.

Hill returned to Presidio and approached the case from another perspective. He returned to the store, which remained closed, and examined Kalamore's records. He discovered that

Alma Rico's husband, Roberto Rico, had sold wax to Mr. Kalamore on several occasions. Hill suspected that Roberto Rico was *La Cochina* and that Martinez claimed ignorance to protect the identity of his brother-in-law.

Hill coordinated further investigation efforts with Mexico City authorities and began extradition procedures to bring the suspects to justice in the United States. The Chihuahua state attorney general of justice removed Martinez from Ojinaga to Chihuahua City. With this move to the interior, Hill saw the possibility of extradition and a murder trial in the United States slipping away.

Martinez stood trial in Mexico, receiving a guilty verdict and a sentence of eighteen years in a Mexican penitentiary. Mexico City authorities later arrested Sonora and Roberto Rico, identified as *La Cochina,* based on information provided by Hill and the Ojinaga police.[11]

With the proximity to the border, the flight of criminals into Mexico to avoid prosecution provided constant frustration for Hill.[12] Despite the cooperation of border law officers, higher-level authorities often moved cases away from the border. Suspects rarely came to trial in Mexico, and those who did seldom received a guilty verdict or lengthy sentence. Mexican trials did not allow for a jury, and judges were easily influenced.[13] Mexican law also did not typically permit the extradition of Mexican nationals charged with first-degree murder to the United States, as Mexico did not recognize the death penalty.

Occasionally, however, local Mexican officers provided for "unofficial" extradition of a criminal to the United States. In one of many similar cases, Hill received word from a Mexican officer through an informant. The officer suggested Hill "check out" a remote section of the border.

Hill exited his patrol car and walked the final mile to the designated site along the river. He looked up and down the sediment beach and in the brush along the bank. There, tied to a small tree, Hill found a Mexican citizen whom he had pursued into Mexico. Sunburned and thirsty, the man appeared glad to be in the custody of a Texas Ranger.

The prisoner had outstanding warrants in the United States. Apparently, the Mexican officers agreed that the man should pay for his crime regardless of nationality. This practice of "pushing out" those wanted for crimes in the United States was commonplace.[14]

Northern Mexico, *la frontera,* was far removed from Mexico City, as was the Big Bend country from Washington, D.C., both geographically and ideologically. Officers and officials worked closely with Hill to resolve issues of mutual concern affecting citizen safety and property along the border. At this time, before the wholesale corruption of the illegal drug trade, Hill viewed the Mexican officers with whom he worked as respected colleagues.

Hill's case files contain evidence of various forms of contraband, including limited investigations of peyote transport in Big Bend Park, marijuana smuggling to supply a small ring on the college campus, and the transport of "black tar" heroin in small amounts.[15] Drug smuggling at this time did not reach the volume of later years. But the groundwork for the illicit drug trade, which had begun before Prohibition, continued to be laid in the remote border region.

5

Brush Country Ranger

In that rough rural terrain, no officer excelled like the Texas
Ranger. He knew his prey and his territory, but tenacity was his
greatest asset. . . . A Ranger was a Ranger because he was bred for
the prairies and the backwoods. He personified the frontier and
lived by its rough-hewn ethic.

Robert Draper, "Twilight of the Texas Rangers,"
***Texas Monthly,* February 1994**

OTHER products of the smuggler's trade created challenges for
border Rangers and U.S. Customs. Transporting cattle and other
livestock across the river constituted the primary type of smuggling that Hill encountered during the 1947–1957 period. This
practice also became problematic for animal health officials as
smuggled animals evaded not only customs but also quarantine
and thus disease inspection.

The River Riders of the U.S. Department of Agriculture's Bureau of Animal Industry (BAI) performed mounted patrols along
the Rio Grande from Brownsville to El Paso in these years. The
patrols attempted to prevent foot-and-mouth disease, common in
Mexican herds, from spreading to animals in the United States.[1]

As they had no real policing powers, the River Riders primarily guarded against the entry of trespass stock; they also quaran-
tined animals and pastures that had been exposed to infected
livestock that wandered across the border. Because of their reg-

ular patrols, River Riders often were the first to observe illegal activity.

Livestock smuggling took on many forms. Smugglers typically herded livestock from Mexico into the United States, bypassing customs, and sold the animals to area ranchers. Livestock traffic moved south as well, with thefts from American ranches making their way across the border for sale to Mexican meat packers/butchers and ranchers.

The same stories had played out a century before as frontier and border Rangers fought cattle raiders. Famed Texas Ranger Captain Leander McNelly shared the results of a cattle-smuggling case with Texas Adjutant General Steele. After pursuing bandits into Matamoros, Mexico, McNelly wired Steele briefly describing the events, "Had a fight with raiders, killed twelve, and captured two hundred and sixty five beeves." He added wryly, "Wish you were here."[2]

In January 1952, Hill received word through an informant that cattle crossed the Rio Grande from Mexico at an "old smuggler's pass" near Santa Elena Canyon. Hill and Brewster County Sheriff Jim Skinner loaded Hill's horse trailer and headed for the border. At Castolon they met Wayne Green, the leader of the BAI River Riders. The three continued toward the river and then stopped where the dirt road dead-ended at the riverbank.

Hill opted to start the search in Mexico. Farther upriver toward the pass, the ground grew rocky. By intercepting the trail in Mexico, Hill hoped to find readable tracks in the sandy soil. With prints to follow into the rocks, the group stood a better chance of identifying the exact crossing site.

The men mounted their horses and forded the shallow river. They fanned out and scanned the terrain. Each studied the ground from both sides of his horse, plodding along. Soon, they discovered tracks. The prints indicated approximately thirty calves driven by riders on horseback.

They tracked the cattle along the riverbank to a point where they crossed to the American side, near the canyon. Fortunately, the ground remained relatively sandy. Hill turned his horse toward the river and coaxed him into the water, crossing as the calves had the previous night. The murky water came up to his stirrups. Hill followed the tracks from the crossing point to a location where the animals apparently were loaded onto a truck.

He climbed down from his horse and examined the scene. Cut sotol leaves and heads lay scattered by the wind, evidently used for feed. Hill walked around the tracks, which disappeared where truck tire marks began. He noted baling wire and scraps of insulated wire in the dirt beside the truck marks. Sheriff Skinner followed the tire tracks up from the river but they disappeared in the rocky terrain.

Deciding to begin the investigation at the source, Hill and Skinner turned their horses back across the river. Green returned to Castolon. They rode into the small village of Santa Elena, Chihuahua, on the main dirt street. Adobe brick and plastered buildings blended with the soil of the mountains surrounding it. Some had a thatch roof, others corrugated tin. Hill pulled up his horse to a man tending goats in a pen. A few well-placed questions later, and they had a place to start.

Hill placed great importance on the role of informants on the Mexican side of the border. In this case, an informant indicated first that smuggling had occurred, and another informant provided the intelligence the Ranger needed to proceed. Hill learned that Antonio Valenzuela had received the smuggled calves and loaded them in a truck. They returned across the river, trailered their horses, and drove toward the Valenzuela Ranch near Terlingua.

As they neared the Valenzuela Ranch, Skinner noticed a large pen (trap) that contained thirty-five black calves. The calves fed on cut sotol heads. Hill stopped, looked over the calves, and walked around a small feed barn located within the trap. There he found tire marks matching those seen at the river. He also discovered a large quantity of cut sotol feed stored within.

The ranch property belonged to Clinton Fulcher, a Brewster County commissioner, and thus Skinner's boss. This fact did not give pause to either man.

They continued on to the Valenzuela Ranch, where Hill questioned the suspect. Valenzuela's contradictory statements convinced Hill of his guilt and of the involvement of others. He left to gather more evidence.

Skinner and Hill returned to the Fulcher Ranch, this time going to the residence. Hill eyed Fulcher's truck, parked in front of the home, as he made his way to the door. The tires matched the tracks at the feed barn and the river. In the back of the truck sotol heads, baling wire, and insulated wire, matching the gauge and casing found at the river, lay strewn about.

Hill watched Fulcher's expression as he answered the door. His first reaction would speak volumes. Fulcher's appearance indeed reflected the surprise and fear that Hill expected. Hill questioned Fulcher casually, but did not press him until he had more information in place. Fulcher adamantly denied involvement, claiming to have raised the calves on his ranch.

With some pieces of the puzzle falling into place, Hill and Skinner spent the next few days working both sides of the river. They questioned people and reviewed livestock and local theft records for the areas in and around Castolon, Terlingua, and Santa Elena, Mexico.

Their efforts proved fruitful. Another interview, at La Harmonia Store in Castolon, revealed the name of an accomplice, Ramon Lujon, who assisted Valenzuela and Fulcher on the American side. Hill also discovered that the incident was not an isolated one. Fulcher and Valenzuela frequently organized cattle "shipments" from Mexico.

Hill and Skinner quickly located Lujon, who admitted his involvement and confirmed the identity of his associates. Hill arrested Lujon, Valenzuela, and Fulcher on smuggling charges, a federal offense. "After lengthy interrogation," according to Hill, Fulcher and Valenzuela also admitted their involvement in that instance and others. Hill delivered the men into the custody of U.S. Customs in El Paso.[3]

The investigation, however, did not end with arrests only on the U.S. side of the border. Hill traveled again to Mexico where he requested that Mexican rangers Pila Rivera and José Alemán, in Ojinaga, collaborate in the investigation. Together the Texas Ranger and the Mexican rangers ultimately uncovered the two men who acted as drovers in the smuggling scheme.

The investigation followed a typical process for cases involving livestock smuggling in the Big Bend and demonstrated common interoffice cooperation. Officers involved represented local and state law enforcement and two federal agencies, as well as Mexican state officials. Despite the "one riot, one Ranger" tradition, Hill readily acknowledged the importance of such collaboration.

One of Hill's primary responsibilities as a Ranger involved rendering assistance to local law enforcement. He forged close working ties with officers in the towns and counties in his region of responsibility. One of the men with whom Arthur worked most frequently and closely was the Brewster County sheriff, Jim Skinner.

Skinner, born in 1905 in Seymour, Texas, worked as a ranch hand near Marathon before his involvement in law enforcement. Brewster County Sheriff Clarence Hord solicited Skinner's help to clean up the wild ranch town.

Skinner gained a reputation for his tough, no-nonsense approach as he quickly "whipped the town into shape." He reputedly could "track a criminal, from the scene of a crime to right where his shoes rested under his bed and arrest the man while he slept." A deputy in Brewster County from 1945 to 1948, Skinner was elected sheriff of Brewster County on January 1, 1949.[4]

Arthur and Jim worked many cases together and came to trust, respect, and depend on one another. Hill said of Skinner, "He was one of the best sheriffs I ever worked with. We went through a whole lot together."[5]

In cattle smuggling and theft cases, Hill called on his cowboy skills as much as his investigative skills. Hill saddled up again after a U.S. Customs agent, Tom Wagner, requested his assistance in a smuggling and cow theft case at Presidio. Hill, along with Rangers White and Hardin and Captain Cowsert, responded to the request.

The Rangers arrived at the Clark Ranch, twenty-five miles west of Presidio, in two state cars with bumper-pull horse trailers

Brewster County Sheriff Jim Skinner.

attached. Hill and the other Rangers rounded up all cattle on the large ranch and moved them through smaller pens and chutes to identify brands and other markings, which was called "close work."

Ten head of Mexican cattle were identified by the Rangers and impounded and released to U.S. Customs. Hill set out to determine the source. The brand did not match any of those registered in Presidio County. He left for Ojinaga, Chihuahua, to contact officials and check Mexican brand records.

Hill found the brand registered to Cruz Gonzales of Ojinaga. Hill, along with Mexican officers, drove to the Gonzales Rancho, where they questioned the ranchero, or ranch owner. Gonzales revealed that he had been missing cattle for several months. He and Hill rode through the stock on his ranch. Hill easily identified the brand and earmark on Gonzales's stock as matching those of the impounded cattle.[6]

With Gonzales's branding iron in hand, Hill returned to Presidio. The brand exactly matched that of the cattle, as suspected. Gonzales traveled to the United States to identify and claim his stock.

In another theft and smuggling incident, carcasses rather than live animals comprised the illegal imports. In December 1954, Hill and Presidio County Sheriff Ernest Barnett were working in Pilares, Texas, investigating an assault case. Moody Bennett, a local rancher, located them in town and reported a theft on his ranch.

Bennett told them that Mexican nationals had butchered three head of his sheep. Hill and Barnett traveled to the ranch, where they interviewed workers and determined the names of three Mexican nationals believed to be involved.

Hill alerted Mexican official Lazaro Begas, who arrested the men identified and placed them in the Guadalupe, Mexico, jail. The incident seemed isolated, but new information soon led Hill to believe otherwise.

Hill and Barnett returned to Marfa, where they contacted District Attorney Travers Crumpton. Crumpton coordinated with Hill to prepare complaints on the three subjects for sheep theft, as required by Mexican law, in order to proceed with formal charges in Mexico.

Hill and Ranger Jim Nance took the complaints to Guadalupe, Mexico, and filed them with the *presidente municipal* (mayor) of Guadalupe, whose name was Obregon. Obregon advised that all three suspects would stand trial in Mexico for sheep theft and for the smuggling of stolen meat into Mexico.[7]

Hill and Nance learned of butchered sheep on the McSpadden, Rooney, and Livingston Ranches as well. After interviews on the area ranches, the Rangers received information that implicated Juan Terragano, a resident of Los Fresnos, Mexico, in the butchering.

Working with Sheriff Barnett, Ranger Nance, and two Mexican officials, Hill traveled to Los Fresnos. The officers discovered that Terragano fronted a widespread smuggling operation, consisting of Terragano, a group of smugglers, and a local Mexican official, Carlos Apadoca, who covered up their activities.

"They had a pretty good setup to smuggle in meat and other items," Hill explained in his report to Captain Cowsert, "but I think we have it broken up now." Hill, Nance, and Mexican officers arrested Juan Terragano and Carlos Apadoca and delivered them to the jail in Guadalupe, Mexico.[10]

Smuggled livestock traveled both directions across the border. Sometimes incidents were based locally, sometimes with ties farther "inland." Ranger Jim Nance received notice from an informant about smuggled burros coming in from Mexico. He contacted Hill to assist. Nance learned that a rancher named Tinsley Means planned to drive burros from the Rio Grande to stock pens near Valentine, Texas.

Hill and Nance rode to the pens on horseback to avoid detection. They intercepted Means and the burros. Under questioning by the Rangers, Means revealed the entire smuggling scheme. He agreed to cooperate with U.S. Customs and the Texas Rangers in providing information to lead to the "principal in the venture," Harold Starr of San Angelo.

Nance and Hill contacted U.S. Customs in El Paso and arranged to allow Means to deliver the burros to Starr on the evening of June 13, 1955, as planned. Rangers Nance and Hill, along with U.S. Customs agents, waited patiently out of sight of the transfer. Officers arrested Elda and Roy Starr and seized a 1955 Ford half-ton pickup truck, trailer, and nineteen burros.[11]

In a letter of thanks to Homer Garrison, U.S. Customs supervisor Lawrence Fleishman commended Hill and Nance on their work. He also praised the cooperation received from the Ranger Service: "This [case] is only a continuance of the excellent cooperation this office receives from Ranger Nance and Ranger Hill, in a difficult area, which is greatly appreciated."[12]

In addition to international smuggling, domestic livestock theft was widespread as well. With miles of remote rangeland, the practice of rustling thrived on Texas's Last Frontier. Occasionally, however, the guise of rustling provided an excuse to cover up a more personal agenda.

In response to a request from Captain Cowsert to look into a report of sheep theft on the Henry Willbanks Ranch near Sanderson, Hill began an investigation. Hill, along with Terrell County Sheriff Charley Baker, arrived at the Willbanks Ranch on the morning of March 23, 1948. Together with Willbanks, they rode the pasture that had held the allegedly stolen sheep. Hill and Baker worked the area until late that afternoon, but they found no evidence that vehicles had loaded sheep, or that any riders had driven sheep off the property.

As the men loaded their horses and prepared to leave, Willbanks requested that Hill stay behind. "I stayed for about an hour after Charley left," Hill explained, "during which time Willbanks did much talking." The conversation shed light on the situation.

Willbanks propped his arms atop the bed of his pickup truck. He began to question Hill about his investigation findings. Hill was not forthcoming with information. Willbanks then asked if the loan company would investigate. He questioned Hill about the procedures that an investigation would follow, growing more anxious with Hill's terse responses and stare.

Apparently, the rancher had attempted to dupe his insurance company and now had second thoughts. Livestock insurance fraud occurred frequently, especially in times of drought or low prices. There is nothing like the presence of a Ranger to make the guilty sweat. Hill reported back to Captain Cowsert, "I am of the opinion that Henry Willbanks's 800 head of sheep have not been stolen."[11]

The western proverb, "Good fences make good neighbors," holds true. Livestock theft or the perception that it has occurred between neighbors can lead to very bad relations. In late 1949, accusations by Bud Roark that Burl Sauls had stolen sheep from him escalated to the point where Rangers intervened.

Captain Cowsert notified Hill to work with W. L. Barler to inspect the brands and marks of all the sheep on the Sauls Dove Mountain Ranch. Barler had served as captain of Ranger Company E from 1917 to 1919, during the period of the State Rangers. Barler continued to live and ranch in the area, retaining his Special Ranger commission.[12] Although Barler had long since retired, Hill and the other Rangers of Company E, as a mark of their respect, continued to refer to him as "Cap."

On the morning of November 14, 1949, Hill met Cap Barler at the Sauls Ranch headquarters, and then saddled up and rode to corrals two miles east. There Hill found the Roarks family and three of their hired hands sitting atop the pipe rails of the working pens, awaiting the inspection. According to Bud Roark, at the invitation of Captain Cowsert they had assembled on the Sauls property to claim their stolen sheep. The Saulses would arrive at the corrals soon, and Hill knew that a confrontation would ensue.

The sounds of sheep and the sight of dust rising over the horizon in the morning light gave the first indication of their approach. Soon after, the Saulses and two hired hands appeared, driving three hundred head of sheep toward the corral. When Burl Sauls spotted Bud Roark sitting on the top rail, he broke from the herd, pulled his rifle from its case, and rode hard for the corral. Hill mounted quickly, spurred his horse into a gallop, and intercepted Sauls in the pasture.

"What the hell is Roark doing on my place?" Sauls demanded. Hill explained that Captain Cowsert had invited the Roarks to claim any sheep that belonged to them during the inspection. Sauls insisted that he had no knowledge of this, nor, incidentally, did Hill. Sauls wanted the Roarks off his ranch immediately, or he said he would force them off. Sauls added that he trusted only Hill and Barler to work the stock and resolve the dispute.

Hill felt sure that Cowsert did not understand the deep-seated hatred that festered between the neighboring ranchers. Otherwise, he would not have orchestrated such a potentially explosive situation. Hill asked the Roarks to leave Saulses property and assured them that he and Barler would account for any of their sheep.

Over the next four days, Hill and Barler worked from daylight until dark, checking over 2,800 head of sheep on the large ranch. They found no animal bearing the Roarks' brand. The animosity that had developed between the neighbors seemed unreasonable. Hill added after reporting the events to Cowsert, "I feel sure that the Roarks are not satisfied with what happened."[13]

Hill enjoyed the combination of "cowboying" and investigation in his Ranger experience. The work of a cowboy, like that of law enforcement, was unpredictable and not without risks.

While rounding up a herd of cattle for brand inspection, Hill discovered that dealing with horses is sometimes more difficult than dealing with criminals. On a border ranch, Hill, riding flank, helped to move a herd of cattle down a steep hill toward holding pens where they would be inspected. The pace of the herd quickened as the front-runners hit the flat. Hill's horse stumbled in the rocky terrain, throwing Hill headlong down the mountain ahead of his mount.

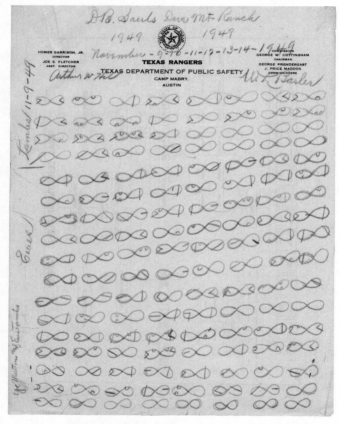

Captain W. L. Barler's working notes on the earmarks of
Sauls Dove Mountain Ranch sheep (1949).

Hill rolled end over end against rock and cactus, mesquite and cedar. He could hear his horse tumbling just above him. Not wanting the horse to roll over him, he grabbed a cedar tree as he fell past and "scooted up around it."

The horse landed squarely on top of the same cedar tree with all four legs directly up in the air. "I didn't know if she was dead or not," Hill described. "I wasn't sure I was going to make it." Both horse and rider lay stunned, trying to catch their breath.

After a few moments passed, Hill slowly moved and began to check his body for injuries. The horse, unconcerned with such things, still lay with legs straight up and merely turned her head to eat some grass beside the tree. Hill later laughed, "I never saw one eat upside down in my life."[14]

Hill used horses frequently in manhunts, livestock roundups for inspections, and his own ranching sideline. In another incident, Hill was working a young horse in an inspection roundup. Some of the cattle cut back quickly on Hill. He reacted as he would if he were on his older, more reliable mount. "I whirled around and put the spurs to him," Hill explained. When he did, the startled "green" horse started to pitch. Hill added, "I rode him too long. If I would have fallen off it wouldn't have hurt me near as bad, but I rode him a good long while and he threw me anyway."[15]

Hill received his only major injury in the line of duty as a result of using unpredictable equines. Taking a fall from a horse during another brand inspection roundup, Arthur ruptured a disc in the lumbar region of his back. The injury required back surgery and bed rest.

Somewhat unwillingly, he traveled to Dallas for the surgery. Frequent visits and the hospitality of the Rangers of Company B made an uncomfortable situation bearable. Captain M. T. "Lone Wolf" Gonzaullas personally handled all of the paperwork and made his home available for Ruby Hill during their stay in

Dallas.[16] Rangers have a close brotherhood and a dedicated commitment to "take care of their own."

A friendly distinction between rural, or "brush country" Rangers and their urban, or "concrete," counterparts has existed for generations. This distinction has nothing to do with the proficiency with which the two groups perform their assigned Ranger duties. The designation refers to the environment in which they work.

The remoteness of the Last Frontier resulted in different types of cases, limited law-enforcement support, and extraordinarily long response times due to the distances covered. One border rancher summed up the situation, "The Rangers ain't much on fast, but they are hell on sure."

6

"They Rode for the Brand"

They made no braggadocio demonstrations. They did not gallop through the streets and shoot and yell. They had a specie of moral discipline which developed moral courage. They did right because it was right.

Captain John S. "Rip" Ford, Memoirs,
John Salmon Ford Papers, Barker Texas History Center,
University of Texas at Austin

BURGLARY is a common crime encountered by law enforcement officers everywhere. Hill investigated many burglaries in homes and businesses in towns throughout the region. Burglaries on remote ranches and camps, however, added a different dimension to Hill's responsibilities. The more remote the property, the more time the criminal had to perpetrate the crime, and the less likely he was to be discovered in doing so.

Few dwellings were more remote than the Bureau of Animal Industry River Rider camps. BAI River Riders built camps along the border to accommodate their foot-and-mouth disease patrols. Although rudimentary, the camp dwellings provided shelter for the riders and housed their supplies.

In July 1950, Hill investigated a typical remote burglary perpetrated by an atypical burglar. River Rider Rastus Caveness came into Alpine to report to Hill the burglary of his camp at Black Gap. Caveness explained that he spent one night away from camp on the river and upon his return discovered the crime.

Hill loaded the horse trailer, drove to the ranch headquarters from which the riders were based, and followed Caveness on horseback to Black Gap. Hill surveyed the camp. With no door or windows, no mystery existed as to the means of access. The interior appeared disheveled, but that may or may not have been out of the ordinary. Caveness indicated that a bolt-action .22 rifle, three boxes of .22 long-rifle shells, some clothing, canned food, and a small amount of money appeared to be missing.

Hoof prints around the camp led along the trail toward the next River Rider camp belonging to Bill Saunders. Hill and Caveness mounted up and followed the tracks. Hours later, they arrived at Bill Saunders's camp. Saunders greeted them with, "I've been waiting for y'all."

Saunders turned to point out a man, his hands tied with a lariat, sitting on a rock at the center of camp. Saunders explained that the man, Myron Schmidt, rode into his camp the previous day. Saunders recognized the rifle and clothing. He easily captured Schmidt and patiently awaited the help he knew would eventually arrive.[1]

The case solved itself. Tracks led straight to the suspect. He had in his possession some of the stolen goods, and Saunders had already captured the prisoner. The unusual story of how Schmidt arrived at the remote camp provided an interesting addendum to a routine investigation.

Schmidt had left his wife and his job selling magazines in St. Louis, Missouri, on May 29, 1950. He drove his 1941 Ford to Presidio, Texas. There he sold the car and bought a horse from Juan Ochoa and a saddle and boots in Ojinaga, Mexico. He started down the river toward Lajitas along what now is the "river road." He rode into Big Bend Park and through Boquillas before arriving at the River Riders' camp.

Along the hundred-plus-mile trip down the Rio Grande, Schmidt encountered no fences, few people, and quite a western adventure in 1950s' Texas. Schmidt received a five-year sentence for burglary, to be served at the state penitentiary in Huntsville.[2]

Schmidt's wild and woolly western adventure did not end there. One month after his sentencing, Schmidt broke out of the Brewster County Jail. The *Alpine Avalanche* reported, "After trailing Myron Schmidt, escaped convict, all night through the Christmas Mountains west of Big Bend National Park, Ranger Arthur Hill and Sheriff Jim Skinner captured Schmidt who broke jail here Friday night while awaiting transfer to Huntsville." The account continued, "Schmidt was in a hideout popular with outlaws when Judge Roy Bean was the only 'law west of the Pecos' and was heading for the Mexican border eighteen miles distant."[3]

Proximity to the border and the regional economic disparities contributed to many of the ranch burglaries in the area. Ranchers frequently maintained a line shack, or "Mexican" shack, for undocumented Mexican nationals passing through to find food and shelter. Some did so for philanthropic reasons; others to ensure that such people avoided the main house. Regardless, word spread among those who traversed the border about shack locations.

On most border ranches, the labor force was composed largely of Mexican aliens. It was advantageous for ranchers to maintain positive relationships with Mexican laborers. Unfortunately, certain people on both sides of the river took advantage of this interaction.

On the afternoon of September 24, 1956, Jake Nutt, owner of the Kincade Ranch near Marathon, Texas, reported a burglary at his residence to Sheriff Jim Skinner. Nutt informed Skinner that the theft involved approximately three hundred dollars' worth of jewelry and cash.

Skinner asked Hill to work with him on the investigation, and the two left for Marathon with little daylight remaining. Hill and Skinner examined Nutt's home. They encountered footprints leading off in the direction of the neighboring Roberts Ranch in line with a path toward Mexico.

They arrived at the Roberts Ranch house just before dark and spoke with Mrs. Roberts. Hill was told that she fed a Mexican man lunch that afternoon. He left afterward, bound for Mulato, Chihuahua, Mexico, through the Del Norte Mountains. Hill and Skinner checked for tracks, which they found leading off toward the mountains. The route continued to the Nevill and Kokernot Ranches on the southern slopes of the Del Norte Mountains. With darkness encroaching, Hill and Skinner returned to Alpine for the night.

They arrived at the Nevill Ranch at daybreak on horseback, where they picked up the trail of the suspect and tracked him onto the adjacent Kokernot Ranch. The tracks appeared fresh; evidently, he spent the night at trail side and had only begun his trek again at daylight. Hill spotted the man ahead on the trail. Because they were riding into a strong wind, the man did not hear them approach. Hill and Skinner apprehended Juan Rodriguez Velasquez and recovered all of the "loot" taken in the burglary.[4]

The plight of impoverished people coming from Mexico was not lost on Arthur Hill. He sympathized with men attempting to make a better life for their families by seeking work in the United States. However, he would enforce the law to the letter, believing that, regardless of circumstances, nothing justified theft.[5]

Once back at Hill's office, Velasquez gave his account of the crime. He told Hill that he had worked for Nutt since early September, earning two dollars per day. He planned to obtain a visa and passport allowing him to immigrate legally to the United States. For that purpose, he needed to appear in court in Monterrey, Chihuahua, Mexico, in October. Velasquez asked Nutt for the remainder of his wages due so that he could return to Monterrey. Nutt paid him by check.

Without a bank account or real understanding of the process, Velasquez believed he needed cash or something of value to fund his walk to Monterrey. He knew that the Nutt family went into town on Saturday night, so he waited for his chance.

He worked outside milking and feeding the cow, until he saw the family drive off. He then entered the ranch house through the front door and gathered several items, worth more than his wages paid by check, in a blanket.

Velasquez then walked into Marathon, where he slept in the cemetery. He continued on to the ranch of Blas Mariscal, where he ate breakfast. Eluding the Border Patrol, he continued to the Nevill Ranch en route to Mexico. He stopped in a Nevill line shack to eat and sleep. The next morning, he started off again, but "a short time later, the officers arrested me."[6]

Not all burglaries were as benign. In 1955, Hill received a phone call from Jeff Davis County Sheriff Tom Gray requesting his assistance on a burglary case at the Fitzgerald Ranch, thirty miles west of Fort Davis. The Fitzgerald Ranch, like most in the region, lacked a phone and had only a generator to provide electricity. The sheriff did not receive notification of the theft until a worker could drive into town. Hill arrived at the sheriff's office, where he met Gray and discussed details of the case.

Gray explained that an undocumented Mexican, José Ortiz Garcia, had arrived at the Fitzgerald Ranch the previous day seeking work. Fitzgerald told Garcia that he had no work available. Garcia then left the ranch and began walking into the adjoining mountains.

Gray added that as soon as Fitzgerald left the ranch to go into town, Garcia returned. He attempted to steal Fitzgerald's car, but ranch employees pulled him from the vehicle. Garcia broke away from the employees and ran to the ranch house, where he armed himself with Fitzgerald's .30-30 rifle. He fired out the window at the employees in the ranch yard, and they quickly scattered. Garcia then took a .22 revolver, .22 rifle, and shells, and left the house. He ran back into the mountains near the residence.

Hill, briefed on the chain of events, took over the investigation. The suspect, now armed and considered dangerous, was on foot in rugged terrain. Hill hoped that if he could quickly get a mounted search team in pursuit, they could intercept Garcia before he crossed the border.

Hill, Sheriff Gray, Deputy Jones, Highway Patrolman Bolinger, and Border Patrolman Newsome, along with Fitzgerald, mounted ranch horses and began pursuit. The posse searched on horseback from the Fitzgerald Ranch, through the mountains, and forty miles south, near the Mexican border. Garcia's trail disappeared in the rocky terrain. Officers discontinued the search, redirecting their efforts to questioning possible witnesses and contacting Mexican officials.

The occurrence appeared to be another case of a criminal's flight to the southern sanctuary. Two days later, however, Fitzgerald appeared in Gray's office while Hill and Gray were reviewing the case. With no telephone at the ranch, Fitzgerald drove thirty miles into town to notify the law officers that Garcia had struck again.

Hill and Gray set out in Hill's state car to the Fitzgerald Ranch. Arriving at the ranch, Hill and Fitzgerald took stock of stolen items, which included more .30-30 shells, a radio, clothing, and food. Garcia also took Fitzgerald's house and car keys.

"We believed," said Hill, "that Garcia would attempt to steal Fitzgerald's car, which we left in the front yard near the house." The next time Garcia descended to the ranch, Hill would be there to greet him.

Hill, Deputy Jones, Fitzgerald, and two ranch employees, Nievez and Manuel Venegas, stood guard surrounding the home as darkness fell. Hill positioned himself against the side of the house in close proximity to the vehicle, with a view of the mountains, and with access to the home through a side window. The Venegas brothers watched the ranch yard from the wool barn, and Deputy Jones and Fitzgerald covered the other side of the house from a machine shed.

At 2:00 a.m. Jones and Fitzgerald left their post to go into the house to make coffee. Hill watched Deputy Jones walk across the yard toward the wool barn where the Venegas brothers stood guard, bringing them fresh coffee. He heard a movement in the wool barn. Hill stood, drew his weapon, and started toward the barn. He watched the deputy shine his flashlight into the barn to determine the source of the sound. The suspect, Garcia, stood up from his hiding place between the woolsacks and charged the front of the barn with his pistol drawn.

Hill broke into a run. He did not have a clear shot, as Jones stood between him and Garcia. Nievez Venegas quickly drew his .30-30 rifle and fired into the darkness. When Hill arrived at the barn, he found Garcia's body among the woolsacks with a gunshot to the head.

Hill searched Garcia's hiding place and found Fitzgerald's .30-30 and .22 rifles. The .22 revolver lay beside the body, and in the man's pockets Hill found rifle shells and the keys to the car and house.[7]

Although the year was 1955, ranchers such as Fitzgerald often worked alongside law enforcement to protect their property and families, as in the frontier days. However, Hill was selective of any he allowed to be included in the process.

It was said of ranch hands in this remote country that "they rode for the brand," meaning they were loyal to their ranch and would fight to defend it. With law enforcement typically several hours away, and telephones not yet commonplace, those who inhabited remote ranches and villages had to rely on their own ability to defend themselves. This mentality persisted well into the mid-twentieth century and beyond.

Law enforcement and court system authorities understood this fact of rural life and supported it. Justice of the Peace Barry Scobee exonerated Nievez Venegas of any wrongdoing in the Garcia shooting, returning a verdict of "justifiable homicide."[8]

But sometimes the stakes proved higher, such as in 1948 when burglars targeted Fort D. A. Russell, outside Marfa. The burglary of a U.S. military installation fell under federal jurisdiction. Hill received a phone call at his home early Sunday morning, December 18, from John B. Blackburn of Marfa. Blackburn managed the Marfa Air Base and Fort D. A. Russell as an employee of the War Assets Administration (WAA). Requesting assistance, Blackburn notified Hill that several buildings at Fort D. A. Russell had been burglarized.[9]

The U.S. Army established Fort D. A. Russell as protection against border raiding parties during the Mexican Revolution. The post also served as the base for Army Signal Corps biplanes that patrolled the Rio Grande during the Revolution. After changing its name and duty assignment several times over the next quarter of a century, the army deactivated the fort in 1945 and closed it the following year.[10]

Hill arrived at Blackburn's office joined by Presidio County Sheriff Ottis "Blackie" Morrow and his deputy Ernest Barnett. Blackburn informed the officers that the ownership of the burgled buildings remained in question, as the WAA had begun the process of transferring the buildings over to a private concern. Therefore, the federal government may or may not have had jurisdiction in the case.

Hill, who was concerned more with solving the crime and finding the perpetrators than with the question of jurisdiction, moved on to examine the buildings. A total of forty-three porcelain toilets were stolen from the inventories of nine buildings.

Hill searched outside of the Quonset hut structures and found clear tire tracks near each of the nine buildings. The tracks indicated a truck with dual tires on the rear axle; the inside, right rear tire was flat.

Hill and Morrow also discovered footprints of at least three persons believed to have taken part in the burglary. They photographed the tire tracks and prints and then made plaster of paris casts of them.

With the information on the tires and type of truck used in the theft, Hill and Morrow began a meticulous search of the vehicles in town. Knowing that the truck had dual wheels proved especially helpful.

Hill drove slowly through parking lots and down city streets, starting in Marfa. Finally, the search paid off. At the Yucca Motor Court in Marfa, Hill spotted a truck that had tires exactly matching the casts taken. However, the truck had only one right rear tire. Hill searched the area and found a flat tire on the ground near the truck that matched the flat tire track at the burglary scene.

Hill and Morrow determined the identity of the truck owner, Woodie Baker, who worked at Marfa Air Base. Upon telephoning Blackburn, Hill learned that Baker had just left the base and headed into town. Morrow and Hill awaited his arrival behind the Yucca Motor Court and arrested Baker and three other occupants of the vehicle when they parked at the Yucca Court Café.

After Hill collected written statements in which the suspects admitted their guilt, he traveled to El Paso along with Sheriff Morrow and District Attorney Crumpton to recover the stolen toilets, which had been sold there. They were able to recover all of the stolen items.

Hill added the following: "When we arrived back in Marfa from El Paso, we were informed that the W.A.A. had finally determined that the stolen property did, in fact, belong to the U.S. Government. Two F.B.I. Special Agents, Allan M. Oppen and Willard D. Wharton, were waiting to take the case. . . . The four subjects were taken to El Paso, Texas jail by a U.S. Marshall and were charged with conspiring to commit an offense against the U.S. Government."[11]

Gambling was widespread throughout the state in the affluent postwar period. Hardly unique to the Big Bend country, gambling was prevalent in the region since at least the time of the Frontier Battalion. In addition to being illegal after the war, the resurgence of gambling paralleled the growth of the oil industry in West Texas. Much like alcohol consumption during the Prohibition years and in dry counties thereafter, gambling often had the unspoken support of many in the usually law-abiding communities of the region.

Typical equipment for makeshift gambling halls included marble machines, punchboards, and slot machines. Locations of these activities ranged from the back rooms of small cafés and beer parlors to American Legion halls and country clubs. Frequently these operations received support from larger gambling rings out of San Angelo, Abilene, El Paso, or Odessa.

Twentieth-century Rangers worked to rid the state of gambling. From Galveston to Fort Worth, the practice thrived. Communities across the state hosted socially accepted gambling halls targeted by frequent Ranger raids. With so many in the community supportive of the practice, gamblers had an extensive network of informants, and thus Ranger raids often failed.

In 1956, Texas Attorney General Will Wilson made good on a campaign promise to close down illegal casinos in Galveston using the Texas Rangers. Under the direction of Johnny Klevenhagen, captain of Company A, Rangers secured search warrants, organized raids, and destroyed confiscated gambling equipment. However, Company A did not have the manpower to address the widespread problem effectively, so additional Rangers from around the state were called in to assist. Hill reported to Captain Klevenhagen on several occasions and stayed a week or two at a time at the makeshift Ranger headquarters in the Buccaneer Hotel, assisting Company A in this endeavor. Ultimately, after three and a half years, the Rangers succeeded in shutting down organized gambling along the Texas coast.

Gambling establishments in Galveston posed a unique problem. The facilities stretched out into the Gulf on piers. The entry faced Seawall Boulevard, but a bouncer and a long walkway stood between the front door and the gambling activity. With the pressing of a concealed button, the room at the end of the pier received notice to shut down gambling operations. By the time Rangers covered the length of the pier, no evidence of the illegal activity remained. Several such establishments existed in the Galveston area.

In one operation, Hill and another Ranger procured a rowboat and fishing gear. Acquiring the boat proved difficult. The gamblers had "eyes and ears" up and down the coast. Finally, they obtained a boat from a retired law officer. "We were so glad to get a boat," Hill laughed, "we didn't even question what the coffee can was doing in the bottom of the boat."

The Rangers soon found out. The boat leaked and the coffee can served as a great bailer. They rowed to a spot not far from the end of the gambling room. Posing as fishermen out for a night of fishing, they put out their lines but drifted slowly toward the pier.

Gamblers also posted a guard on the bay side of the facility. Hill knew the guard eyed their movements, but he patiently bailed and fished hoping to assure the guard of their innocent activity. He also hoped to get his seasickness under control before stepping up the action.

After several hours the Rangers, assured that the guard did not regard them as a threat, got close enough that they cast a line under the facility and intentionally caught the hook on one of the wooden piers. Bumbling around trying to get the line unhooked, they rowed the boat up close to the water level dock built onto the end of the pier.

The guard came down to meet them. They began their ruse about needing to go under the pier to unhook the line. Once the boat was close enough, Hill stepped onto the small dock, grabbed the guard before he had time to punch the alert button, and pushed him into the bay.

The two Rangers, in their fishing hats and tackle vests, quickly climbed the ladder into the back end of the gambling facility where activities were in full swing. Other Rangers and local officers moved in from the front. The Rangers arrested all the patrons and shut down the facility.[12]

Hill had gambling operations in his own territory to concern him as well. Making a case against gamblers was a difficult proposition. Gambling, like prostitution, proved difficult to prosecute unless the perpetrators were caught in the act. Consequently, gambling hall entrepreneurs constructed elaborate means by which to hide their equipment quickly during a raid.[13]

The district attorney of Pecos County, Travers Crumpton, notified Hill of suspected gambling at the Fort Stockton Country Club. Hill verified Crumpton's information and obtained a search warrant. Assisted by Houston White, Hill planned a raid on the country club.

Hill and White entered the clubhouse through a back door. When they arrived at the dining area, no gamblers remained. But the transformation from gambling parlor back to dining hall had not been entirely complete. The Rangers confiscated three slot machines, four punchboards, a dice table, thirteen decks of cards, and three boxes of poker chips.

Hill arrested the club manager, Jack Sharp. No other club members remained in the building. The local newspaper editor and publisher served as club vice president. Not surprisingly, the paper carried a different account of the event.[14]

Hill had a lengthy correspondence with Captain Cowsert regarding his efforts to shut down gambling in the area. Locations changed frequently, and the clientele proved elusive, despite Hill's tips from informants. In a typical letter to Cowsert, dated July 5, 1948, Hill commented on an ongoing effort to curb gambling in his area. "I was unable to make a marble machine case at the Best Café in Marfa, however, I got two large punch boards there. I checked all of the other places in Marfa and made two marble machine cases and four punchboard cases."[15]

Cowsert and the other Rangers of Company E had their hands full with the oilfield towns of West Texas. In April 1949, Ranger Ralph Rohatsch and Captain Cowsert led a gambling raid at the St. Angeles Hotel in San Angelo. While the raid was under way and Rangers were arresting gamblers and destroying gambling equipment, the telephone rang. Captain Cowsert answered the phone with a casual "hello." A nervous female voice asked if Tommy Brown (a gambler from Abilene) was there. Cowsert had already arrested Brown, but played along, hoping to obtain additional information and for the fun of it.

Cowsert informed the woman that Brown could not come to the phone, but that he would be glad to take a message. The woman pleaded, "Tell him that Captain Cowsert and the Rangers are in town and they are going to raid the gambling room." Cowsert assured her that he would relay the message. He then identified himself as the Ranger captain. She quickly hung up the receiver without any further requests.[16]

7

The Borderland

The real Ranger has been a very quiet, deliberate, gentle person
who could gaze calmly into the eye of a murderer, divine his
thoughts, and anticipate his action, a man who could ride
straight up to death.

Walter Prescott Webb, *The Texas Rangers:*
A Century of Frontier Defense, xv

WHEN Hill first arrived in Alpine, Ranger Bridge passed certain
information on to him. For example, former Ranger Pete Crawford left word for future Rangers regarding a 1938 murder case:
"no parole."[1] The brief message to future Rangers from Crawford
pertained to his investigation of Mr. and Mrs. Francis Black on
the charge of murder. The couple traveled into the Big Bend along
with a young boy, for whom they were guardians. They had managed to obtain a life insurance policy on the boy and traveled to
the Big Bend, under the guise of vacationing, to "collect their insurance."

"After attempts to drown the boy in an area lake proved unsuccessful," Crawford described, "the couple found a tall cliff
and pushed the boy from the cliff, killing him instantly on impact
with the rocky surface below."[2]

Hill received phone calls from the parole board on several occasions regarding the possibility of parole for Francis Black, who

received a life sentence. Hill wholeheartedly agreed with Crawford's assessment; the hardest cases for Hill were those involving people who abused or mistreated children.[3]

Remote locations seem to provide the illusion of secrecy, anonymity, and protection for those involved in crime. As Captain Barry Caver, Company E commander at the time of this writing, explained, "The terrain is rugged and mountainous, which leads some criminals to believe that this is a safe haven for their activities."[4]

In 1948, Hill investigated such a case—a double murder on a remote stretch of West Texas highway near McCamey. Called in on the investigation by District Attorney Travers Crumpton of Fort Stockton, Hill traveled to McCamey, where he began his investigation.

At McCamey, Hill met with Deputy Sheriff Gant. Gant explained that he found two black men, Gene Robinson and Ben Johnson, shot to death in their car. Another man, Leon Hooper, remained in critical condition in the local hospital.

Hill left for the hospital to question the wounded man. Hooper explained that he was in a "negro café" in Odessa when two "Mexican men" approached him and offered him fifteen dollars to take them to McCamey. Hooper accepted the offer and asked two of his friends, Ben Johnson and Gene Robinson, to ride with them.

When the group saw the lights of McCamey coming into view, the Mexican men asked Hooper to stop the vehicle. They got out of the car and started shooting. "Then they robbed us and walked off," Hooper added.

At the crime scene, Hill picked up the trail. He borrowed a horse from a nearby ranch and began tracking the murderers. He followed the trail until dark and then bedded down for the night. Ranger Houston White joined him at daybreak the next morning from a nearby ranch. Hill said, "We followed suspects' tracks into the mountains northeast of McCamey but lost them in the rocky cliffs."

Hill and Houston, now joined by Captain Gully Cowsert, redirected the search. They began to work the ranch country in the direction of the criminals' flight. Along with local law enforcement, they visited every ranch in the vicinity to warn residents of the suspects at large.

"We checked all of the watering places for signs," Hill described the strategy. On foot in the August heat with no food or water, it was only a matter of time until the suspects showed themselves. Hill got word that the suspects had approached an area rancher for food. From there, the Rangers had a new starting point for following their trail.

Rangers, along with the Reagan County sheriff's posse, soon captured the two men, who were nearly dehydrated. The same remote conditions that made possible the concealment of their crime also helped lead to their capture.[5]

An unusual communication method notified Hill of another homicide. In June 1954, Hill spent a rare day in his office at the Brewster County Courthouse, completing paperwork that seemed to increase with every legislative session. For ten years, he shared his small office with the legendary Brewster County justice of the peace (JP) Hallie Stillwell. She arrived in the area with her family in a covered wagon at the age of twelve. Hallie and husband Roy worked a ranch south of Marathon from 1918 until his sudden death in 1948. Hallie continued ranching with her sons and daughter, taking work as a justice of the peace and a columnist for the *Alpine Avalanche* to help support the ranch through lean times.[6]

Sheriff Jim Skinner convinced Stilwell that she should take on the position of JP. "Jim Skinner approached me about being the J.P. I told him I didn't know anything about the law. He said I would do fine," Hallie said. "I enjoyed every minute of it. . . . I didn't exactly like being a coroner, but it was part of the job."[7]

Hallie and Arthur became good friends, as they shared not only an office, but also affection for the Big Bend country and a desire to see justice served.

One day, Hill was pecking away at his Underwood typewriter at an unusually fast cadence considering he used only his index fingers. A telephone call interrupted this undertaking.

The Civil Aeronautics Administration (CAA) radio station at the Marfa Air Base called to relay a message from Game Warden Frank Hamer. Hamer radioed from his airplane to the station to request that they advise Hill of a shooting at Lajitas.[8]

Hamer was the son of famed Texas Ranger Frank Hamer, Sr., remembered for his role in tracking down Bonnie Parker and Clyde Barrow. The younger Hamer also had a distinguished law enforcement career spanning thirty-four years, serving as a Texas Ranger and as a game warden with the Texas Parks and Wildlife Department.[9]

The caller explained that Hamer, while patrolling Lajitas by air, landed after noticing a man waving wildly in the roadway. Lajitas, located 112 miles south of Alpine on the Rio Grande, had no telephone. The man informed Hamer that a Mexican national had shot Jim and Luther Watters. Hamer's aviation radio, via the Marfa Air Base, offered the fastest communication to law enforcement.

Hill immediately contacted Sheriff Skinner, and they rushed toward Lajitas to investigate. Two men lay shot, and the culprit was at large, most likely en route to Mexico. Time was of the essence.

In his state-issued car, Hill flew down Texas Highway 118. Over the great distances he routinely covered, Hill's only "cruise control" was the accelerator to the floorboard. Approaching Study Butte, Hill noticed a swerving vehicle in the oncoming lane of traffic. He slowed. The driver flashed the headlights and waved an arm out the window before pulling over to the side of the road. Hill did the same on the opposite side, parking across from the pickup truck.

Hill started across the highway on foot, believing the driver may have important information. He soon realized that Clinton Fulcher sat in the pickup. Fulcher, the former Brewster County commissioner Hill helped convict for cattle smuggling (see Chapter 5), was currently serving a suspended sentence from the federal court in El Paso.

Fulcher shouted at Hill questions about what he had learned in Lajitas. Hill replied that had Fulcher not created the unnecessary stop on the road, he and Skinner might already be in Lajitas. Fulcher blasted Hill and the Rangers, adding, "You come down here and arrest me for smuggling and let a murderer get away." Hill saw that Fulcher's face was very flushed. He also spoke with a thick tongue and smelled strongly of alcohol.

Hill opened the door to the pickup and directed Fulcher to get out. He informed Fulcher that he was under arrest for driving while intoxicated. Fulcher refused to get out of the truck, squeezing the steering wheel and setting his jaw. Hill deftly extracted Fulcher, handcuffed him, and placed him in the backseat of his state car.

An exasperating disruption to more important business, Fulcher nevertheless posed a safety hazard to himself and others if left to drive down the highway. The only jail in the area was eighty miles north in Alpine. With a gunman on the loose in Lajitas, twenty miles away, Hill and Skinner proceeded with their prisoner in tow.

Hill pulled up to the Lajitas Trading Post, the hub of activity in the border town. The temperature had soared to 110 degrees. Fulcher could not safely remain in the vehicle. Hill spotted a workshop behind the trading post. A porch provided shade to the front of the building. Salt blocks stacked by the corner post created makeshift seating. Hill handcuffed Fulcher to the post and began his investigation.

Fulcher fell asleep soon thereafter. "We had several occasions to pass Fulcher while investigating the shooting," Hill explained, "and he was asleep each time."[10]

Handcuffing Fulcher to the post, in Hill's mind, presented a commonsense solution to the problem at hand—one that would not stand up in today's courts. Hill believed Fulcher was comfortable, given his condition, the location, and the circumstances that precipitated his arrest.

Hill and Skinner determined the identity of the gunman, Hector Cota. As suspected, Cota had escaped into Mexico. Hill filed the proper warrants and notified Mexican authorities. This event exemplified another frustrating incidence of the flight of criminals across the border.

In this instance, however, Hill's tenacity saw justice served. In 1961, Hill received news from an informant that Cota resided in Ensenada, Baja California. Hill believed that Cota would attempt a border crossing there and notified California authorities. The Los Angeles County Sheriff's Department arrested Cota and extradited the prisoner to Texas.[11]

Hill and Skinner returned with Fulcher to Alpine. Hill booked Fulcher on DWI charges. Though Fulcher pled not guilty, he was convicted and fined. He then filed a complaint against Hill that his civil liberties had been violated in Lajitas. Authorities investigated and dismissed the complaint.

Hill's responsibility as a Ranger included the investigation of local officials on suspicion of wrongdoing. In 1951, Hill investigated the Presidio County justice of the peace, J. C. Pool, on a charge of murder. The case began when Hill, along with Presidio County Sheriff Ernest Barnett and District Attorney Norman Davis, were called to investigate a shooting at Presidio. Hill interviewed and took statements from six witnesses, each of whose testimony corroborated the others' stories.

Outside the Grill Beer Parlor in Presidio, Deputy Sheriff Mack Tarwater noticed a truck without a license plate. Tarwater questioned the owner, Jack Jennings, about the missing plate. Jennings argued that Tarwater had no authority to work license plate violations. Several accounts of the event added that bad blood existed between Tarwater and Jennings, escalating the situation.

Deputy Tarwater told Jennings that he was under arrest. Jennings cursed Tarwater, pulled a knife from his pocket, and challenged the deputy. Officer Tarwater grabbed an ax handle from the rear of a pickup truck parked nearby, and the two started fighting.

Jennings overpowered Tarwater, took the ax handle from him, and threw him to the ground. Tarwater called for help. Justice of the Peace J. C. Pool then took the ax handle from Jennings.

Twenty-two-year-old J. C. Pool was the youngest JP in Texas at the time. Pool was a small man: five feet five inches and 105 pounds. Jennings dwarfed Pool, with 190 pounds packed onto his six-foot frame.

Jennings's brother "Boomer" then entered the picture, taking the ax handle from Pool and striking him on the shoulder and neck. Pool drew his .38 revolver from his belt and fired one shot near Boomer Jennings. The bullet missed Boomer, striking an onlooker in the arm.

Simultaneously, Jack Jennings disarmed Tarwater, taking the deputy's pistol from its holster. Jennings fired at Tarwater, striking him in the hand. Attempting to protect Tarwater, Pool then shot Jennings in the neck.

The charge of attempted murder against Pool changed to murder when Jennings died of his wound. After hearing the testimony of onlookers, Hill became convinced of Pool's motivation to defend a third party, by protecting Deputy Tarwater from another shot by Jennings. A jury, after Hill's rare testimony for the defense, acquitted Pool.[12]

Alcohol was often involved in crimes of passion and anger, resulting in murder and attempted murder charges. Reports on many homicides that Hill investigated list the place of the crime as outside a beer parlor.[13]

The beer parlor served as a social gathering place, especially for Hispanic men. Numerous case files report the death of a young Hispanic man after an alcohol-influenced altercation at a beer parlor. Hill regarded the loss of these young lives as a tragic waste. Such cases, combined with his experiences with whiskey runners and DWIs in Seymour, confirmed Hill's strong belief that alcohol was destructive and served no good purpose.

At 3:00 a.m. on August 10, 1950, Hill received a phone call informing him of a murder in southwest Brewster County. Juan Salgado and Martin Ramos, of Marfa, had driven to the Terry Ranch the previous night to visit with friends. They talked and drank beer until 1:00 a.m., when the pair decided to return to Marfa.

Ramos picked up a .30-30 rifle from the corner of the small room where they visited. He decided to take it with him back to Marfa. Ramos's friends, employees of the Terry Ranch, told Ramos he could not take the rifle as it belonged to the ranch. Ramos was enraged—he yelled that he would take the rifle and no one could stop him. With the ineffable logic of the inebriated, he asserted that he might want to kill an antelope on the way to Marfa.

One of the ranch employees, Ramon Gonzales, climbed into the car with Ramos and Salgado as they left. He hoped to claim the rifle and return it to the ranch when possible.

When the three arrived at a gate that blocked the road, Ramos, with gun in hand, stepped out and opened the gate. Salgado drove through the opening, and Ramos closed the gate behind the car. He then walked up beside the driver's window, raised the .30-30, and shot Salgado through the head. He turned the rifle on Gonzales and shot him in the arm. Gonzales managed to get control of the car and drive back to the ranch. Ramos made his escape toward Mexico.

Once word finally reached Hill, only a few hours remained until daybreak. Hill assembled all the law officers and resources available in the area. He knew only too well that the criminal's flight to the border would be swift. With a large search team in place, Hill hoped to intercept Ramos before he reached the border, sixty miles to the south.

Hill explained the scope of the effort: "We notified Department of Public Safety, U.S. Border Patrol and secured airplanes, jeeps and bloodhounds and a posse of approximately thirty men." Before dawn, Hill met with DPS Troopers to set up roadblocks and to position other resources.

Hill, Skinner, Barnett, and the posse picked up the trail at the scene of the crime at daybreak. The officers covered the area from the crime scene to the Mexican border about sixty miles away. Border Patrol officers dotted the border and headed north in an attempt to box Ramos in. Aircraft combed the region looking for signs of the suspect, while runners waited by the radio communications post at Marfa to relay any messages to the posse on the ground. Bloodhounds and their handlers worked with the posse scattered across the area of the trail headed southward.

They trailed Ramos toward Mexico, picking up the trail and losing it again through the mountains. Hill ended his case report as follows: "Ramos was able to elude the posse and cross into Mexico. Extradition procedure was begun in an attempt to bring Ramos back to Texas for trial."[14]

Hill would have another opportunity to apprehend this criminal after Ramos made the mistake of seeking work on the American side of the border.[15]

The Big Bend has historically been a haven for fugitives from the law. Hill worked several cases that involved the search for criminals wanted in other parts of the state, who risked the harsh conditions in an attempt to evade capture.

In a typical incident, a man wanted for attempted murder in

Van Horn, Texas, escaped jail and took his chances in the Big Bend. On February 3, 1949, Hill received a phone call from Sheriff Capehart of Van Horn requesting Hill's assistance in finding Jimmie Barrow, believed to be hiding at the Dunagan Ranch or the Evans Means Ranch, both near the border.

Hill, Sheriff Capehart, Rangers Bob Coffey and Earl Stewart, and Presidio County Sheriff Morrow drove to the Dunagan Ranch on the Rio Grande. Upon arriving at the ranch, Hill questioned workers at the stock pens. The workers had seen Barrow at a line shack downriver. They directed the officers to a ranch road—in reality, more of a cow trail—that headed to the destination.

When the officers arrived at the line shack, which rested on a small bluff above the Rio Grande, it was empty, but recent tracks indicated one person on foot headed north. Hill knew that Barrow had set out for the Evans Means Ranch, fifteen miles to the north. "The Evans Means Ranch is a very isolated place back in the mountains and is impossible to reach by car," Hill explained. The officers started the drive in cars but soon abandoned them. They walked the remaining miles in rocky, mountainous terrain.

As they finally approached the Means ranch house, they saw a man astride a galloping white horse dart out of the barn and up a nearby canyon. Capehart recognized the rider as Barrow.

Hill stepped onto the wooden porch of the house. Evans Means opened the door before Hill could knock. Means eyed the visitors and addressed Hill, asking what they wanted. Hill questioned Means about his knowledge of Barrow. Means indicated that he had not seen or heard from Barrow since before his incarceration in Van Horn.

Cold, tired, and in no mood for the runaround, Hill addressed Means more sternly when he asked about the rider on the white horse. Means again denied any interaction with Barrow, claiming to know nothing of a white horse. Hill responded that they would have a look around and form their own conclusions.

The officers easily followed the fresh horse tracks, which ended in the narrow canyon where "the trail became too rocky and steep for even a good rock horse." There they found the white horse tied to a bush. Footprints continued up the canyon.

Hill, irritated at Means's lies, untied the horse and led him the short distance back to the house. He walked the horse up onto the wooden porch and banged on the door. When Means finally answered, Hill held up the coiled reins in his hands and curtly asked, "Does this jar your memory?" Means, stunned, quickly admitted that Jimmie Barrow had left his house on the white horse as the officers walked up.

One officer stayed at the ranch after having arrested Means for harboring a known fugitive. Hill and other officers began to track Barrow on foot into the mountainous terrain. "We followed Jimmie Barrow's trail, on foot, until late the next afternoon, February 5, 1949," Hill explained.

The trail led to an abandoned house near the Mexican border. Jimmie Barrow was asleep inside when officers arrived. He awoke and drew his weapon, but seeing four officers drawn down on him, he "did not attempt to fight."[16]

The remoteness of the borderland served all too often to disguise the crimes and flight of criminals in the 1940s and 1950s as it had in the previous century. When Hill was asked in later years about the case that stood out most from his years of service as a Ranger, one event invariably came to his mind. The possibility of death in the career of the law enforcement officer always exists, typically unstated but understood. That possibility became a tragic reality for Presidio County Sheriff Ottis "Blackie" Morrow. Morrow was not only a colleague of Hill's, but also a friend. Morrow's murder and the ensuing investigation would torment Hill for years to come.[17]

8

"El Corrido de José Villalobos"

It is like going into the jaws of death with only twenty-six men in a foreign country where we have no right according to law, but as I have went this far, I am going to the finish with it.

———

Captain Leander McNelly,
from "The Memoirs of William Callicott,"
ed. Chuck Parsons (Texas Ranger Hall of Fame)

THE NEWS came by phone, awakening Hill at 3:00 a.m. on March 12, 1950. Sheriff Ottis "Blackie" Morrow of Presidio County was dead. Hill dressed quickly in the dark, not certain when he would return home. For the moment, he knew only that the search for answers would begin on the side of a dark highway, ten miles north of Presidio.[1]

Morrow had worked closely with Hill on many cases. The people of Presidio County elected him sheriff in 1947, the same year that Hill arrived in Alpine. Morrow had lived in the area since 1932. He fought fires at Marfa Army Air Field and worked as a mail carrier on the Presidio route before venturing into law enforcement. He knew everyone in the small community and was well liked and respected.

Morrow enlisted in the navy during World War II and returned home with his sights set on serving as sheriff. After winning a reelection bid in 1949, he did not live to serve out his second term.[2]

Arthur Hill, *left,* **and Presidio County Sheriff Ottis Morrow
in front of Presidio County Courthouse, Marfa, Texas (1949).**

Passing through Marfa and turning south toward Presidio, Hill encountered the flashing lights of the ambulance returning to Marfa with Morrow's body. He could only help Morrow now by capturing his killer.

Hill completed the seventy-five-mile trip, arriving at the scene at 4:20 a.m. He could see Morrow's patrol car in the ditch on the east side of the road. The vehicle faced south, and the driver's door was wide open.

Hill greeted Border Patrol chief Calvin Darst, who had command of the scene until Hill's arrival. Along with Presidio County deputies Mack Tarwater and Ernest Barnett, Darst briefed Hill on the current findings.[3]

Darst explained that four Marfa teens discovered Morrow at approximately midnight. The four boys—Jimmie Plubly, Otis De-Volin, Bill Wheeless, and W. A. Oatman—were driving home from Presidio when they saw headlights shining from the ditch into oncoming traffic and stopped to help. When they saw Morrow, close to death, two of the boys returned to Presidio to call for help, leaving the others with Morrow.[4]

Hill walked around Morrow's car to the opened driver's door while he listened. Blood was visible along the hood, the doorframe, and the front seat of the vehicle. Darst, the first officer on the scene, had found Morrow lying on his back across the front seat with his head against the closed passenger-side door.

Darst said that ambulance personnel examined two wounds. Morrow's forehead showed blunt trauma that split the skin to the skull. In addition, he had a bullet wound in the left chest in the region of the heart.[5] Hill saw the corresponding blood on the seat, forming the scene in his mind as the details unfolded.

Tarwater added that the sheriff's holster was empty and his handcuffs were missing. They searched the area but did not find Morrow's gun. Tarwater had worked that night in Presidio with Morrow until 11:00 p.m. when Morrow left to go home to Marfa. Deputy Tarwater indicated that the sheriff's nightstick, which lay on the front seat all day as they worked in Presidio, was also missing.

Darst handed Hill a black pocketbook. The wallet, Darst revealed, was found under Morrow's body. Hill opened the leather wallet. Inside he discovered a paper identification card bearing the name José Villalobos. Another paper ID bore the name Manuel Villalobos and had a crudely cut photo attached.

The photo on the card showed a young, smiling Hispanic man with slicked-back black hair and a thin mustache. He was dressed fashionably in suit jacket and tie.

Another photograph found in the wallet was a nightclub photo showing a man and woman dancing. The man's face, identified on the back as José Villalobos, was cut out. The photo cut from the nightclub picture was attached to the identification for Manuel Villalobos—apparently an attempted fabrication of an ID.[6]

José Villalobos and unknown woman. Villalobos's picture
was cut from this larger photograph and adhered to a false ID. Found at
the crime scene, this evidence gave Rangers the name of their suspect.
Courtesy Marfa Public Library Junior Historians Collection.

Darst handed Hill other papers found near the scene in a preliminary sweep of the area. Hill reviewed another identification
paper, this one bearing the name Juan Carrasco Navarette. The
identification bore the same fold marks as a letter addressed to
the priest of a Catholic church in Pecos, Texas. The letter requested a copy of Navarette's birth certificate.[7]

Initially, it appeared likely that a prisoner overcame Morrow or
that a traffic stop yielded fatal results. The murderer or murderers
already had a five-hour head start. Waiting on daylight, Hill began
to cast a wide net for the primary suspect, José Villalobos.

He immediately notified Ranger Captain Gully Cowsert, Highway Patrol Captain George L. Morahan at Pecos, and sheriffs of all
adjacent counties. He ordered roadblocks thrown up on all roads
in Presidio and adjoining counties. All available Border Patrol
and BAI personnel mobilized to search the Rio Grande border.[8]

With the distances and the number of people involved, a central command center would prove invaluable. Hill called Austin to request use of the portable DPS two-way communications unit. The DPS acted quickly, moving the unit into the Presidio County Courthouse at Marfa. Highway Patrolmen from Van Horn operated the communications center throughout the manhunt.[9]

Hill also notified Homer Garrison of the murder. Garrison sent Worth Seaman, a fingerprint and ballistics expert from Austin, in the hope his expertise might prove helpful.[10] Seaman planned to fly from Austin in the DPS plane. Weather conditions made air travel impossible for Seaman, who ended up driving the ten hours to the scene. The same conditions made aviation support unavailable to the manhunt in the first days.

With all available resources in place, Hill awaited the coming dawn. He stood in the middle of the gravel highway examining each shadow as the sun began to illuminate the scene. With the tracks visible, Hill and other officers slowly retraced Morrow's trail from the previous night.

One mile up the highway, Morrow's trail U-turned, showing that the car had stopped previously at the end of four long skid marks pointed northward in the direction of Marfa. Evidently, Morrow braked heavily at this point. Here officers found Morrow's nightstick as well as additional evidence, which began to paint a clearer picture.

"A trail of blood led from the west side of the road to the fence on the east side of the highway," Hill stated. The barbed wire fence on the east side of the highway noticeably sagged above a point where a pool of blood lay drying on the rocky ground. A wounded Morrow had probably supported himself against the fence before returning to the west side of the road.

Another trail of blood evidenced Morrow's return to the vehicle, likely after the assailant had gone. Blood along the hood of Morrow's car showed that Morrow had supported himself in a desperate attempt to get in the car and seek help.

Hill initially reported, "Evidently, the sheriff had been

wounded here, went across the highway, then came back to his car and attempted to drive back to Presidio."[11]

From Morrow's wounds and the fact of the missing firearm and handcuffs, Hill theorized that Morrow had arrested Villalobos. Then, Villalobos must have disarmed Morrow and shot him with his own weapon. More questions remained.

By midmorning Hill's posse consisted of Captain Cowsert, Ranger Forrest Hardin, Sheriff Jim Nance of Sanderson, Sheriff Charley Baker of Fort Stockton, and Deputy Sheriff Ernest Barnett of Marfa.[12] Hill assigned "three of the most experienced trail men" to the scene to find footprints or other evidence. The rocky terrain, however, revealed no signs of the murderer's flight. Officers also checked the U.S. customhouse at the International Bridge. After questioning twenty-five people who crossed the river that day, they had found no useful information. A day was lost and time was crucial.[13]

**Sheriff Morrow's Smith & Wesson .38 on .44 frame used in his murder.
Courtesy Richard Morrow.**

Hill had an ace in the hole—BAI River Rider Juan Ochoa. Ochoa's reputation and experience as a tracker were renowned in the region. Born in 1894, Ochoa was the great-grandson of Ben Leaton, a Chihuahua Trail freighter who established Fort Leaton.[14] Ochoa learned his craft growing up on the Ochoa Ranch, twelve miles up the river from Presidio. "Juan could tell one horse track from another and determine the weight of a rider," Hill said.

Beginning in 1919, Ochoa served as a scout and tracker for the Eighth Texas Cavalry stationed in the Big Bend. His first assignment was to gain information on Pablito Villa, Pancho Villa's brother. Ochoa's commanding officer during this time was a young captain by the name of "Captain Harry," Harry Truman. Decades later, when President Truman's train made a whistle stop in Marfa in 1949, he remembered Ochoa and inquired about him.[15]

Ochoa's expertise had him in demand by all branches of area law enforcement. He worked with U.S. Customs, Border Patrol, Mexican officials, and other officers. According to the *El Paso Times,* officers would simply decide, "We need Juan, go pick him up."[16] Ochoa worked under a special commission as a Presidio County deputy sheriff held since 1932.

Ottis Morrow's
Presidio County sheriff's badge.
Courtesy Richard Morrow.

Hill contacted C. M. Wikes, of the BAI headquarters office in El Paso and requested permission to "borrow" Juan and his unique services. Wikes granted Ochoa a temporary leave to participate in the search for Villalobos.[17]

Monday, March 13, the second day of the search, began with a promising development. Ochoa discovered footprints three-quarters of a mile from the crime scene. Hill, Ochoa, and the posse of officers followed the tracks to a point about seven miles away where they disappeared into the rocks and animal tracks at a goat camp.

With the trail obliterated, Ochoa began a new search south of the camp. He walked his horse slowly and scanned the country-side ahead of Hill and the other officers who trailed behind, giving him room to work. Ochoa stopped and dismounted. He bent over, picked something up off the ground, and walked back to Hill. Ochoa looked up at Hill and opened his hand to reveal an unfired cartridge. The shell was identified as one of Morrow's hand loads. They were on the right trail.[18]

Hill believed that the suspect still wore Morrow's handcuffs. Tracks showed elbows striking the ground as the suspect tripped in his nighttime flight across the rough terrain. Captain Cowsert described the findings of the manhunt to the press, "There was evidence that he [Villalobos] had terrifically hard going. He had fallen into ocotillo [cactus] bushes. The marks made in the ground where he fell among the rocks and cactus, indicated he was handcuffed."[19]

From the goat camp, Ochoa once again picked up Villalobos's trail. The tracks led due south to a canyon in the Rio Grande about twelve miles upriver from Presidio. Hill and the posse followed the tracks and soon found where the trail had "cut"—gone into Mexico.

Hill sat on his horse, staring in disbelief at the footprints in the sand descending into the river. The cold now penetrated as sleet

began to fall. Unfortunately, the strain of the near freezing temper-
atures and days of strenuous tracking on foot and horseback
through rugged terrain took a toll on Ochoa's bad heart. Moments
after identifying the killer's trail into Mexico, Ochoa collapsed.

Hill and the posse quickly gathered Ochoa and rode as hard as
possible back to the highway. Officers loaded Ochoa in a vehicle
and delivered him to the nearest medical assistance. Hill and the
others returned to Marfa.

Overall, an estimated fifty officers searched some five hundred square miles of borderland in a pursuit described by Sheriff
Joe Campbell of El Paso as the "biggest border manhunt in history." The search included horseback patrols, jeeps, and airplanes
from all branches of law enforcement in the area and from as far
away as El Paso and Uvalde.[20]

The *El Paso Times* reported, "Participating in the border manhunt were: Arthur Hill, Forrest Hardin and Gully Cowsert of the

Investigators involved in the Villalobos manhunt,
left to right: Captain Gully Cowsert, Juan Ochoa, Ranger Arthur Hill,
Sheriff Ernest Barnett, Ranger Forrest Hardin (1950).

Rangers; Sheriff O. Capehart of Culberson County; Sheriff Jim Skinner of Brewster County; Sheriff Jim Nance of Terrell County; Sheriff Tom Gray of Jeff Davis County; Lake Webb of the U.S. Customs Service at El Paso; all of the border patrolmen of the Marfa–Alpine–Fort Davis area; State Highway Patrolmen from Uvalde, Pecos, Kermit and Fort Stockton; City Marshall Floyd Williams of Marfa; Deputy Sheriff Ernest Barnett of Marfa, and Deputy Sheriff Mack Tarwater of Presidio." The list, although incomplete, showed the scope and scale of the investigation.[21]

Arriving at the Crews Hotel in Marfa, Captain Cowsert made a statement about the posse's findings and fielded questions from the regional press. "A few men are staying on," Cowsert said, "but it is up to the Mexican police now. Chances are lessening hourly for a quick capture. We fear that some of the man's friends may have given him aid." Cowsert's fear proved to be well founded.[22]

Hill met up with Mack Tarwater and Calvin Darst, the small contingent of American officers who would "stay on." The men continued into Ojinaga, where they joined Mexican rangers José Gonzales and Carlos Chavez, as well as Ojinaga city police, in the investigation.

Mexican rangers quickly discovered the trail from the Mexican side of the river. Their investigation provided information that Villalobos had crossed the Rio Grande at dawn the morning after Morrow's murder. Two workers on an irrigated farm adjoining the river claimed to have seen Villalobos cross.[23] "He showed them a pistol," Hill explained, "telling them that he had killed the sheriff at Presidio with the sheriff's own pistol."[24]

From there, Mexican authorities received information that Villalobos continued to the small, remote community of El Paradero, approximately fifteen miles from the murder scene.[25] Gonzales and Chavez searched the community, but found no sign of Villalobos.

Local legend holds that Villalobos obtained help from the residents, some of whom were distant relations. He hid from investigating Mexican authorities by burying himself in some hay. Eusebio "Chibo" Baiza removed his handcuffs, and he obtained a horse to cross the desert and mountains of El Pegüis Canyon en route to his hometown of Cuchillo Parado on the Río Conchos to the east.

Once Mexican officers left El Paradero, and with a horse and provisions, Villalobos was able to make his escape deeper into Mexico.[26] Villalobos, however, would not have an easy trek. Seventy miles of canyonland and desert lay between him and his destination, his hometown of Cuchillo Parado. Villalobos crossed the two-thousand-foot-deep El Pegüis Canyon, the most formidable natural obstacle in the Big Bend region, in his quest for refuge.[27]

Back in Ojinaga, investigators pursued other possibilities. Hill and Mexican Ranger José Gonzales followed a lead that put Villalobos at a local bar with another man just hours before Morrow's murder.

Investigators received a break in the case when they learned through informants that Villalobos likely would return to Cuchillo Parado. Mexican ranger Carlos Chavez, two other Rangers, Presidio County deputy Mack Tarwater, U.S. Border Patrol chief Calvin Darst, and local Ojinaga officials piled into four-wheel-drive jeep pickups and cut across the rough terrain toward Cuchillo Parado.[28]

Villalobos arrived at his mother's home in Cuchillo Parado only a few hours before the group of officers descended on the town at 5:00 p.m. on Wednesday, March 15, almost three days since he began his flight.

Chief Darst recalled, "The Mayor [of Ojinaga, Pascual Valdez,] and a local officer [Chief of Police Francisco Urias] went to the Villalobos home. Mr. Tarwater and I stayed in the jeep, as we had no jurisdiction, and the rest searched the house. About then, Villalobos ran from his sister's home nearby. Ranger Chavez ordered him to stop and he did so. We started to Ojinaga with him."[29]

Officers recalled that Villalobos's coat was marked with a bloody handprint on the left shoulder. His beard had grown out and his clothes were tattered by brush and cactus. He certainly looked the part of a man who had been on the run from the law for three days, on foot and horseback, across some of the most unforgiving terrain in the world.

Hill met up with the group in Ojinaga upon their return. He watched officers pile out of the back of the pickup and eyed Villalobos as he exited, held firmly around the arm by Ranger Chavez. The group moved into the small adobe jail on the courthouse square.

Although outside of Hill's jurisdiction, Ranger Chavez insisted that Hill take part in questioning the prisoner, as Hill had the most familiarity with the crime scene. Hill recounted Villalobos's statement about the events of that fateful night. "He [Villalobos] said that he was attempting to get a ride out of Presidio when Sheriff Morrow drove up and asked him for his citizenship papers or passport. When Villalobos informed Sheriff Morrow that he had no papers, the sheriff arrested Villalobos as an alien."

Villalobos said the sheriff searched him, took his pocketbook, and reviewed the papers inside. Morrow then told him to get in the car. After going about ten miles, Villalobos stated that he grabbed the sheriff's nightstick that was lying on the seat and hit him in the forehead. He then took Morrow's revolver from his holster. The sheriff stopped the car, and they got out on opposite sides of the car. The sheriff came around the car, and Villalobos stated that he shot four times at the sheriff and saw the sheriff grab his chest and run across the road in the darkness.

"Villalobos stated that he ran out into the rough country west of the highway and towards the Rio Grande River where he crossed about daylight on the morning of March 12, into Mexico," Hill recounted.[30]

The *Odessa American* reported, regarding the apprehension of Villalobos, "The capture was a partial climax to one of history's most intense manhunts on the rugged mountain country on both sides of the U.S.-Mexico border."[31] The statement proved to be prophetic. The incident garnered national and international press attention. It had mobilized the largest law enforcement force ever assembled in the remote region, with the exception of military units during the Mexican Revolution.

The story, however, did not end or even climax with the apprehension of Villalobos in the mountain village of Cuchillo Parado. The incident quickly took on international proportions as conflicting perceptions of justice clashed at the border. Villalobos's plight solicited a strong, sympathetic response in the Mexican community, while Hill remained determined to see Villalobos tried in an American court.

Mere hours after Villalobos's incarceration in the Ojinaga jail, at approximately 1:00 a.m. Thursday, March 16, a crowd of "shirt-sleeved onlookers" gathered in front of the jail.[32] Crowds continued to grow in number and in aggressiveness as the days wore on.

Back in Texas, Hill once again called on Juan Ochoa and his unique skills in his attempt to bring Villalobos to stand trial in the United States. Ochoa had completely recovered from the illness he experienced during the manhunt. The *El Paso Times* reported, "Despite a haywire heart, you couldn't keep Juan down. He was soon up and around, carrying on in his very quiet and unassuming way."[33]

Ochoa's familiarity with both cultures, both languages, and officers on both sides of the border made him an invaluable asset. Ochoa worked behind the scenes to try to effect the release of the prisoner into American custody. Hill reported, "We think he can pull the necessary strings for the Villalobos release sooner."[34]

As mentioned previously, the red tape of international procedure and politics was often bypassed through interoffice cross-border cooperation, particularly in the case of those wanted for murder. Mexican officers, satisfied with a prisoner's connection with the crime, would often "push" the prisoner back across the border, unknown to any but those most closely involved.

Coordinating with Hill and Ochoa, Mexican officers made plans to "smuggle" Villalobos across the border. Local stories tell of the officers placing the prisoner in a car trunk for many hours waiting for an opportunity. In the end, the officers got cold feet. Somehow, news of the attempt leaked out, and the growing crowd that surrounded the white stucco jail in the Ojinaga town square grew more agitated.[35]

The mob, and public sentiment against the Americans, continued to grow. Immediately after Villalobos's arrest, American officers and officials were granted the opportunity to speak with the prisoner. Now, with state and national attention focused on the event, government officials allowed no interaction. Hill explained, "Our attempts to fingerprint and interrogate the prisoner were denied by the Mexican government."[36] Presidio County Attorney Norman Davis added, "The situation is very tense."[37]

Immediately after Villalobos's incarceration, County Attorney Davis, along with District Attorney Travers Crumpton of Fort Stockton, began work on extradition. The lengthy process originated in the county attorney's office. Extradition requests then went to the Texas governor, Allan Shivers, and then to the U.S. State Department, U.S. Embassy, Mexican Foreign Office, Mexican Attorney General's Office, and ultimately to the president of Mexico, Miguel Alemán. Crumpton, in an effort to save time, drove the papers directly to Austin himself to deliver to Governor Shivers.[38]

Meanwhile, on the other side of the river, Mexican ranger

Carlos Chavez traveled to Ciudad Juárez, where Chihuahua Governor Fernando Foglio Miramontes was in meetings. Chavez delivered Morrow's .38-caliber pistol, used in the murder, to Miramontes. Chavez reported to the press, "Mexican authorities hope to make an example of Villalobos by giving him the maximum twenty-year sentence. They want to discourage the killing of police."[39]

Governor Miramontes did not share Chavez's sentiment. In a Mexican radio broadcast at the time, a journalist reported, "Gov. Miramontes said in Juárez that Villalobos was not the man wanted for the crime." Miramontes used the flood of anti-American sentiment in the case as a political boost, telling the Mexican media a different story than the one he told American officials.[40]

While local tensions mounted, Governor Miramontes ordered Villalobos transferred to a Chihuahua City jail for "safekeeping." Miramontes assured American authorities that Villalobos would remain in prison until extradition status was determined. However, it is likely that the move was designed to deflect American influence and attention from the case.[41]

The *presidente municipal* (mayor) of Ojinaga, Pascual Valdez, had other ideas. Valdez would not accommodate Miramontes's telegraphed request to transfer Villalobos to Chihuahua City. Valdez claimed that he must have a written order from the state police to allow such a release. The mayor attempted to stall the process to allow for American extradition, and to snub state government interference in local matters.

Valdez responded to the increased tensions and the growing number of "onlookers" by ordering armed troops from the nearby garrison to stand guard on the roof of the white-stuccoed jail in the Ojinaga town square.[42] This precautionary move only added fuel to the fire, however.

With the possibility of Villalobos's move to Chihuahua City, American officers feared the worst. "All we can do now is sit back and let the government red tape go to work," Mack Tarwater commented. "I expect they'll be taking him to Chihuahua City in a few days." A beleaguered Captain Cowsert added, "Then we'd never get him."[43]

Unsatisfied with the course of events, Hill obtained an arrest warrant and personal request for Villalobos's release from the president of the United States to the president of Mexico. "I got a warrant from the President of the United States, the only one I ever got," Hill noted. "But the Mexican President wouldn't honor it."[44] Juan Ochoa likely had some pull in bringing special attention to this case from then-president Harry Truman.

By Friday, Villalobos had changed his story from the one given to arresting officers Wednesday night. Among other inconsistencies with his previous statements, Villalobos claimed that he shot Sheriff Morrow in self-defense, and that Morrow told him to "shut up" and shoved the blackjack (nightstick) down his throat. Villalobos had no marks around his mouth or throat that would indicate this had taken place.[45]

Villalobos's initial statement to officers echoed Hill's theory, based on the evidence at the scene. Exactly what transpired that cold winter night only two men knew, and one of them was dead.

Despite Valdez's attempts to keep the prisoner in Ojinaga, Mexican authorities would soon transfer Villalobos to Chihuahua City. If any efforts to remove Villalobos were to transpire, the time was at hand.

Hill and Cowsert, against protocol and Mexican law, decided to attempt their own "unofficial" extradition. They planned to bring Villalobos back to the United States, with assistance from Mayor Valdez, Police Chief Urias, and others. Once they were back across the river with Villalobos, Mexican law would have no bearing. An American court could then try Morrow's killer. In Hill's mind, this was the only alternative remaining to ensure justice.

Hill, Cowsert, and Ochoa met in a hotel room in Presidio to plan their ill-fated venture back into Mexico to finish the job they started. Hill could see the river and the outskirts of Ojinaga out the window—so close and yet so far. He recommended using Ochoa to contact Mexican officials informally to ensure a low profile for their common objective. Captain Cowsert, however, had other ideas.

Frustrated at the likely move of the prisoner inland and determined to get the man who killed a sheriff in his region, Cowsert tired of waiting and playing the political game. He was ready to play his heavy hand and damn the consequences.

Cowsert laid out his plan to enter Ojinaga, quickly get Villalobos, and get back across the river without confrontation. Elements of surprise and speed minimized the threat posed by any resistance. Mexican officers at the jail supported the move. Mexican customs officers at the border created the main obstacle, but Cowsert and the others could run the border stop.

The captain began to bark orders to Ochoa. The more demanding Cowsert became, the more Ochoa withdrew. Hill watched the interaction and tried to defuse Cowsert's approach. He knew Ochoa well enough to understand that Cowsert's gruff manner was counterproductive. When Cowsert poked his finger at Ochoa's chest to emphasize his instructions, Ochoa had had enough.

"Don't you tell me what to do," Ochoa warned Cowsert, pushing his hand away. Cowsert responded, "You can go straight to Hell. We'll go in there and do it ourselves."[46]

Hill watched the screen door slap shut behind Ochoa. The tension-filled room suddenly quieted. Hill knew that losing Ochoa was a mistake. Nevertheless, the job at hand awaited, and he would follow his captain.

Hill secured two Border Patrol officers to help with translations and the carload of Americans headed to the International

Bridge. Gazing out the passenger window, he watched the water pass under the bridge. They entered Ojinaga, the larger of the two border towns, with its narrowed streets, stuccoed storefronts, and colorful signage.

The jail adjoined the town square, with a large church at one side. Many townspeople were gathered in the square. Most milled around in front of the jail. All eyed the approaching vehicle.

Hill scanned the crowd and found a welcome sight. "We got across the river," Hill explained, "and I saw Juan. He beat us over there." Although frustrated with Captain Cowsert's methods, Juan would not abandon his friends. Ochoa had taken up a position inconspicuously in the crowd.[47]

Hill, Cowsert, and the Border Patrol officers parked and entered the jail from the back alley. They began to arrange Villalobos's transfer with their Mexican officer allies. Increasing noise in the plaza caught their attention, and the Border Patrol officers stepped out on the porch to assess the situation.

Word had spread quickly of the Americans' arrival. Some people in the crowd were now wielding weapons. Hill described the restive townspeople as follows: "It wasn't just a little bit, and I bet there were two hundred of them around us."

Tempers had escalated when the pursuit of Villalobos was under way, and only worsened since his incarceration. The people of Ojinaga believed that American officers bribed local officials to remove Villalobos—the "influential Americans" waving money and power. A cause célèbre, Villalobos had come to represent the poor worker, defending himself against American prejudice.[48]

Soon the mob's frenzy reached fever pitch. The two Border Patrolmen came back into the jail, bolting the door behind them. "Arthur, we don't like the looks of this," one spoke breathlessly with wide eyes. "We're going back across the river. If you're smart, you'll do the same. I think they're going to kill you."[49]

The Mexican and American officers watched out the window as the crowd turned violent. A photographer for *Life* magazine who was covering the international incident climbed up on the fender of a bus and took pictures of the crowd surrounding the jail. "It wasn't long after he snapped his camera that they had him down," Hill reported. "There were about ten or fifteen people on top of him."[50] A Mexican immigration officer seized the camera, taking it from the angry crowd, claiming that "the film must be developed and censored."[51] After the mob ripped the camera from the photographer, they left him and surged closer to the jail.

The camera incident fueled the mob's fury and resolve, which were now directed at the Texas Rangers inside the jail. Hill watched the sea of rifles and fists turn toward the jail. Enraged shouts in Spanish needed no translation.

Out of their jurisdiction, with an armed mob bent on their removal, Hill and Cowsert realized that they would be lucky to get themselves out, much less with Villalobos. "We'd better get away from here," Cowsert said. "I expect that would be a good idea," Hill agreed.[52] But how could they get away unseen?

With the help of Mexican officers, Hill and Cowsert bundled up in serapes to disguise themselves. They waited for an opportunity to escape to their vehicle unnoticed. The crowd was concentrated at the front of the building, but some people had spilled over into the back alley. One sighting of the Rangers would incite chaos.

The throng began beating on the front door and walls of the jailhouse. More moved around to the rear of the building, attempting to surround it. Hill and Cowsert had run out of ideas. They readied their weapons, prepared to go down fighting.

A sudden commotion caught the attention of the group outside. They turned and stepped away from the jail back into the square. Those from the alley ran to the square to see the activity.

Unforeseen help came from within the crowd to make it possi-

ble for the Rangers to get away. "We got down to our car because
Juan stirred them [the crowd] up so we could go," Hill explained.
"I don't know what he did, but it got us out of there."[53] Ochoa's
diversion created a small window of opportunity for Hill and
Cowsert to make their escape.

A Presidio resident reported to the *El Paso Times,* "If anybody
had tried to take him [Villalobos] out of the jail, they would have
had a small war on their hands." At times, discretion is the better
part of valor. Despite having two Rangers and only one riot, this
was one of those times.

Hill and Cowsert wasted no time beating a path back to Presidio. Once on the American side of the bridge, they stopped.
They could still hear the mob.

After their escape, the crowd must have turned on the jailers.
Hill watched across the bridge. The horde now made their way
through the streets. American sympathizers were marched to the
bridge where gunmen forced them out of the country to the elation of the remaining crowd.

"They ran every officer that had helped us across the river,"
Hill recalled. Hill and Cowsert helped the Mexican officers reen-
ter their country at Del Rio. They could not return to Ojinaga. Per-
ceived by the populace as giving in to American influence and
taking bribes, they were forced to relocate and start new lives
elsewhere.[54]

Mexican officers lending aid to the Americans were not the
only ones to feel the sting of their involvement in the six-day ordeal. Mayor Pascual Valdez, who emerged as a central figure in
the tug-of-war with Miramontes, was formally stripped of his position. Colonel Antonio Gallegos Landeros influenced the political powers in Chihuahua City to remove Valdez from office.[55] A
local power play came about as a result of the Villalobos uproar,
with far-reaching ramifications for the local political stage for
years to come.

After the Rangers left, and the Mexican officers were ejected, state officials moved Villalobos to Chihuahua to await trial. A Mexican court found Villalobos not guilty due to lack of evidence. "He was tried in Mexico," Hill recounted, "but no evidence was ever requested from Austin and no one in the United States was subpoenaed to appear. They eventually turned him loose."[56]

Today, in the Ojinaga town square, the people still recall the crowd and the day the Americans came for Villalobos. In the village of Cuchillo Parado and throughout northern Chihuahua, they still sing a ballad about this event, "El Corrido de José Villalobos." The song serves as an oral history and lends some insight into the feelings of the Mexican community about the episode. In the English translation, much of the poetry of the original version is missing, but the feelings of the composer are evident:

"El Corrido de José Villalobos"
The Ballad of José Villalobos

Sirs, I am going to sing
To those of you here
What criminal things happened
Of these two brave men

Ottis Morrow was his name
The brave American
It was said that he lost his life
At the hands of a Mexican

Morrow left Presidio
Around eleven at night
Like all of us supposed
He was by himself in his car

On the road he was on
He met Villalobos
He asked for his passport
And his identification

Villalobos answered
Not in a malicious way
That he did not have his passport
Nor papers to present

Ottis Morrow answered
Very disturbed and excited
I'll take you to jail
So they can send you to the other side

Villalobos resisted
In the Mexican way
And very quickly
He grabbed the police stick

He fired on the sheriff
With his taken gun
The American lay dying
He left for the border

Villalobos crossed the Bravo
And once on this side
He went toward his home
That is Cuchillo Parado

Americans came
Local women and men
Asking that he be taken out of jail
So that he could leave

The people were opposed
Some of the law were in agreement

Some pictures were taken
Of the Chief of Immigration

Good-bye brave Ottis Morrow
Your whole town mourned
You were serious in your work
You were a brave man

Good-bye José Villalobos
I'm saying good-bye to you
If they give you liberty
Don't stay around here

The one who wrote these verses
Is not a poet or a songwriter
Just a poor worker
Who works in the fields[57]

Hill continued to contact informants in Mexico inquiring about Villalobos's whereabouts until Hill's death in 1987. He remained determined to bring the fugitive to justice and to serve the outstanding murder-with-malice warrant if Villalobos so much as set foot on American soil again.

Fortunately for Hill, the work of a Texas Ranger in the Big Bend was not all as intense and gut-wrenching as handling the case of Ottis Morrow. In the early 1950s, Hill took a brief break from his Ranger duties. He had the opportunity to tell of his experiences, and of the Big Bend country he loved, to director Stacy Keach, who was then bringing the work of the Rangers to life on the small screen in homes across America in his *Tales of the Texas Rangers.*

The Texas Ranger legend has served as the topic of mystery and adventure in works of poetry, fiction, film, and song. As early as the Mexican-American War, news dispatches chronicled the

heroic exploits of Rangers, laying the basis for the enduring legend. Soon the image of the Rangers as fearless fighters, securing
justice on the frontier, permeated popular culture.[58]

The legend continued to grow in the twentieth century, gain-
ing its greatest popularity in the character of the "Lone Ranger."
Created in 1933 for Detroit radio station WXYZ, the masked rider
immortalized the Ranger image in radio, movies, and television.[59]

The Tales of the Texas Rangers, starring Joel McCrea, aired on
NBC radio from 1950 to 1952. The popular radio show made a
successful transition to television with a program of the same
name starring Harry Lauter and Willard Parker. The televised
Tales of the Texas Rangers aired on CBS from 1955 to 1957 and
were rebroadcast until 1959.

The success of the series stemmed in part from the fact that
episode story lines were based on actual case files of the Texas
Rangers from 1830 to 1950.[60] Adding to the credibility, retired
Texas Ranger Captain M. T. "Lone Wolf" Gonzaullas served as
technical adviser. Producers submitted each script to the DPS for
review prior to filming.[61]

In August 1951, at Homer Garrison's request, Hill hosted the
Tales film crew during their Big Bend excursion. Director Stacy
Keach, Sr.; a writer; and a camera operator needed background
shots of the West Texas landscape for their preliminary filming
schedule.

Hill escorted the crew down into the Big Bend and along the
border. He brought them to the ghost town of Shafter and to the site
of an unmarked grave currently under investigation. Captain Gonzaullas and Captain Bob Crowder accompanied this excursion.[62]

Keach wrote a note of thanks to Ranger Hill: "We certainly did
enjoy being with you and appreciated your taking us through the
Big Bend country. I'm sure that without you to guide us out, we
would still be down there." The drama of real crimes all too soon
replaced the staged ones.

Rangers and guests examining human bones, evidence in an investigation.
Sitting: Captain Bob Crowder, Arthur Hill. Standing, *left to right:* Stacy Keach Sr.,
unknown cameraman, and Captain M. T. Gonzaullas (ret.).

In 1957, Hill had served as a Ranger for ten years. His girls
were grown and in college. He began to look toward new challenges. He completed the test for Ranger sergeant, received the
promotion, and transferred to the only opening at the time, in
Company B. Hill went from horseback pursuits, and the border
culture of the Rio Grande, to Mafia investigations and labor
strikes in one of the largest, fastest-growing cities in the nation,
Dallas.

9

Doin' Time in Big D

A Ranger is an officer who is able to handle any given situation
without definite instructions from his commanding officer, or
higher authority.

———

**Captain Bob Crowder, TRHF, "Texas Ranger Robert A.
'Bob' Crowder: 1901–1972"**

THE YEAR 1957 was one of transition for the Ranger Service
and for Texas Ranger Arthur Hill. For the first time since their association with the Department of Public Safety in 1935, the
Rangers underwent broad-based reorganization. Hill, now sergeant of Company B in Dallas, adjusted to his new position and
new surroundings.

The DPS had grown in size and scope since its inception in
1935. Every legislative session brought the agency new functions
and responsibilities. Texas's postwar growth and urbanization resulted in rising crime and traffic. The DPS continued to maintain
public safety by meeting these needs as they arose.

The 1950s in particular saw drastic increases in departmental
responsibilities. Beginning in 1951, the DPS assumed the task of
tracking and maintaining records on known communists in
Texas. In 1953, the DPS added a narcotics branch, funded for the
first time since 1937. Initially, the unit assigned only one Texas

Ranger to the detached duty. By 1955 the narcotics branch consisted of ten agents, as it would remain until funding was increased to add ten more agents in 1968. Before the existence of the narcotics branch, Rangers handled all drug-related investigations. And with the number of agents dedicated to narcotics limited, most Rangers continued to do so throughout the 1950s and 1960s.

By 1957, the DPS infrastructure consisted of fifteen branches, many with overlapping functions. The department needed a more efficient organizational structure. As a result, a major reorganization plan went into effect on September 1, 1957.[1]

Regional headquarters offices for the DPS were established in Dallas, Houston, Corpus Christi, Midland, Lubbock, and Waco, with a limited crime lab at each site. A DPS major served as chief administrator at each headquarters location.

The Texas Rangers were then organized into six companies under regional commands headquartered in the same locations as those of DPS. This move increased the Ranger companies from five to six, as well as moving headquarters all over the state from Austin. The Rangers had been organized into five commands and all headquartered in the capital city since the Rangers' initial association with DPS.[2] A Ranger captain still headed each Ranger company, now assisted by a sergeant.

Ranger companies (A through F) were located at the following DPS regional headquarters: Company A (Houston), Company B (Dallas), Company C (Lubbock), Company D (Corpus Christi), Company E (Midland), and Company F (Waco).[3] Rangers were assigned posts in various towns in each company's region.

Originally, in the reorganization scheme, Ranger captains reported to DPS majors in charge of their respective region. This chain of command did not last long, however. The Rangers' activities varied greatly from those of the Highway Patrol. Rangers needed to have the flexibility to perform their duties without conferring constantly with higher authority. By December 1957, Ranger captains in each company again had direct responsibility to the director of the DPS.[4] Reorganization not only changed some Ranger company boundaries and headquarters locations, but also added paperwork and protocol for Rangers in the field, historically not a favorite part of the job description for any Ranger.

The most publicly visible change that came about because of reorganization, however, has since become a Texas tradition. In 1958, all DPS uniform designs were consolidated into a single one, creating the tan uniform with blue tie and blue and red stripe down the pants as is in use today. A vendor created the new color, "Texas tan," exclusively for the Texas DPS. Various divisions within DPS now wore the same uniform differentiated by shoulder patches.

The department reported, "Since its adoption, the Reorganization Plan has shown to have accomplished its purpose. It has brought better Department services closer to the people and has proved to be more economical and efficient than the previous operating structure."[5]

In March 1957, Hill began his assimilation into the position of sergeant of Dallas's Company B. Ten years previously, when Hill started as a Ranger, Houston White informally mentored him into the position. This process allowed him to demonstrate ability with on-the-job oversight.

Hill went through a similar training process prior to assuming the post of Ranger sergeant. This training was more formal and academic, placing greater emphasis on the administrative duties that Hill would assume. On April 1, 1957, his first day as a Ranger sergeant, Hill reported to Acting Chief Bob Crowder in Austin for his "special assignment" (i.e., training for his new responsibilities).

Crowder arrived in Austin in October 1956. He assumed the position of acting chief of the Rangers while awaiting confirmation and legislative funding for the new position planned under the upcoming reorganization. The legislature, however, neglected to appropriate funds for the Ranger chief position. Crowder then reluctantly accepted the position of DPS Region V commander in Lubbock.[6]

Chief Crowder's "training school" included familiarization with all aspects of DPS entities with which the Rangers interacted, including Identification and Records, Criminal Laboratory, and Criminal Intelligence Service. Hill worked closely with Sergeant J. L. Rogers of Headquarters Company, acquainting himself with the responsibilities of the position. He attended seminars and conferences, including the DPS Safe Burglary Conference, Means of Combatting Organized Crime, DPS Homicide, and the DPS Criminal Investigation Seminar.[7]

Texas Rangers Company B (1957). *Left to right:* **Captain E. J. Banks, Ernest Daniel, Lewis Rigler, Jim Riddles, Red Arnold, E. J. Wimberly, Bob Badgett, Byron Currin, Jim Ray, George Roach, Sergeant Arthur Hill.**

Acting Captain E. J. "Jay" Banks headed the Texas Ranger Company B in 1957. In addition to Captain Banks and Sergeant Hill, Company B had eight Rangers posted within its region: Jim Riddles (Breckenridge), Byron Currin (Vernon), George Roach (Stephenville), R. L. "Bob" Badgett (Forney), Ernest Daniel (Dallas), Lewis Rigler (Gainesville), R. M. "Red" Arnold (Mt. Pleasant), and Jim Ray (Athens).

Captain Banks received his appointment to the Ranger Service on the same day as Hill, September 1, 1947. A native of Munday, Texas, Banks had spent the majority of his career as a Highway Patrol officer and as a Ranger stationed in and around the Dallas area. Banks had served as Company B sergeant since 1955, under then-Captain Bob Crowder. He became acting captain of Company B when Crowder moved to Austin to assume the position of Ranger chief (for which the legislature ultimately failed to provide funding). Banks assumed the captaincy post on September 1, 1957, six months after Hill's appointment as sergeant.[8]

Hill moved into his office in the Company B headquarters building on April 25, 1957. Built in 1936 as part of the Texas Centennial celebration, the Texas Rangers post was featured on many newsreels shown in movie houses across the nation at that time. Texas Ranger headquarters for Company B was referred to as the "Fair Park Station."

The log cabin structure looked much like a Ranger outpost of the previous century. Snakeskins, deer heads, and buffalo hides adorned the walls. Rifles, pistols, knives, canteens, and other equipment were on prominent display throughout the building, representing the Ranger history that linked the officers of the day with their storied past. The building, located on the state fairgrounds, seemed to be an architectural anachronism tucked away in the sprawling urban frontier of the Dallas–Fort Worth metroplex.[9]

Hill may have felt much the same way as he began his adjust-

Sergeant Arthur Hill in his Company B Fair Park Station headquarters office (1957).

ment to the facts of city life—buildings that obscured the horizon and people who outnumbered cattle. Hill joked that it was a good thing the office had such a tall radio antenna, or he would have had a hard time finding his way to work every day in the big city.[10]

On his first full day of work in the Dallas office, Hill became involved in a case that made headlines and sent shockwaves throughout the criminal underworld. The Rangers had previously received information from an informant that Gene Paul Norris and others planned the theft of a $500,000 payroll delivery at Fort Worth's Carswell Air Force Base on April 30. As the base was a federal installation, the FBI worked with Rangers on the investigation.

Hill and Banks left Dallas for Fort Worth on the morning of April 27, 1957. There they met with Tarrant County Sheriff Harlan Wright and FBI agents, led by Agent Bill Murphy, to set up electronic surveillance on Gene Paul Norris, William Carl Humphrey, and James Papworth.[11] FBI agents wired the suspects' hotel room. Officers assembled in a nearby room awaiting their return.

Hill and the others sat in silence, listening. Finally, voices broke the stillness as Norris and his partners discussed the details of their plot. Norris's calculated plan to achieve his ends was chilling. "We knew when they were going to rob it," Hill explained, "and that they were planning to kill one of the employees, a woman and her young son."[12]

The murderous scheme held no surprise to those familiar with Gene Paul Norris. Considered one of "gangland's chief executioners," it was estimated that Norris had killed more than forty people in his career in organized crime.

A native of Oklahoma, Norris made a name for himself in the North Texas underworld. He allegedly took part in the sensational robbery of $258,000 from Cuban nationals who were staying at the Western Hills Hotel in Fort Worth. The men were awaiting an arms sale to support the revolution in Cuba. "Gene Paul was one" of the robbers, Captain Banks insisted, "but he was never convicted."[13]

Norris changed his modus operandi from robbery and theft to murder for hire. He worked as an assassin for and within the world of organized crime in Fort Worth. The Rangers and area officers knew of many of these killings, yet lacked sufficient evidence or witnesses to prosecute them. The motivation to solve these crimes was not very high either, as the victims were known gangsters as well.

Officers knew of the plot to rob the bank at Carswell Air Force Base before the fact. This time an innocent woman and her child were in danger. The woman, Elizabeth Barles, lived in a secluded area on Meandering Road, not far from the base. Norris planned to enter the woman's home, kill her and her son, and obtain keys and credentials to enter the bank unnoticed. "Norris was going to get her car and drive through the base gate before the bank opened," Hill explained. "He'd use her door keys and be there waiting for the delivery when they got there with the soldiers' payroll."

The woman's car displayed a base sticker that allowed easy entry to the gated compound. During the morning rush, gate guards typically waved cars with stickers in without stopping them. Norris hoped the same would be possible to enable escape.[14]

In addition to the detailed plans of the robbery, officers also learned of Norris's practice run the day before, April 29. "The day before the robbery, they were going to have a dry run," Hill revealed, "and we were going to be there waiting for them."[15] If officers were to have a chance to capture the elusive Norris before innocent lives were lost, the time was at hand.[16]

Norris kept busy in the weeks leading up to his arrival in Dallas for the Carswell heist. He and "Silent" Bill Humphrey conducted business in Houston before arriving in Dallas. There, among other activities, they brutally murdered local gambler Johnny Brannan and his cancer-stricken wife in their home. A shotgun blast to the head killed the Brannans—the shotgun was Norris's weapon of choice.

Company A Ranger Captain Johnny Klevenhagen previously warned Norris to stay out of Houston. "If there are any shotgunnings around here, I'll be coming after you. Get out of town and stay out." Klevenhagen investigated the Brannan murder and knew that Norris had not heeded his warning. Soon there was evidence to support his assumption.

A Houston police officer reported to Klevenhagen that on the night of the Brannan murder he pursued a green 1957 Chevy matching the description of the vehicle seen in front of the Brannan home. The vehicle eluded the officer, but he added that the occupants threw something out of the window during the chase. Klevenhagen searched the area indicated and found two pistols in the grass on the side of the road. Both pistols were traced to Norris.

Klevenhagen now had enough evidence to obtain an arrest warrant for Norris and Humphrey. He and the Rangers of Company A turned Houston and surrounding areas upside down looking for the suspects, but to no avail.

Cato Hightower, Fort Worth police chief, contacted Captain Klevenhagen after learning of the outstanding warrant issued on Norris. Hightower informed Klevenhagen of Norris's plans in Fort Worth on April 30. Captain Klevenhagen joined the Rangers of Company B, the FBI, and local authorities as they put into motion the chain of events that ultimately led to the end of Norris's reign of crime.[17]

Officers devised a plan to minimize public exposure and maximize the possibility of trapping Norris and Humphrey. The plan involved catching the pair on the day of their practice run as they approached Elizabeth Barles's home. When asked about letting the pair carry out their plans and catching them in the act, Chief Hightower responded, "No! These men were too dangerous. We had to prevent this."[18]

The plan was set into motion. Rangers and FBI units patrolled the area where Norris was expected, intending to radio other units into position when they spotted the suspects.

Hill rode in his assigned state car, 96-B, with Ranger Jim Ray driving, as Ray was more familiar with the roads in the area. Chief Detective Andy Fournier joined Hill and Ray in their surveillance of the Casino Beach area, watching for Norris.

When the FBI radioed that they had spotted Norris, in a green 1957 Chevy, and had a tail on him, the Ranger units moved into position. Along with the FBI, three DPS vehicles participated in the surveillance.[19] Captain Banks, Captain Klevenhagen, Chief

Hightower, Detective Captain O. L. Brown, and Sheriff Wright occupied the first car, located on Meandering Road near the home of the woman. Officers also were situated inside the woman's home and around the property to ensure her safety.

Ray positioned the vehicle in the parking lot of the Beachcomber Inn at the intersection of Meandering Road and the Jacksboro Highway. There he, Hill, and Fournier waited. In a third DPS vehicle, Ranger Ernest Daniel, along with George Brakefield and Robert Morton of the Sheriff's Department, patrolled near Carswell AFB, farther out on the Jacksboro Highway.

Banks also posted Rangers at all Red River crossings, into Oklahoma, in case Norris made an escape. Sharpshooters manned the gates of Carswell AFB.[20] The trap was set.

Ideally, Norris and Humphrey would start driving on Meandering Road toward the woman's house, practicing their route for the following day. Hill and Ray would pull in behind and block off Meandering Road from Jacksboro Highway. Norris then would meet Banks and Klevenhagen, boxing in the criminals. The best-laid plans went awry.

Hill, Ray, and Fournier waited for Norris's green Chevy at the intersection where Norris would make his turn. At 4:00 p.m., the FBI radioed the Rangers, pinpointing Norris's position as he made his way toward the Rangers' trap.

Hill watched the green car draw closer. When he could positively identify the vehicle, he radioed that he had Norris in sight. The FBI discontinued their tail.

Norris's Chevy turned onto Meandering Road. Hill and Ray waited briefly, and then pulled in behind Norris, blocking exit to the Jacksboro Highway as planned. Norris and Humphrey continued up Meandering Road, toward the woman's home, as expected. Captain Banks pulled out into the road to complete the blockade, but Norris and Humphrey quickly realized what was happening.

Humphrey gunned the Chevy, cut across a muddy field through two fence lines, and made his way back out to the Jacksboro Highway. Captain Banks's Dodge sped down Meandering Road to the highway, passing Hill and Ray, whose vehicle faced away from the highway. Banks turned onto the Jacksboro Highway and caught up with the pair as Humphrey maneuvered the vehicle out onto the road from the muddy field. The men in the two cars exchanged gunfire as they raced down the road.

Hill and Ray quickly turned around in the narrow road and accelerated back onto the highway, following close behind Banks. All three cars soon exceeded speeds of 115 mph with frequent exchanges of gunfire in both directions. Chief Hightower described, "Every time the car would turn right, Gene Paul would fire at us from his window in the front seat. We'd see the flash and we'd return fire."[21]

The trio of vehicles flew twenty-one miles down the highway before Norris turned off on a dirt road topped with crushed caliche. Rain had turned the road slick with mud. "We were crowding them pretty close," Hill explained. "They tried to take a corner too fast, slid, and got stuck in some bushes in the ditch lining the road." The road followed a rain-swollen Walnut Creek, three miles east of Springtown in Parker County.[22]

Norris and Humphrey piled out of the wrecked car, headed toward the bank of the river for cover, and opened fire on the officers. Banks, Klevenhagen, and local officers quickly exited their car and returned fire. Humphrey, although already hit, began staggering across the creek, while Norris turned to run up the bank.

Hill and Ray slid to a stop almost immediately behind Banks's car. Before the vehicle completely stopped, Hill hopped out and opened fire. "They got out of the car and started shooting and so did we," Hill remembered. Ray exited and prepared to fire when Klevenhagen yelled, "He's getting away, give me a gun!" Klevenhagen had depleted his ammunition in the ongoing pursuit. "I had my shotgun in my hands," Ray explained, "and I just tossed it to him. We heard Norris give a scream like a banshee and then came a full burst from Jay's [Banks's] M-3."[23]

When the smoke cleared, the criminals lay dead—Humphrey on a sandbar in the middle of the creek with twenty-three gunshot wounds; and Norris, with sixteen, closer to the water's edge. With the chaotic barrage of gunfire now silenced, only the sound of the creek remained. Hill stepped into the running water, grabbed hold of Norris, and pulled him up onto the bank of Walnut Creek.

When asked years later about his reaction to the event, Hill responded, "These people were killers. It was either some of us or them. It hasn't worried me one bit because they needed killin' and they got what they deserved."[24]

The investigation did not end at Walnut Creek. While Rangers pursued Norris and Humphrey toward Jacksboro, the FBI arrested

Ranger Sergeant Hill, *center* **(wet pants legs), pulls Gene Paul Norris from Walnut Creek (1957). Courtesy** *Fort Worth Star-Telegram* **Photograph Collection, University of Texas at Arlington Library.**

James Papworth at his home on the charge of conspiring to rob a Federal Reserve Bank. Norris had moved from Papworth's Cadillac into the passenger seat of his 1957 Chevy, prior to initiating the dry run to the Barles house. While one car of FBI agents tailed Norris to the Rangers' trap, the other picked up Papworth, following him to his home.[25]

The following morning, Rangers Hill, Banks, and Badgett returned to Fort Worth to question Papworth. Initially, the FBI attempted to gather information from Norris's accomplice to no avail. Captain Banks next met with Papworth—still nothing. Papworth remained frozen with the fear that Norris would kill him if he revealed any incriminating information. Although officers tried to convince him that Norris was dead, Papworth remained convinced they were lying to get him to "roll over" on Norris.

"They wanted me to get a statement out of him," Hill explained. He had watched a nervous Papworth evade questions posed by the FBI and Banks. He entered the interrogation room and studied Papworth. Attempts by other officers to convince him that Norris was dead had already proven futile. The solution seemed obvious—let him see for himself.

Hill exited the room with a handcuffed Papworth in tow. "I took him to the morgue," Hill explained. "He was real afraid of Norris. He was afraid to talk because Norris would kill him—and he would have if he wasn't dead."

The coroner pulled Norris's body out of the cooler. Hill unzipped the body bag and stepped back. Papworth peered in at Norris. He saw for himself that no threat remained from Norris. "After that," Hill explained, "he told me . . . everything."[26] Papworth began revealing information on the spot, over Norris's dead body, at a speed that made Hill's note taking difficult.

Organized crime activity became widespread during the late 1950s. Hill's records during this time show numerous leads followed in the investigation of such activity. Typical cases related to gambling, drugs, or illegal alcohol, and were principally based in Fort Worth.

Fort Worth's reputation as a gambling playground began not long after the Texas Centennial celebration in 1936. Amon Carter, a chief promoter and benefactor of Fort Worth, pushed the city as the ideal site for Texas Centennial festivities. When Dallas was selected to host the celebration, Carter set out to make Fort Worth the place where visitors came to play.[27]

In the years that followed, many drinking and entertainment establishments popped up along the Jacksboro Highway, a main artery to "dry" West Texas. Not only did bootleggers come to Fort Worth and purchase liquor to sell in the western part of the state, but oilfield workers and ranchers came to frequent Fort Worth's entertainment venues to "paint the town."

Nightclubs such as the Chateau Club, Ringside Club, 3939 Club, Rocket Club, Sportsmen's Club, Top of the Hill, Four Deuces, and Carter's Casa Ma?ana lined the Jacksboro Highway. Most of the establishments were legal enterprises, but more than a few were fronts for illegal gambling and drug and alcohol trafficking.

The most difficult barrier to success in closing down an illegal club was catching the illegal activity in progress. Club owners usually knew of impending raids through leaks at all levels of local law enforcement. District Attorney Howard Fender turned to the Texas Rangers to try to "clean up" the Jacksboro Highway, thereby limiting local officials' knowledge of his efforts. Hill and the Rangers of Company B staged raids and investigations on area clubs with sporadic success.

Coordinated investigations of Fort Worth gambling intertwined with those of other organized crime activities. Hill, local officials, and the FBI completed extensive investigations into the doings of Dallas and Fort Worth crime bosses Nick Casio, Jett Bass, Andy Carteiss, Kenneth Davis, and other known members of the "Dixie Mafia." Investigations that began before Hill's arrival in Dallas would continue long after his departure.

From organized crime to organized labor, Hill faced new challenges unlike those found in the brush country and mountains of the Big Bend. In the fall of 1957, Lone Star Steel workers in the East Texas town of Daingerfield instigated a wildcat strike that resulted in beatings, bombings, sabotage, intimidation, and other violence, immobilizing the region's economy. The Rangers, led by Hill, descended on the town to maintain law and order amid the turmoil.

10

The Lone Star Steel Strike

They were men who could not be stampeded.

Colonel Homer Garrison

THE STRIKE began on September 21, 1957. Before it was re-
solved, it affected 3,600 employees and left the small East Texas
communities in Cass and Morris Counties paralyzed with fear.[1]

Built in 1943 to support war mobilization, Lone Star Steel encompassed multiple locations. The main plant near Daingerfield
produced steel ingots and pipe. Open-pit mines for limonite and
other ores used in the manufacture of steel were scattered
throughout the region.[2]

Lone Star Steel was the principal employer in the rural area.
Before the plant opened, whiskey and sweet potatoes were the
area's main products. Nine of ten workers were recruited locally,
most from farms and small sawmills. Area workers gained their
first experiences with industrial jobs and with a labor union at
Lone Star. The plant revolutionized the economy and standard of
living in the area. With families, friends, and neighbors divided
on the issues underlying the strike, emotions ran high.

As a "wildcat strike," it did not have the union's formal sanction. In fact, the contractual agreement between the United Steelworkers Union and Lone Star Steel prohibited strikes. Therefore, Lone Star Steel obtained an injunction banning the mass picketing of gates and other entrances to the plant.

While not officially sanctioning the strike, the union did encourage it. At issue was the procedure for filling temporary vacancies. Certainly, other grievances and circumstances, as well as emotions on both sides, clouded the matter.[3]

The protests began without incident. Captain Banks first reported to Daingerfield to assess the situation on September 25. Banks returned to Dallas the following day, instructing Hill to maintain surveillance on activities and to suppress any trouble that might develop.

Hill immediately drove to Daingerfield and contacted Rangers Red Arnold, Jim Ray, and Byron Currin. Rangers patrolled the striking area throughout the night. They found that strikers complied with the injunctions against mass picketing, issued by Judge Robertson. Initially, demonstrations were peaceful and nonviolent.[4] This assessment would soon change.

Hill and the other Rangers returned to their posts while continuing to monitor the situation. In the following weeks, tensions in Daingerfield and surrounding areas mounted as many of the striking workers returned to work. Those still striking were fired and new workers—"scabs"—were hired. Many of the new workers came in from as far away as Alabama and Pennsylvania, where steel plants had closed.

Threats became prevalent on both sides of the strike line. Cars and homes were vandalized. Fights broke out. Fires were set, and shotgun blasts pelted homes and businesses. The area was a pressure cooker about to explode. An area newspaper publisher wrote that "unbridled chaos" reigned in the counties surrounding the Lone Star Steel plant.[5]

It became evident that the Rangers must intervene. However, the DPS chain of command was now more involved. In the past, Rangers had worked under direct order of the Ranger captain, the director of the DPS, the governor, and even the attorney general of Texas. With reorganization precariously in place, Rangers now received orders and instruction from the DPS regional commander—in this case, Major Guy Smith.

When the time came to take action, Captain Banks remained in Dallas. Among other issues, Banks resented the new chain of command under reorganization. He described Smith as a "fine man," but did not believe he had the training or qualifications to take on the "special powers that Rangers had always assumed in cases of emergency, insurrections, etc."[6] As a result, Major Smith dealt directly with Hill to get the job done.

By October 17, on orders from Major Smith, Hill returned to Daingerfield. This time, he remained for the duration of the strike, directing the Rangers and Highway Patrolmen involved. Hill called on Rangers Ray, Arnold, Wimberly, and Daniel to join him in Daingerfield. From the beginning of their involvement, the Rangers maintained a neutral position in the matter of the strike. They made clear their purpose: the "protection of life and property and the enforcement of laws in the wildcat strike area."[7]

By the time the Rangers arrived, the tension within the community was palpable. Along with Highway Patrol sergeants Evans and Robertson, they met to devise a plan to address the mounting violence. Hill established a command post at the Daingerfield Motel. From there he developed the plan of operation, which involved patrols of the area, periodic roadblocks to check for firearms and explosives, surveillance of company gates for violence toward workers at shift changes, surveillance of union hall activity, and response to emergency calls.[8]

Rangers and Highway Patrolmen were on duty in rotating shifts, working twenty or more hours a day. The motel room had become the "Ranger Camp" of the modern time, serving as a command post, makeshift dining room, and sleeping quarters for Rangers working in close proximity under stressful conditions.

Rangers also took statements from those who were involved in or witnessed acts of violence. They collected evidence and investigated violent incidents in order to prosecute those involved. Perhaps most important, the Rangers' presence represented the hope for law and order. In fact, violence in the towns and at the gates of the plant was quelled as a result of their visibility. Aggressors, however, then focused their attacks in rural areas.

So it went for the next three weeks. Reinforcements, including Rangers Rigler, Krueger, Currin, and Horton, soon joined other Rangers and Highway Patrolmen assisting local authorities. A total of seven Rangers and twenty-five Patrolmen, headed by Hill,

Rangers at Lone Star Steel strike, Daingerfield, Texas (1957).
Left to right: Red Arnold, Sergeant Arthur Hill, and Byron Currin arrive at Daingerfield to deter strike violence.

served an area of 5,000 square miles with a population of two hundred thousand.[9]

After the beatings of two plant workers, nonstriking workers began to illegally carry concealed firearms for protection. Plant security, overseen by Rangers, began collecting firearms from nonstriking workers as they came to work, to gain a handle on a combustible situation. "We've given no one the right to carry a gun," Hill reported to the local paper. "Those found violating the laws concerning the carrying of weapons will be prosecuted."

Despite Hill's warning, the incidence of shotgun blasts fired into houses or cars increased. One such blast narrowly missed the invalid mother-in-law of a plant worker. In response, Rangers increased roadblocks throughout the area, checking for weapons and evidence of explosives.[10]

The violence and threats of violence were not limited to those involved in the strike. Innocents were often threatened or used as pawns. Hill's records of this time include hundreds of statements of threats to children and families of workers and strikers. Children were kept out of school and parishioners stayed home from church for fear that threats would be acted upon or that they would be caught in the midst of violence.[11]

In one example, Ranger Red Arnold was checking on the safety of a woman at home alone with four children. Someone had thrown a large rock into the plate glass window of her home. As a result, the woman and her children spent the night locked in a bedroom, afraid to come out.

Concerned that the safety of the woman and her children could not be ensured because of the limited number of officers, Arnold asked to see her husband's guns. He selected a carbine and instructed her in the proper use of the rifle to protect her home and family. Arnold told the woman that if she had any more trouble, she should aim in the direction of the noise, empty the clip, and call him. He would come and see if she had shot anything.[12]

Rangers discovered the identity of some individuals causing trouble, and arrests were made. But cases such as these would take too long to come to trial for results to have an effect on the growing chaos.

With the increased violence and threats, the public became more leery of talking and sharing information with the authorities. Hill attempted to ease people's fears by reporting his beliefs to the newspaper: "This is the work of a small band of fanatics. You always find them in a situation like this."[13]

In the rural economy, which now relied almost exclusively on the Lone Star Steel plant payroll to drive the cash flow of area businesses, the financial loss hit the entire region hard. Rangers, Highway Patrol, and local law enforcement continued their watch on the plant gates, small towns in the region, and rural homes, but the pressure cooker, fueled by desperation, was about to explode.

Over the next week, events transpired that changed the face of the strike. On the night of October 26, a blast roared through rural Morris County, shaking all area towns with the power of a small earthquake. Saboteurs had blown up two eight-inch gas pipelines, which they believed served the Lone Star Steel plant. "It was definitely sabotage," Hill reported. "It looked like they were blown up by dynamite or nitroglycerin. They were blown up where they were easy to get to, in a ditch where the pipe was exposed."[14]

The saboteurs' target, the Arkansas-Louisiana Gas pipeline, served residential areas as well as a nearby hospital. The blast left thirteen thousand people without heat on the coldest night of the season, which reached a low of twenty-seven degrees. Lone Star Steel, which was served by Humble Gas, was unharmed.

On October 29, another bomb ripped a hole in the loading platform of Irvin Oil Company, blowing out windows and shattering gas pumps. Irvin Oil was a leading shareholder in Lone Star Steel.

Next, a parked truck, loaded with pipe from the steel plant, was destroyed by dynamite thrown through the window from a passing car. A local paper reported, "Ranger Sergeant Hill is pressing a search for bombers who have blasted holes in pipelines and other property."[15] On the evening of October 29, a fourth explosion shook the towns of Lone Star and Daingerfield, coming from the direction of the Union Hall and Lone Star Lake. Hill and other Rangers investigated around the lake but found no evidence. Hill speculated that the explosive material was set afloat on a log and thus the evidence submerged upon detonation. Evidence later would be found at the bottom of the lake that substantiated the theory.

Within a week, four bombings, four shotgun blasts fired into homes, and uncounted telephone threats had terrorized the strike area. Public opinion turned strongly against the extremists and their destructive tactics. Lone Star Steel posted signs promising a $10,000 reward for information leading to the arrest and conviction of anyone causing injury to an employee or an employee's family. A reward of $5,000 was offered for information on anyone causing damage to the property of any employee.[16]

The *Longview Daily News* commented, "Sergeant Hill and his men have done a wonderful job, sleeping only three hours a night or less, but like the men at the Alamo, they need reinforcements." On orders of the governor, Major Guy Smith dispatched additional officers to the strike scene. "We are going to control that situation over there regardless of how many men it takes." Five more Rangers and sixteen additional Highway Patrol officers arrived in Daingerfield on October 31, Halloween morning.[17]

After receiving word that the reorganization plan regarding the Ranger hierarchy would be "scrapped," Captain Banks joined the other Rangers in Daingerfield on Halloween morning. After first informing the *Longview News Journal* of his arrival, Banks met with Hill. Hill and Banks, along with other Rangers and Highway Patrol officers, studied a large aerial photographic map of the eight-county area in which incidents, threats, and dynamite explosions had occurred. They reviewed existing plans for patrols, roadblocks, and duty assignments.[18] With Halloween

night approaching, the Rangers wanted to make clear the serious-
ness of the situation. Banks announced, "Anyone found outside
their property wearing a mask would be arrested."

The children of Daingerfield had no Halloween. There was no
trick-or-treating, no jack-o-lanterns in the windows. The streets
were deserted. Teachers warned students that the slightest disturbance outside a house might scare the occupants into acting
hastily and firing their weapons. Ranger Lewis Rigler hosted a
get-together for teens at the community center.[19]

In stopping cars at roadblocks and on patrol throughout the
night, Rangers found that the citizens of the area were ready for
the strike to end. Captain Banks remembered, "Most didn't ap-
prove of the violence. Everyone we talked to seemed ready to get
back to work."[20]

Finally, negotiations between Lone Star Steel and the United
Steelworkers Union achieved results. Lone Star's owners agreed to
rehire strikers without prejudice, with the exception of the strike
leaders. The union called a meeting, and soon thereafter the
Rangers received notice that the forty-three-day strike was over.

Although the strike had ended, work remained for the
Rangers. Lewis Rigler calmed an anxious crowd at the rehiring
station. He assured them that each would receive a position based
on seniority, not on a first-come, first-served basis.

The throng created a dangerous situation. They had already
pushed out a plate glass window. Ranger Rigler shoved his way to
the front of the crowd. Rigler utilized an unorthodox, yet effective
crowd control tactic. He got up on a chair, raised his bullhorn,
and got the people's attention. "Y'all are all pressing too much,
and there is no need of it—someone might get hurt." Then he
added, "Just think of what it would be like if you were all buck
naked and pressing like that!" Rigler noted that they backed off
considerably after that.[21]

Hill stayed at Daingerfield until November 7, 1957, in a super-
visory capacity as Rangers prepared evidence to present to grand

juries in Cass and Morris Counties relative to the numerous investigations completed during the strike.

The Lone Star Steel strike of 1957, despite many acts of violence and threats of more, ended without fatalities. Unfortunately, this would not be the last strike at Lone Star. The strike of 1968 saw even more violence and ultimately several deaths before its resolution.[22]

Ranger Lewis Rigler reminisced with Hill about that time, "You were sergeant in the fall of 1957, at that Lone Star Steel strike. We all stayed there in that hotel in Daingerfield and caught hell night and day. You learn what a man is like when you put him under pressure, and we found out you were a good one."[23]

Strike situations were, for many years, the difficult responsibility of the Ranger force. Caught between labor and management, many Rangers compared working a strike to being in the middle of a war. Most Rangers experienced that unenviable position at least once during this era of the labor movement's resurgence amid civil rights legislation and industrial development.

During the turmoil of the next decade, the Rangers found themselves embroiled in controversy relating to the handling of labor strike situations. The United Farm Workers strike in Starr County, in the Rio Grande Valley of South Texas in 1967, and the Lone Star Steel strike in 1968 left the Rangers taxed logistically and legally. The DPS took the opportunity to reassess the Rangers' duties in such cases.

Rangers no longer shoulder the responsibility of maintaining order in strike situations.[24] DPS policy changed so that Rangers are now involved exclusively in criminal investigation. They no longer police labor disputes, a duty that now falls to the Highway Patrol in addition to local law enforcement officers.

Coordination with other departments remained an essential element in Hill's Ranger experience in Dallas. In his years along the border, he had worked frequently with U.S. Border Patrol, U.S. Customs Service, and occasionally National Park Service rangers, in addition to local law enforcement. Hill enjoyed the tight-knit cooperation, support, and camaraderie among the area's officers.

In Dallas, Hill maintained close interaction with local authorities as well, although there were far more entities and individual officers in the region. He also interacted with various federal agencies, working more frequently with FBI and Justice Department special agents than had been the case along the border. What remained the same was the necessity for interoffice communication with all branches of law enforcement. This process was much more formal in Dallas and often more difficult owing to the number of people and offices involved.[25]

Dallas Rangers were much less likely to work closely with local law enforcement on everyday cases. Local sheriff and police departments had many more resources and personnel available than those in the Big Bend. Hill's caseload in Dallas consisted primarily of organized crime and gambling, labor disputes, narcotics, burglaries, murder, and racial disputes.

Because of their position as state law officers, Rangers can work effectively across city, county, and state lines in the investigation of crime. After discovering reports of mercury theft in a four-state area, Hill was able to pursue these leads across Texas and the Southwest. In September 1957, Hill began to receive reports from oil and gas companies throughout the state of mercury thefts from gas meters. By December it became apparent that such crimes had increased enough to "indicate that these thefts were committed by a gang."

Identifying the lawful owners of mercury was impossible. Because mercury was used in oil-field meter switches, availability and opportunity for theft were widespread. For these reasons, a law was passed in 1941 that made it illegal to possess liquid mercury without a bill of sale or other proof of ownership.

Hill contacted the agents of the various oil companies, sheriff offices, and police departments throughout the state and obtained all reports of mercury thefts. He then correlated the findings and notified Mid-Continent Oil and Gas Association investigators of his findings. The Association then issued a press release that warned operators of the wave of mercury thefts.

Hill worked closely with Mid-Continent investigators and Rangers in other parts of the state to identify the culprits behind the coordinated thefts. The investigation began by contacting businesses that purchased mercury. Rangers Zeno Smith (San Antonio), Byron Currin (Vernon), and Jim Ray (Tyler), plus Rangers in Corpus Christi and law enforcement agencies from Texas, Louisiana, New Mexico, and Mississippi, compiled lists of individuals who had sold quantities of mercury to receiving companies.

Soon a pattern was detected. Ranger Currin found one of the suspects in possession of 140 pounds of mercury. Ranger Hill found traces of mercury remaining in the trunk of another suspect's car. Ranger Zeno Smith arrested a suspect on a drunk-and-disorderly charge, and the man soon confessed to his involvement during questioning.

As more arrests were made, the scope of the thefts was determined. "We figured out the operation of two gangs. One that operated in Texas, Louisiana, New Mexico and Mississippi and one that operated out of Fort Worth."[26]

Activities for Hill at Company B Headquarters also included frequent "locate and apprehend" requests. Ironically, because Dallas was a large and growing city, it served as a place to hide for fugitives, similar in that way to the remote reaches of the Big Bend. Hill's weekly reports include numerous requests from other agencies across the country to locate wanted individuals believed to be in the Dallas area.

A substantial narcotics trade existed in Dallas and Fort
Worth in the late 1950s, linked closely with gambling and organized crime. Many of Hill's daily reports involve collaboration
on narcotics investigations with the newly formed DPS Narcotics unit and with local law enforcement in the Dallas area
and in some of the small, outlying communities served by the
Rangers.[27]

Twelve years after disbanding in 1939 due to budget cuts, the
Narcotics Division of the DPS was reorganized, in 1951, to address the growing illicit drug trade. By 1957, the Narcotics Division had grown to ten agents who focused their efforts primarily
in urban areas, including Dallas.

In the position of Ranger sergeant, and certainly after reorganization, Hill encountered increasing administrative demands.
Although he did not like it, Hill approached deskwork as he did
any other responsibility. One of the administrative tasks for
which he was now responsible was the completion of Ranger
performance evaluations. Hill disliked the idea of judging other
Rangers and their job performance. He certainly would not hesitate to talk to a Ranger in his company if he believed the man
was not performing up to the standard. Nor would he hesitate to
dismiss one who continued substandard performance or who
failed to comply with the ethical or moral standards expected of
the position.

However, he did not like being in a position to judge the men
he led and to record those judgments on paper for others to view.
Hill felt that this undermined the communication and cooperation that should exist between Rangers and a Ranger company's
leaders. Leaders in the company could and should address any
problems "in-house."

The times were changing. After reorganization, the Ranger
Service administration now completed formal evaluations of the
Rangers under its command. These reports required a scaled

score in the following categories: quality of work, quantity of work, job knowledge, personal qualities and demeanor, relationships with others, and care and use of state property. Hill completed the task, but he would rather have faced down an angry mob, unarmed.[28]

In 1954, after the milestone *Brown v. Board of Education of Topeka* decision, social upheaval gripped the South, including East Texas. In September 1957, the National Guard escorted the "Little Rock Nine" to their classes in the previously all-white Little Rock (Arkansas) Central High School.

As racial tensions increased throughout the South, so did incidents in Texas that threatened the peace and required the attention of the Rangers. In one such case, Hill received information that a local chief of police had distributed Ku Klux Klan propaganda, inciting racial unrest.

An informer, Horace Miller, notified the Company B office that Chief Aaron Stephens of White Settlement used his office to disseminate racist materials. Hill, along with Rangers Daniel and Ray, left for White Settlement to investigate racial unrest and possible misuse of public office.

Hill, Daniel, and Ray questioned local residents, police department employees, and the chief. They reviewed the distributed material, the *Aryan View* newspaper. Delivered to every home in the small community, the *Aryan View* bore the name of Police Chief Aaron Stephens as the distributor.

Through further questioning, however, the Rangers discovered an interesting twist. Horace Miller, who reported the chief's supposed racist activities, was active in the Aryan Knights of the Ku Klux Klan and "other organizations in which the Internal Security division of the DPS will be interested."

Upon further investigation, and with the arrest of Miller, Rangers discovered that Chief Stephens had no association with the flyers or the Klan. Miller had tried to implicate Chief

Stephens in such activity in order to stir up racial unrest in the community.

Miller's wallet revealed his racist credentials: "Imperial Passport Number 8, Citizen of the Invisible Empire, Knights of the Ku Klux Klan." Hill noted that he referred Miller's information to John Fain of the FBI for further investigation.[29]

During his time in Dallas, Hill kept in close contact with officers in Alpine and surrounding areas. He continued to collaborate on outstanding cases in the region. In June 1957, Hill received a request from Brewster County Sheriff Jim Skinner to assist in the apprehension of Martin Ramos, wanted in Alpine for the 1950 murder of Juan Salgado. Ramos escaped across the Mexican border after leading Hill and Skinner on a lengthy and ultimately futile manhunt [see Chap. 7]. The two Rangers shared a strong desire to see the suspect brought to justice in the United States.

Skinner had received information that Ramos lived in Mulato, Mexico, and worked on the Chinata Ranch near Presidio. Hill obtained permission to follow up on the outstanding murder investigation. He left Dallas at 10:00 a.m. and arrived in Alpine by 9:00 p.m., covering 525 miles in his state unit 96-B.

Upon his arrival in Alpine, Hill met with Skinner and Ranger Charlie Miller to make plans for their apprehension of Ramos. Ranger Miller was no stranger to the border. He wore his first Ranger badge in 1919, stationed at Del Rio. He was back in his old stomping grounds, having worked at Presidio in 1921. For a half-century, Miller served Texas as both a regular Ranger and Special Ranger. With his Special Ranger designation, Miller headed security for all YO Ranch properties for the Schreiner family of Kerrville.

No one knew his actual age as he had "doctored" his birth certificate several times to remain below the mandatory retirement age of the Ranger Service. In 1951, Miller rejoined the ranks of the regular Rangers, serving at Mason until his retirement in 1968.

Hill admired Miller and enjoyed his stories of the old Rangers and the border country.[30]

Hill, Skinner, and Miller set out at 4:00 a.m. for the Chinata Ranch near Presidio. Not knowing what to expect, they had their horse trailer in tow.

Pulling into the ranch yard, Hill questioned a Mexican worker about Ramos. The worker indicated that Ramos worked in the pens. Hill, Skinner, and Miller surrounded the area and quickly had Ramos in custody. "Subject Martin Ramos apprehended in pens on Chinata Ranch without incident," Hill reported. "Ramos was returned to Brewster County jail on charge of murder."[31]

Beginning in late May 1957, Hill again worked in Alpine with Ranger Jim Nance, reviewing and preparing evidence for trial in two murder cases. In both cases the fugitive escaped into Mexico; one was later captured by Hill, and the other stood trial in Mexico. Hill and Nance worked with prosecutors in Mexico and with the district attorney in the United States.

Hill returned to Dallas to investigate the activities of the KKK and their involvement in racial disturbances in Grayson County. Days later, Hill worked with the Tarrant County Sheriff's Department in the investigation of "known underworld characters" operating in the Fort Worth area.[32]

Hill's ability and job performance prompted DPS major Guy Smith to recommend him for promotion in December 1957. Smith wrote to deputy DPS director Joe Fletcher, "I have observed Sergeant Hill for the past six months, his work, his ability to organize and take hold of a situation, to supervise personnel and conduct the business of the Ranger function are outstanding, and I believe him to be qualified to be a Captain of that function. I therefore recommend that he be considered and interviewed by the board for that position."[33]

Hill, however, had other plans. By early summer of 1958, he

decided that his home was back in the Big Bend. In June, Hill called Colonel Garrison and requested a conference. Hill met with Colonel Garrison in Austin on the following day for eight hours behind closed doors.[34]

Hill recounted, "I stayed in Dallas a year and three months as Sergeant of Company B. I decided I would rather be back and work the border area in Alpine and he [Colonel Garrison] was good enough to let me return to my home station [Alpine]."[35]

From June 1958 until his retirement in June 1974, Hill again maintained the Ranger outpost in Alpine as a Ranger private—dubbed by the *DPS Chaparral* as the "mile high Ranger."

Hill's decision to transfer back to Alpine involved more than his desire to be back in the remote Big Bend country he loved, although that certainly played the major part. A strained relationship existed between Hill and Captain Banks. Hill and Banks had personality and perception differences that made interactions difficult, especially on Hill's part as sergeant.[36]

One year after Hill returned to Alpine, Banks resigned from the Ranger Service—or was fired, depending on which version of events is to be believed. Colonel Garrison made a public statement explaining the move: "For failure to carry out Department orders, Captain Banks has been relieved of his command and dismissed from the Ranger Service." Garrison continued, "When Banks was notified of this action, he requested permission to resign, which, in view of the many years of service to the Department, was granted."

Garrison's statement indicated that Banks had not performed his duties as they related to the handling of gambling in Fort Worth, among other issues that would remain private. Banks claimed that he had no notice to that effect and that higher authority prohibited him from pursuing the matter in Fort Worth as it involved prominent people in the government and business. He claimed DPS leaders targeted him in order to make a place for then-DPS regional commander Bob Crowder to return to his previous station as captain of Company B.[37]

Hill, back at home in the Big Bend, far removed from the interaction, never spoke publicly about it or any difficulties or disagreements that he had with Captain Banks.

During the time Hill spent in Dallas, *Sputnik* began its orbit around the Earth. At Texas Instruments in Dallas, Jack Kilby had begun work on the first integrated circuit, the silicon chip, which fueled the budding computer industry.[38] The 1960s would bring other social and technological changes that eventually spread even to the far reaches of the Big Bend.

11

Times Are a-Changin'

Texan fighting men could be led but not commanded. . . . Only a gifted leader, one who led by example and who understood the Texan makeup, could mold such mulish freemen into a cohesive team.

Robert M. Utley, "The Texas Ranger Tradition Established," *Montana: The Magazine of Western History* **52 (Spring 2002): 2–11**

"HOLA MI AMIGO, this letter finds me back in the far west, where the deer and the antelope play and the sun shines again." Hill's elation at his return to the Big Bend was evident. He wrote to the men in his Company B command, thanking each for his co-operation and fine work as well as extending an invitation to visit.[1]

In the Big Bend, country life and law enforcement remained straightforward. The period from 1959 until 1969, however, marked great changes in society and in law enforcement across America. The Big Bend could not continue to remain isolated.

Slowly, the generation of Rangers who made the transition from horseback to automobile, from the Adjutant General's Office to the DPS, retired. They left behind a new generation of Rangers, trained by those who lived the old ways, now immersed in changing times.

Technological advances of the time aided law enforcement efforts. By the end of the 1960s, the DPS had seven helicopters and five airplanes stationed throughout the state for department use. A new communications station, established in Del Rio in 1965, helped to bridge some, though not all, communication gaps in southwestern Texas and the Trans-Pecos. The old manual teletype received an upgrade to a fully computerized system. Local departments could now access driver's license, vehicle registration, and criminal history data. Issued Ranger gear improved to include bulletproof vests and infrared night scopes.[2]

Hill's inventory of April 3, 1959, included no such innovations, although they later became available to him. In his state inventory report to Captain Frank Probst, Hill claimed a Sirchie fingerprint kit, binoculars, GE transceiver, Corona portable typewriter, file cabinet, fan, handcuffs, .38 Colt revolver, Smith & Wesson .357 Magnum, .351 Winchester rifle, .30-30 Winchester rifle, federal siren, 1959 Ford sedan, and Hobbs horse trailer.[3]

Hill's Smith & Wesson, nickel-plated, K-frame .357 Magnum with split-leather speed holster.

Even the symbol of a Ranger, the badge, changed during this time. This change, however, was actually a return to the old ways. In a 1962 press release, Homer Garrison announced that the Texas Rangers "are going back to the tradition steeped Mexican silver badge worn by their predecessors during frontier days." Garrison added that the new badge, issued to all sixty-two active Rangers, was a replica of the original badges that old-time Rangers carved or had made out of a Mexican five-peso silver dollar when Texas became a state and their duties changed from a military force to that of law enforcement.[4]

The change came about thanks to Ranger G. W. Burks of Fort Worth. Burks, a history buff, particularly of Ranger history, read about the badges of the frontier Rangers, many of which were fashioned from Mexican five-peso coins. He approached Company B Captain Bob Crowder and requested permission to have a replica of the original badge made. Crowder agreed, and Burks commissioned Halston's Jewelry in Fort Worth to make one to his specifications.

Ranger Glenn Elliott recalled, "At a company meeting we were shown the badge. We all loved it and naturally wanted one. We had to furnish our own coin, which if memory serves me right, cost about six or seven dollars." The new design replaced the "bottle cap" badges that had been issued in 1957 and were not very popular among the Rangers.[5]

The new badge's five-pointed star, symbolic of the Lone Star State of Texas, sits within a "wagon wheel." The oak leaves, carved on the left side of the badge, represent strength; and the olive branch, on the right, peace—the symbols derived from the Texas Great Seal. Variations in the badges—including rank, company, or name—must meet DPS guidelines. The design is still in use by the Ranger force today.

The state did not issue an "official" Ranger badge until 1935 when the Rangers began their association with the DPS. Prior to this time, many individual variations existed. Rangers of the

Hill's first Ranger badge (1947), *left,* and "bottle cap" badge (1957–1962).

Frontier Battalion originally carried only "warrants of authority," official paper documents issued by the Adjutant General's Office. These were kept in the Ranger's pocket as a means of identification.[6]

Changes in the DPS during the 1960s included a new area of responsibility, the coordination of the state's disaster relief program. In 1961, Hurricane Carla demolished the Texas coastline. Before Carla even crossed into Matagorda Bay, the Texas DPS, along with local authorities, helped evacuate five hundred thousand people from coastal areas. The DPS quickly set up mobile communications centers in Houston and San Antonio. Two-thirds of the Ranger force, including Ranger Hill, and Highway Patrol units from all over the state, were dispatched to the coastal region to handle traffic problems and deal with looting.[7]

The DPS, with infrastructure and communications systems already in place, became the most likely candidate to coordinate natural disaster emergencies. To meet this need, the DPS Office of Defense and Disaster Relief was formed.

The sixties also brought change at the highest level of DPS ad-

ministration. In 1968, Colonel Homer Garrison, DPS director
since 1938, passed away after a long illness. Garrison had guided
the department and the Ranger Service through three decades of
growth. He ensured that the Rangers did not become obsolete by
structuring them as a skilled crime analysis core agency trained
in state-of-the-art investigative and forensic techniques.[8] Retired
Alpine Ranger Joaquin Jackson, the last Ranger Garrison hired,
mused, "The Rangers would never have survived the modern era
if not for him."[9]

Assistant Director Wilson Spier ascended to the position of di-
rector, and the head of the Criminal Law Enforcement Division,
Leo Gossett, received promotion to assistant director. Changes in
leadership closer to home affected Hill as well. Two Highway Pa-
trol school classmates attained the rank of Ranger captain in
Hill's Company E. Captain Frank Probst took over command of
Company E in 1958, serving until 1967 when he transferred to
Lubbock to command Company C.[10]

Captain Jim Riddles succeeded Probst. Under his command,
Company E Rangers soon became known as "Riddles' Rangers."
According to Hill, "I don't believe that any company ever had a
better captain than Jim Riddles." Riddles led by suggestion and
consideration. He expressed his hands-off leadership style thus:
"My Rangers don't need supervision in the field; if they needed
field supervision, they wouldn't be Rangers."[11]

Upon Hill's return to the Last Frontier, his caseload remained
much as it had been in the previous ten years. Livestock theft,
burglaries, murder, and smuggling were still the most prevalent
cases he investigated. Toward the end of the 1960s, this, too,
began to change.[12]

The region's proximity to the border and the remoteness of
ranches and small communities had not changed. Livestock theft
therefore remained a common call for Hill. With three hundred
miles of ranch land adjoining the border, many a bandit could be

well into Mexico before his crime was even discovered. As a result, Hill once again worked closely with Mexican officials in ongoing investigations.

In one such investigation, Hill traveled to the Adams Ranch, seventy-five miles south of Marathon, along the border. Ranch workers had discovered eight horses stolen. Hill arrived at the ranch and spoke with workers to determine where the theft had occurred. He rode off, on horseback, to investigate the scene.

Hill examined the tracks. Three riders had come across from Mexico. They returned to the river with four riderless horses. He crossed the river to examine tracks south of the border. Only six sets of tracks came up out of the water.

He returned to stateside and found that a lone set of tracks broke off from the group at the river's edge. Boot prints indented the sand by the hoof prints. Hill followed the animal, which did not appear to be mounted. He soon found a sorrel horse grazing in the grass along the water's edge.

Sweat marks indicated that the animal had recently worn a saddle and bridle. As Hill approached, the animal turned and he could see that the horse was lame in one front leg. When the animal turned sideways, he also saw that the brand on its hip showed deep cuts and bleeding. Apparently, when the horse could not keep up due to the leg injury, the bandits unsaddled the horse and left it on the U.S. side. They mutilated the brand to prevent identification of the owner.[13]

In a similar case, thieves rounded up eight burros from a border ranch. Used as pack animals, the burros transported candelilla wax plants off the mountains down to wax camps. Hill tracked the stolen animals into Big Bend National Park and across the Rio Grande into Mexico. "Mexican officials have been contacted," Hill reported, "and have promised their assistance in attempting to recover stolen animals."[14]

Thefts moved both ways across the river. In the summer of

1961, Hill received a report from Rutillo Martinez, group com-mander of the Chihuahua State Police. In the process of investi-gating a livestock theft, Martinez had discovered that it was part of a smuggling operation that implicated a rancher on the U.S. side of the border.

Martinez arrested two Mexican rustlers in Ojinaga for stealing cattle from the Los Rincones del Guaje Ranch. One of the rustlers admitted that the stolen cattle were smuggled into the United States.

Martinez sent a copy of the rustler's confession to Hill. The man stated that he and his accomplices drove cattle across the Río Bravo. The rustlers arrived at La Ternera Ranch outside of Presidio. He added, "We had already agreed that Amador Estrada would purchase the stolen cattle."[15]

Attached to a copy of the rustler's statement, the Mexican officer added a brief note, "I was in Ciudad Ojinaga to make an investigation of cattle theft. I think you should desire to make an investigation in Presidio, Texas."[16] For the time being, interna-tional law enforcement cooperation remained strong and amiable. The growth of the drug trade later strained this relationship.

Burglaries in the Big Bend began to increase in number during the late fifties and throughout the sixties. Small residential and business burglaries, as well as thefts from remote ranches, contin-ued to be the mainstay of burglary cases for Hill. In a typical case of 1963, a rider crossed the Rio Grande and went to the Terragano residence where he broke the lock on the front door. The burglar took two saddles and blankets, two bridles, two rifles, one shot-gun, a pair of chaps, a radio, and some clothing.

The thief had the luxury of making two trips on horseback across the border to transport the spoils. But with each step, tell-tale signs linked him to the crime: the thief rode a horse with half of the right rear shoe missing.

When called to the scene, Hill followed the unusual imprint

to the border. He contacted Mexican officials and met them at the burglar's crossing. Hill and Captain Lupe Gonzales of the Chihuahua State Police trailed the criminal to his home. As the men rode up to the house, Captain Gonzales hollered to the man, who came out with his hands up. Hill recovered most of the property and returned it to Terragano.[17]

In the 1960s, safecrackers appeared on the scene in the small towns of the Big Bend region.[18] New technologies in security had made many of the more lucrative targets in urban areas difficult to access. Small-town banks and other businesses tended to have old safes and limited security.

Hill detailed the procedure of "knob knockers" who burglarized a local bank. The burglars entered the Fort Davis State Bank by the side door, near the rear of the building. They used a pry bar to break the night lock and gain entry into the bank, and then "knocked knobs" and "pushed pins" to open two vaults. This process involved using a sledgehammer to knock off the combination knob and then punching out the securing pins back into the safe. Burglars netted $2,600 in silver in the bank vault and an undetermined amount from seventy-five safe deposit boxes.[19]

Hill investigated the following morning, but found no latent fingerprints—the safecrackers used gloves—and no tire marks on the paved parking area. He did find slight indentations of a tennis shoe in the dirt around the concrete entry.

In February 1965, only days after the Fort Davis Bank robbery, safecrackers were back at work in the sleepy towns of the Big Bend. This time they targeted the Presidio County Courthouse in Marfa. The burglars again knocked knobs and pushed pins to access three walk-in safes. After investigation, Hill found a similar pattern. No fingerprints, no tire marks, but a slight tennis shoe imprint was discovered matching the one found at the Fort Davis State Bank.

Hill contacted Captain Probst. Similar activity in and around

Odessa had Company E Rangers at Midland looking into possible suspects. By comparing evidence and combining efforts, Hill and other Company E Rangers soon solved the case and arrested three safecrackers in Odessa. Items found in their possession confirmed their involvement.

Hill's case reports of the 1960s show a substantial increase in forgery cases and several cases of extortion. One extortion incident involved a fifteen-year-old girl, the daughter of a local pastor. Hill explained that the plan to extort money from the girl and her family started with a telephone call. The caller told the girl that he had nude photos of her. He claimed to have placed hidden cameras in her bathroom while she was out. The caller claimed that through trick photography, he "placed her picture in sexual

Texas Rangers Company E (1962). Sitting, *left to right:* Sergeant John Wood, Captain Frank Probst. Standing, *left to right:* L. Hardy Purvis, Ralph Rohatsch, Earl Stewart, Gene Graves, Dudley White, Forrest Hardin, Jim Nance, Arthur Hill.

acts with men and that she must submit to his demands or he would expose her pictures."

When the girl, horrified, handed the phone to her mother, the man hung up. The family notified Sheriff Skinner. Skinner explained that the only way to catch the caller would be to set up a meeting and catch him in the act.

A few days later, the extortionist called back, listing his demands. He stipulated that the girl pay him one hundred dollars and "submit sexually to his demands." Hill added, "These proposals were made in the most vulgar language."

Following Skinner's advice, the girl agreed to meet the man. He threatened the girl not to tell officers or anyone else or he would kill her and anyone who came with her. He also stated that he would blow up her father's house. If she complied with all of his demands, the caller claimed, he would give her the pictures and leave town.

Sheriff Skinner requested Hill's assistance, and along with other officers, they tried to identify and locate the caller prior to the arranged meeting, but were unsuccessful. The only chance to capture the man was to ensure the girl's safety first, have her go through with the meeting, and attempt to capture the extortionist.

Hill and Skinner evaluated the alley where the exchange was to take place. Hill picked a place where he could conceal himself and await the girl's car as she pulled into the alley to meet the caller. Skinner planned to ride in the trunk of the girl's car. Other officers would position themselves nearby in unmarked cars.

Hill and Skinner met with the parents and the girl to review the plan. She was to drive into the alley where Hill hid and to stop her car with all of the doors locked. She should leave the window only slightly down to permit her to hand the marked money to the extortionist. When he took the money, the girl was to say, "Now you have my money, give me the pictures." Hill instructed that she immediately lie down in the floorboard of the car. This would signal Hill and Skinner to action.

The actual event did not go quite as planned. Hill concealed himself in the alley and waited in the darkness for the girl's car or a sign of the extortionist approaching. As Hill watched her car's headlights turn slowly into the alley, he also began to hear the clamoring of an approaching train. Train tracks run right down the middle of Alpine. They had not anticipated the train schedule.

Hill watched the girl's car enter the alley. He could not hear anything but the train, which was sounding its whistle as it rolled into town. Hill watched a man run out of the darkness from the far end of the alley and pound on the car, causing the girl to stop far from the point the officers had recommended.

The man circled the car and tried to open the passenger door, but instead took the money the girl offered from the slit in the window. "Now you have the money, give me the pictures," the girl yelled. Although he could not hear the words she uttered, Hill sprung from his hiding place and, with weapon drawn, approached the car at the far end of the alley.

The trunk flew up and Skinner emerged. The extortionist, seeing Skinner, began to run. As Hill arrived at the front of the car, the train had passed. He heard Skinner say, "Stop or I'll shoot!" The suspect immediately ducked around the corner, into the main street. Both officers began to chase the fleeing extortionist.

With Skinner ahead of Hill by the length of the car, he arrived at the corner and turned onto the main street ahead of Hill. "I heard three shots and came around the corner to see Sheriff Skinner and the wounded extortionist," Hill explained. The wounded man handed Sheriff Skinner the five twenty-dollar bills.

Hill and Skinner loaded the man in the sheriff's patrol car and drove him to the Brewster County Hospital. The man died of his wounds. Hill and Skinner returned at daylight to search the alley and found a discarded .25-caliber Beretta that Hill submitted to the DPS laboratory for ballistic testing.[20] Upon further investigation, Hill discovered that the man had successfully pulled off a similar scheme in the nearby town of Valentine.

The financial stakes increased in a case involving an area landowner who, over the course of several years, paid $75,000 to an extortionist. The landowner, James Henderson, was indicted for murder with malice aforethought in the death of his girlfriend and her father. While out on bond, awaiting trial, Henderson met Sullivan Ross Jones at a bar in Juárez. The two struck up a conversation, and Henderson discussed his need to get money for a good defense attorney. Henderson told Jones of his various landholdings and financial assets resulting from inheritance of his mother's estate. The two men parted, and Henderson returned to stand trial.

Henderson received a guilty verdict and was sentenced to fifty years in the Texas State Penitentiary at Huntsville. While awaiting transport to Huntsville at the El Paso jail, Henderson had the misfortune of meeting Jones a second time. Coincidentally, Jones was also awaiting transport to Huntsville on a conviction of armed robbery.

Henderson learned that Jones's real name was Paul Knapp. Knapp had an extensive criminal record, dating back to 1924, including time served in the San Quentin and Folsom prisons in California.[21]

Knapp and Henderson served time together in Huntsville from 1945 until 1956. As Knapp's release date approached, he began pressuring Henderson for money with a threat of violence or death to Henderson's daughter and grandchildren. At first, the payments were small, in the hundreds of dollars, but as the time for Knapp's parole grew closer, the larger the demands and the more violent the threats became.

In 1956, the Texas Department of Corrections released Knapp

to the State of California to serve out parole violation charges. The same year, Henderson received parole, after only nine years served on his fifty-year double-murder sentence, and he moved back to Jeff Davis County. He sold his ranch and purchased the Holland Hotel in Alpine.

Upon his release in California, Knapp returned to Alpine and picked up where he left off with Henderson. With threats of parole revocation and violence, Knapp, over the course of several years, conned Henderson out of all his cash, his car, the Holland Hotel, his remaining land, and crops.

Finally, Henderson fearfully approached Hill to conduct an investigation. As an ex-con, he was worried about receiving fair treatment. At this time, however, he was more fearful of the possibility that Knapp would resort to violence against his family if he did not come up with more money, which he no longer had.

Hill completed an extensive investigation, following the paper trail of financial evidence. The Brewster County Grand Jury returned six indictments against Paul Knapp, alias Sullivan Ross Jones, charging him with extortion by threats of violence.

By this time, Knapp was incarcerated once again, this time in Pennsylvania for a three-year sentence. Hill requested notification from the federal penitentiary at Lewisburg, Pennsylvania, regarding Knapp's release, so he could be extradited to Texas to stand trial.

The case finally culminated two years later. Hill received notice in March 1963 from the Lewisburg penitentiary that Paul Knapp would complete his sentence there. Hill immediately began extradition procedures. On April 5, 1963, Knapp was released into Hill's custody from the Pennsylvania institution. Hill returned Knapp to the Brewster County Jail in Alpine, to await trial on the extortion charges.

On the nonstop drive back to Texas from Pennsylvania, Knapp intrigued Hill. Although a lifetime criminal, he was intelligent, polite, and well read. Even after Knapp's incarceration, Hill received lengthy letters written in Knapp's unique, perfect script.

The Alpine jury returned guilty verdicts on all charges, and Knapp received a sentence of five years on each of six counts. Imprisoned at age sixty-two to serve out the thirty-year sentence, Knapp maintained correspondence with Hill into the late 1970s.[22]

12

A Harsh Land

Practically all of the mobile army of the United States is stationed along the international border and still it is impossible to patrol the entire area.

———

General Frederic Funston, U.S. Army Commander
Big Bend District (1916), Museum of the Big Bend,
Sul Ross State University

VIOLENT crimes are as varied as their motives. Throughout the 1960s, Hill's caseload included a large number of such investigations. Unfortunately, whether lost to the border or the harsh landscape, even a Ranger does not always "get his man."

When Hill first arrived in the Big Bend area, phone coverage was sparse, with many towns and most ranches without service. By the 1960s, although many ranches still lacked telephones, the small communities along the Rio Grande had a means of communicating with law enforcement and emergency services.

Hill received a phone call from Ben English of Lajitas informing him that a body had been discovered. Hill, along with Sheriff Williams of Brewster County, Justice of the Peace Hallie Stillwell, and Dr. W. E. Lockhart, drove to Lajitas, where they met English at the site described.

Hill viewed the charred remains of the corpse. A gasoline can, discarded at the scene, held the fuel used to burn the body. The body was not identifiable, due to its "bad state of decomposition due to climate, varmints, and vultures."

Dr. Lockhart knelt by Hill to examine the remains. The body appeared to be that of a young white woman. The hair remaining on a scalp fragment was fine and light brown. The doctor pointed to a small hole in the woman's left breastbone and looked up at Hill. Both recognized the mark as a bullet hole.

Hill knelt down by the doctor and surveyed the remains more closely. A bullet hole likely also contained a bullet. He spotted a .38-caliber bullet hidden in bits and pieces of scorched clothing. Hill also found four zippers near the remains, and fabric remnants "chartreuse in color."[1]

The doctor estimated that the death occurred sometime in the previous month. Hill examined the scene and found tire marks, but weather had eroded any detail. The gasoline can and the body provided the only physical evidence of the crime.

Hill collected the evidence and submitted it to the DPS laboratory for testing, while his investigation continued. The most likely lead was provided by a gas station attendant who said that a piano tuner from Houston had come through the gas station at Marathon with a woman, and days later without her. The attendant described the man as very nervous. When the station attendant asked the man about his wife, he stated that his wife was in a sanitarium in Houston. Hill's follow-up on this vague information proved unproductive.[2]

The *San Angelo Standard Times* reported, "The people of this remote village on the Rio Grande possibly hold the key to unlocking the truth about one of the state's most baffling murder mysteries. One of them may have seen a woman dressed in a chartreuse outfit."[3]

DPS lab results showed that the woman was enclosed in a plastic bag when burned. The lab report indicated the cause of death as a bullet wound to the chest, and that the woman was dead before the body was incinerated.

Desperate for witnesses who might contribute clues as to the woman's identity, Hill re-created the hair color and clothing style on a Barbie doll. Hill believed, however, that someone had murdered the woman elsewhere, brought her to the Big Bend, and burned her body to cover up the evidence. The unidentified victim became known as "the woman in the chartreuse dress," and the killer was never found.[4]

But even in cases where the killer was readily identified, the result was no less devastating. Hill investigated such a murder case in Presidio. Once he arrived on the scene, all that remained was to collect testimony and confirm what everyone in the area had feared would eventually happen between two cantankerous county commissioners over the issue of a bridge.

Tempers flared with talk of installing a new international bridge between Ojinaga, Mexico, and Presidio, Texas, the only official port of entry in the 450 miles between El Paso and Del Rio. Harold Dupey of El Paso had owned and operated the wooden toll bridge across the river since the 1930s. The U.S. Customs Service maintained a checkpoint at the border, but Dupey had the contract on the commercial crossing.

Presidio County commissioners, led by Dr. Clyde Vought, pushed to make changes. Dr. Vought advocated a new international bridge between Presidio and Ojinaga. This would replace the old toll bridge owned by Dupey. Several intense arguments arose between Dr. Vought and Dupey, each ending with mutual threats of murder.

On the afternoon of October 2, 1959, Dr. Vought made a house call near the Presidio public schools. As he left the house and walked toward his car, Dupey drove by. After a brief exchange of words, Dr. Vought reached in his car and pulled out a .44-40 rifle. He shot Dupey in the face, killing him instantly. "Dupey was not armed," Hill confirmed.[5] The rickety fifty-year-old bridge remained in use until the 1980s, when the current International Bridge was completed.[6]

Any law officer's fulfillment of duties involves inherent risks. In 1959, two U.S. Border Patrol agents were patrolling along the Rio Grande, searching for illegal immigrants. What they found was animosity on the part of a local employer of illegal aliens.

Border Patrolmen Thurston McCutchin and his partner, Carrey Whittman, walked their horses onto the turn row of a cotton field owned by Moody Bennett. The officers sought to apprehend illegal aliens working as cotton pickers for Bennett.

As they entered the field, workers started running toward the nearby Rio Grande. McCutchin and Whittman apprehended three illegal Mexican workers while the majority fled to Mexico, essentially halting the picking operation.

A car flew up the road adjoining the field and into the turn row. Moody Bennett jumped out of the vehicle and started cursing the Border Patrolmen. Bennett wielded a rifle, pointing it to emphasize each statement.

McCutchin and Whittman were mounted. Their prisoners stood nearby, in the line of fire. Before the officers took any action, Bennett raised the rifle and fired at McCutchin. He hit McCutchin's horse, killing it instantly.

As the horse hit the ground, McCutchin slid off to the side away from Bennett and returned fire, hitting Bennett. Not slowed by his injury, Bennett then directed his attack at Whittman, who also drew his weapon to return fire. When Bennett stopped to reload, McCutchin rushed him and took the rifle away from him.[7]

Hill arrived at the scene and questioned the Border Patrol agents and their prisoners regarding the incident. While waiting at the hospital for Bennett to receive treatment, Hill received a phone call from an FBI agent named Pickens in El Paso, the closest FBI field office. Pickens advised that the government would press charges against Bennett for assaulting a federal officer with a deadly weapon. Pickens and Hill arrested Bennett, who was soon convicted of the federal charges.

In three of the four decades that Hill served as a Ranger in the Big Bend, a sheriff was shot. Two officers gave the ultimate sacrifice: Presidio County Sheriff Ottis Morrow in 1950, and Presidio County Sheriff Hank Hamilton in 1973. In 1965, Terrell County Sheriff Bill Cooksey was critically wounded, but survived.

Cooksey was investigating a rash of burglaries in Terrell County. He received information from Alfredo Gallegos, a ranch worker who had discovered household goods hidden in a remote cave. Sheriff Cooksey, along with Deputy Lewis Cash, went to investigate. The two officers met Gallegos and Benny Ross at the Bill Goodwin Ranch. The workers opened the gate and directed Cooksey and Cash to the cave.

Rangers Hill and Nance would later begin an investigation of the incident. They pieced together the following events through testimony and evidence at the scene. Cooksey, Cash, Gallegos, and Ross drove in two vehicles to the top of a hill above the site of the cave. Gallegos led the way down the steep hill to the cave opening. As Ross and the officers approached, a Mexican man stuck his head out of the cave.

Gallegos asked the man, surprised at his unannounced visitors, what he was doing there. After no response came, Deputy Cash repeated the request. The man in the cave mumbled noncommittal responses. Cooksey, tired of the runaround, told the man, through Gallegos's translation, that he was there to investigate some thefts and needed to speak with him.

The Mexican man finally came out of the cave. He put on a green-crowned hat and began walking down the hill toward his campfire, ignoring Cooksey's request. Deputy Cash told Cooksey that he believed the man would try to run. Cooksey walked up close behind the man to stop his retreat so that he could question him.

The man had not appeared to be armed, so Deputy Cash was shocked when he heard two shots in quick succession. "When I next looked up," Cash said, "Bill [Cooksey] was on the ground." The man shot Sheriff Cooksey in the leg and through the back, perforating his lung.

Unarmed at the time, Deputy Cash stood with Gallegos and Ross, held at gunpoint by the sheriff's assailant. The man motioned to a rifle leaning against a rock near the campfire, not visible from the cave. He told Ross to take the .30-30 rifle and toss it to him. Ross picked up the gun but instead of tossing it to the assailant, he threw it to the deputy. Cash explained, "I caught the gun, took aim on the man and pulled the trigger. . . . It snapped on an empty cartridge."

The Mexican then directed his pistol at Cash. He ordered Cash to throw the rifle aside or he would die, "like the sheriff." The man ordered Gallegos, Ross, and Cash to carry his supplies and the items in the cave up the hill. He checked each of the two vehicles parked there and took the one with the most gasoline.

He forced the men to load the supplies into the truck. He then instructed Gallegos at gunpoint to tie the hands of Ross and Cash. He took the keys to the other vehicle and rode off with Gallegos driving, a gun pointed at his head.

Once the vehicle was out of sight, Cash and Ross managed to untie each other. They hurried down the hill to check on Cooksey, whom they believed to be dead.

To their surprise, Cooksey was alive and able to talk. "I'm hit twice," Cooksey uttered. He was alive, but they had to get him out of there quickly. Cash went to the remaining pickup and cut a piece of wire from the taillight to use it as a "hot wire." He got the pickup started, drove it to the road, and cut the fence to allow an ambulance to reach Cooksey. Ross walked down to the railroad tracks to stop the next train in order to get word to town of the sheriff's condition.[8]

The railroad brought word into town of the sheriff's critical injuries. Given that an ambulance was not available, Sanderson resident Dalton Hogg drove his station wagon to the scene. He and Ross lifted Cooksey and laid him in the back of the vehicle. Ross rode with Cooksey into Del Rio, where the sheriff was treated for his injuries, while Cash returned to Alpine to notify Hill of the shooting.

While en route to the hospital, Cooksey talked with Ross and Hogg. "The Mexican came and put a .30-30 rifle in my neck and turned me over," Cooksey reported. "I played a little game with him, I played dead. He got my gun and my pocket book. I've got news for him, there isn't much money in that billfold." Cooksey's sense of humor boded well for his recovery. "You know, Dalt," Cooksey asked the driver, "I think he violated my civil rights, don't you?"[9]

Hill began a manhunt at the scene of the abandoned pickup. Other Rangers involved in the search included Jim Nance, L. Hardy Purvis, Forrest Hardin, and Alfred Allee, Jr. The Terrell County sheriff's posse, Brewster County lawmen, and Border Patrol agents assisted the Rangers.

One posse of officers followed the tracks of the fugitive. Other groups checked area ranches and patrolled the border. The search utilized dogs initially, but the dogs could not maneuver around the cactus that covers a large portion of that area. Officers traveled by jeep and on horseback into some of the rough country and then had to continue on foot. Hill recalled the roughness of the terrain, "I wore out a good pair of boots." Hill's group followed tracks that eventually washed out because of recent rainshowers.[10] Hill added, "It is unbelievable the wildness and vastness of the terrain that we covered. It would take a thousand men a hundred years to search all of the caves, canyons, and hiding places in this big country."

The *El Paso Times* reported, "Texas Ranger Arthur Hill has returned to Alpine after an eleven day search of the vast wild territory along the Rio Grande between Langtry and the mouth of Mar-
avillas Creek for the suspect who gunned down Sheriff Bill
Cooksey."

After a short break in Alpine, Hill returned to the cold trail to
question anyone who might have information leading to the suspect. Only one person, Isidro Blanco, saw the assailant after the
shooting. Blanco rode fence between the Billings and Harrison
Ranches. He said the man wearing a hat with a green crown rode
along the Rio Grande, and that he believed the man would cross
into Mexico since sightings of Mexican travelers were common.
Blanco watched the man for some time, and he never crossed the
river.

The suspect had many opportunities to cross over into Mexico
but did not take them. Hill believed that the man probably faced
charges in Mexico as well. With weapons, provisions, and binoculars, the man had all the supplies he needed to survive by hiding under the cover of the vast, wilderness expanse.[11]

In April 1968, the remote terrain again served as an accomplice, concealing a heinous crime. Hill assisted Ranger Alfred
Allee, Jr., in an investigation involving a mass murder, seemingly
random in nature. A ranch hand found five members of the Arellano family murdered along a mile-long section of U.S. Highway
277, north of Del Rio and south of Sonora, Texas. Family members were left shot, stabbed, raped, and robbed.

The Arellanos left their home in Villa de Fuente, Coahuila, to
travel 190 miles to visit family members in San Angelo. The Arellanos traveled frequently in the United States and spoke English
well. Manuel and Monica Arellano, both twenty-five, traveled
with their children—Manuel, Jr., five; Leticia, two and a half; and
Eduardo, fifteen months—and Manuel's sister, Rosa Elia, nineteen.[12]

Forty miles north of Del Rio, their 1958 Buick Special had a flat. Manuel Arellano changed the tire, and the family continued on their way. A few miles farther on, they had a second flat. Another motorist stopped and offered the family a ride into Sonora, thirty miles north. They accepted and had their tires fixed at Rex's Gulf Station, ordered hamburgers to go at the Park Inn Café, and rode back to their vehicle with their Good Samaritan driving.

At daybreak, when a ranch hand came upon the carnage, he found Manuel lying by a water trough, inside a barbed wire fence. The children were scattered in the pasture near their father. Monica was found in a ditch about a mile south with Rosa Elia lying nearby.

Manuel, Jr., and Leticia, although shot in the head and stabbed, survived. Leticia died two days later, leaving Manuel, Jr., the sole survivor of the ordeal.

Witnesses in Sonora described the man who rendered aid to the family. He stood six feet tall or more with a heavy build and sandy blond hair. He had large freckles and a ruddy complexion and wore a straw cowboy hat. Artists provided officers with a sketch of the suspect that circulated around area communities. As the last person known to have seen the Arellano family alive, he became the primary suspect.

Hill, Allee, and other officers spent countless hours questioning and investigating, yet had no definitive suspects.[13] Hill later reviewed the events repeatedly, wondering what they could have missed, what might have led to the killer. He thought of the young boy without a family. "Some of the worst things were the terrible murder cases which we were unable to completely clear. I think of the Arellano family. They were murdered. I think of it quite often. It bothers me because I think there should have been something that we could have gotten started on, maybe we could have worked it out. Something maybe we overlooked, but, so far the case has never been cleared."[14] The Arellano family slaying remains Texas's oldest unsolved mass killing—its coldest case.

The 1950s and 1960s saw many societal changes, including changes in dress. The change in fashion was much delayed in West Texas, where acceptable attire for men was still limited to long pants—jeans, khakis, or dress slacks—but certainly did not include Bermuda shorts.

In 1963, a traveler from California had car trouble in Alpine. While waiting on his car repair, the man decided to have a look around town. He walked up the main street, casually window shopping and taking in the sights. Dressed as was acceptable in California in the heat of the summer, he had no idea of the effect his dress would have on two West Texas officers.

Hill and Skinner happened to be driving down the main street of Alpine when they spotted the man in "short pants" walking the streets of town! They immediately pulled over and ushered the "indecent" man into the squad car—he could not remain on the streets in sight of women and children.

Skinner wanted to arrest him for indecent exposure, but after talking with the man, Hill believed his offense was inadvertent. They dropped off the man at the service station with his promise to stay out of sight until his car was repaired, after which time he should get out of town—or get properly dressed. This humorous incident demonstrates the quickly changing society and the somewhat delayed, conservative outlook in the Big Bend country.[15]

Another visitor had to shorten his stay as well, but not because he did not comply with the "dress code." Hill's case files during the 1960s show a sharp increase in vehicle thefts, some from local towns, but most from other areas that made their way through the Big Bend.

Hill recounted the story of a stolen vehicle from Lackland Air Force Base in San Antonio. The driver, an escaped psychiatric patient from the Veterans Administration hospital in Waco, and two hitchhikers were in for the ride of their lives.

Sul Ross rodeo parade (1960). *Left to right:* **Sheriff Jim Skinner, rancher Jim Espy, Ranger Arthur Hill.**

Hill was notified that a car drove off without paying for gas in Marathon. After making an escape from the station, the vehicle swerved too close to a concrete post and the passenger door was ripped off its hinges. As Hill's car was in the shop, he joined the Highway Patrol officer in his automobile. The two men sped toward Marathon on U.S. Highway 90 to intercept the vehicle.

Hill and the trooper, now followed by Sheriff Williams, planned to set up a roadblock at the intersection of U.S. 90 and U.S. 67 (the "Y") eight miles east of Alpine. At six miles east of Alpine, Hill saw the vehicle approaching rapidly—so much for a roadblock. He flicked on the lights and siren, but the driver refused to stop. The chase was on.

Hill radioed the sheriff behind them and notified him of the oncoming vehicle, advising him to turn around and prepare to pursue. The stolen vehicle passed the sheriff at upwards of 100 mph. Now the sheriff was ahead of Hill, both officers following the suspect at a high rate of speed and approaching town.

The three vehicles roared through town passing the college campus, churches, courthouse square, post office, and downtown shopping area. Arriving at the west side of town, away from homes and buildings, Deputy Webber, in the sheriff's vehicle, shot out one of the tires on the fleeing automobile. The vehicle went into a wild spin off the pavement and into the dirt.

. "The highway patrolman and I nearly hit them head on because they had skidded around and were then headed back toward town running wide open," Hill recalled. Hill and the trooper spun around and continued pursuit, now immediately behind the suspect's car. Pieces of rubber flying up into the windshield and black smoke from the disintegrating tire partially obscured the fleeing car from view.

The vehicles now made a second pass through town going the opposite direction. Driving at dangerous speeds and approaching the college, Hill made a decision. He would try to stop the vehicle before someone was killed. "I drew my pistol, hung out the window, leveled out, and shot through the back of the car. When I did I saw one of them go down and I knew he was hit alright."

College classes had just let out for lunch. Students now lined the steps outside the buildings watching the pursuit. The group of students included Hill's youngest daughter, Martha. She watched the first car go by, thinking it was going too fast. Then she saw the Highway Patrol car fly by with her dad, hanging out of the window, firing at the fleeing vehicle.[16]

Hill continued to lean out the window, watching and waiting for another clear shot. The wind whipped his face and caused his eyes to water but remarkably, his hat remained in place. Directly across from Sul Ross State University's Lawrence Hall, the suspect's vehicle attempted to make a turn to evade Hill's fire. Hill watched the Plymouth wagon slide sideways over the curb and flip over onto its top.

As the trooper braked quickly behind the wreck, Hill braced himself in the door facing to avoid flying out the window. Both officers jumped out and covered the occupants, the tires on the overturned vehicle still spinning. Hill ordered their evacuation of the vehicle and slowly they emerged. Hill and the trooper took all three occupants into custody.

The driver, Leo Herbert Kidd, was under the influence of narcotics at the time. He sustained a gunshot wound to his shoulder and was taken to the hospital. The two hitchhikers were wanted for burglaries in Caldwell County. One was AWOL from the U.S. Navy at Quonset Point, Rhode Island.[17]

Labor disputes of the 1960s, and the unrest that accompanied them, were not exclusive to East Texas or the Rio Grande Valley. At midnight on January 4, 1969, the national union for oil industry workers, the Oil, Chemical, and Atomic Workers (OCAW), went on strike against Sinclair Oil interests. The strike affected not only the large oil-refining centers on the Texas Gulf Coast but also the smaller switch stations and pipelines spread across West Texas.

Fortunately for law enforcement in West Texas, only a small number of workers participated in the strike, which was short-lived. However, incidents of sabotage on equipment involving high pressures and volatile materials made for some tense moments of potential disaster at Schleicher County's Hulldale Plant, a Sinclair Oil Company holding.

Hill, along with Rangers Alfred Allee, Jr. (Ozona), Ralph Rohatsch (San Angelo), and Captain Jim Riddles (Midland), joined Schleicher County Sheriff Orval Edmiston and Deputy Jack Jones to protect property, guard against violence, and investigate criminal activity throughout the duration of the strike.

Most of the oil and natural gas production in Texas is located in the western part of the state, while refineries for the raw material are primarily in the more populous and accessible eastern coastal region. Oil companies constructed extensive pipeline systems to transport the natural resource to the refinery.

High pressure moves fluids and gases through the pipelines. Booster stations along the route control pressure in the lines. By shutting down the booster stations, saboteurs hoped to stop production.

On the first night of the OCAW strike, union workers tried to make their point with Sinclair Oil. When Hill and other officers arrived at the Hulldale Plant yard, it was immersed in total darkness. Saboteurs had cut off the generator that powered the floodlights illuminating the large storage tanks and pressure booster stations.

The caliche-covered ground, which constituted the yard base, was sticky and damp. The saboteurs had opened hot oil valves on holding tanks, draining the 430-degree fluid over a wide area. The oil was flammable, and the fumes were potentially explosive. Ranger Allee stated, "One little spark could have blown up the whole plant."

The workers struck multiple locations quickly. Hill and Edmiston checked three small booster stations in the remote county. The Tillery booster on the Powell Ranch sustained wiring and radio control damage that rendered the booster inoperable. They searched the area and found tire tracks and boot prints going to and from the station gate. One of the prints showed a unique design in the heel. Officers continued to the Camar booster on the Robert Martin Ranch. There they found the same situation and identical tire and boot prints. The Toenail booster, near Christoval, was shut down but sustained no damage.

Hill and Edmiston met Allee back at the Hulldale Plant. With a gas flame burning off waste product, the yard now had minimal lighting, so officers could reexamine the scene. They discovered more boot prints where two men had climbed the fence to access the Hulldale yard. The same heel track seen at the downed booster stations marked the soft dirt near the fence. Upon examination, the tire tracks also matched those found near the booster stations.

Officers began an investigation to account for all employees of the plant. In a small town in the middle of the night, with few employees to locate, this process did not take long. Only two men could not be located.

As dawn approached, Hill and Edmiston returned to the strike line, which consisted of a few workers and a burn barrel positioned on the side of the county road leading to the plant.

The missing workers appeared at the strike line early that morning. Edmiston, familiar with the men, led the questioning. He tipped back his short-brimmed Stetson and worked his unlit cigar stub in his mouth before speaking, allowing the men to grow more anxious. Under questioning, the pair claimed repeatedly to have spent the night in San Angelo. Edmiston did not push the issue.

The workers moved away from Edmiston and Hill, toward the burn barrel, to warm their hands and evade the officers' scrutiny. There, they stood in the ashes of the previous night's fire, smugly assured that they had convinced Edmiston of their bogus story.

Hill and Edmiston patiently watched the ground beneath the feet of the two workers huddled around the fire. Shortly, they spotted the evidence they needed to link the men to the incidents of sabotage. Boot prints, with a special mark in the heel, stood out in the gray soot. Arrests quickly followed.[18]

13

"Plumo o Oro"

A primary component of Mexico's pivotal role in the trafficking of illegal drugs into the United States is the 2,000-mile porous border. Drug organizations in Mexico have a long history, an established record of poly-drug smuggling for over thirty years, and cross-border familial ties.

DEA director Thomas Constantine, testimony before the U.S. Senate Committee on Banking, Housing, and Urban Affairs, March 28, 1996

ALONG the border, smuggling continued to be a lucrative and prolific industry. Hill saw the enterprise grow and diversify from its established roots. The efforts of Hill and the few other law officers then in the region could not hold back the tide of the drug trade in the 1960s. The result was the entrenchment of an international drug-smuggling corridor that forever changed the character of the Big Bend.

In the early 1960s, narcotics investigations in the region remained the responsibility of the Rangers, U.S. Customs Service, and local law enforcement, as well as U.S. Park Service rangers within Big Bend National Park boundaries.

Underfunded and understaffed, the DPS Narcotics Division had no representation on the border at the time. U.S. Customs agents worked the Big Bend area on temporary duty assignments (TDAs) from the El Paso duty station. By the late 1960s, most of Hill's drug arrests occurred in conjunction with U.S. Customs

agents who had increased their TDAs along the border in response to the increased drug trade.[1] Initially, as the Mexican drug
trade began its exponential growth, only existing officers were
available to combat the onslaught.

Along the Rio Grande, smuggling routes had long been established. Many families had generations of experience in the trade.
Frequently, they worked in agriculture and, out of economic necessity, supplemented their unstable income with sporadic smuggling operations—illegal alcohol, candelilla wax, electronics,
"black tar" heroin, peyote. Hill was familiar with these smuggling
ventures, as were other officers along the border. But the changes
that evolved over the course of the decade were unanticipated
and overwhelming.

The established trade routes and traditions served as a starting
point. However, the new generation of drug traffickers soon developed a culture of violence far removed from that of their predecessors.[2]

One of the first *padrinos,* or drug lords, of the Big Bend–
Ojinaga region, Domingo Aranda, got his start during World War
II. Aranda used mule trains to transport tires, coffee, sugar, and
other rationed items to the United States. After the war, Aranda
turned his enterprise to the smuggling of poorly refined ("black
tar") heroin. As the sixties progressed, Americans' demand for
marijuana increased. Like entrepreneurs everywhere, Aranda di-
versified his operations to meet the increased demand and organized to handle the growing scope of the business.

Hill knew of Aranda's activities through informants and interrogation of traffickers. The telephone switchboard office in downtown Ojinaga served as Aranda's makeshift office. From there he
placed long-distance calls to his contacts from Albuquerque to
Chicago. Local Mexican officers with whom Hill had worked over
the years occasionally tipped him off to an upcoming delivery.

Aranda's reign as *padrino* lasted until the early 1970s when
the more aggressive and well-connected Manuel Carrasco as-

cended to the position. Carrasco later had Aranda murdered and ceremonially burned across the river from Redford, Texas, on the banks of the Río Bravo.

Hill received a phone call from a U.S Customs agent at Presidio informing him of the event and the symbolic change it signified in Ojinaga's drug-trafficking authority. This ruthless act signaled the rise of a new generation of *contrabandistas* and the start of a brutal and violent reign of power in the northern Chihuahuan Desert.[3]

The developing drug trade in Mexico was based on a payoff system involving government and military factions. The concession, or permission, to run drugs in a particular region required that a dealer remit payment to the governmental authority in that region. The local authority then took a cut and sent payment up the line. Everyone participated in the system of bribery (*la mordida,* or "the bite"), or faced consequences. "Plumo o oro," lead or gold, the saying went—take the money or take a bullet.[4]

By establishing his trade and making payments to the proper authorities, a *padrino* was said to have "*la plaza.*" All drug-trafficking operations must then go through him.

Thomas Constantine, head of the U.S. Drug Enforcement Agency (DEA) in the 1994–1999 period, noted three main factors that contributed to Mexico's pivotal role in the trafficking of illegal drugs into the United States during the 1960s and 1970s. The 2,000-mile porous border, an established history of "poly-drug" smuggling, and the existence of cross-border familial ties combined to create the ideal circumstances to foster growth in the drug trade.[5] Arguably, other important contributors were the lack of law enforcement support and the typically slow response at the federal level to combat the meteoric growth of the industry.

Another factor in the success of early *padrinos* was their charitable contributions to the local, depressed economy. By donating food and money and in-kind items for schools, hospitals, windmills, fencing, and churches, the *padrinos* gained the eyes, ears, and loyalty of many of the peasant and working class. Ultimately, however, border residents paid for these "donations" with the peace of their communities, the safety of their children, and the soul of their vibrant culture.

Big Bend National Park also experienced the impact of the increasing drug trade. Former park superintendent Hank Schmidt told of his time in the Big Bend: "Drugs were no problem for the Big Bend in the 1950s. . . . Mexican nationals would come for peyote between Boquillas and the foothills of the Chisos, which they sold across the river."[6]

By the early 1960s, however, this assessment had changed. Park concession official Jim Milburn, who arrived in the Big Bend in 1963, reported that border relations during the sixties reached a low point due to the rise of narcotics trafficking, more incidents of trespass stock and wax production, and an ever-growing migration of Mexicans north of the river to seek employment. Park ranger Robert Arnberger, in 1968, stated, "There have been shootings and drug smugglings," and Arnberger thought that he had returned to "the Texas Ranger days."[7]

In 1969, as the problem of Mexican drug smuggling escalated, President Richard Nixon authorized Operation Intercept. In an attempt to reduce the influx of illegal drugs into the United States from Mexico, the U.S. Customs Service subjected every vehicle crossing the border from Mexico to a three-minute inspection. The operation essentially shut down the border, economically, on both sides, yet accomplished little to influence the illegal flow of narcotics.[8]

The scope of the problem soon became evident. Hill's case reports chronicled a decided increase in narcotics-related investigations in the border counties in his area of responsibility. Cases during this time involved raids and seizures of large- and small-scale drug dealers and the pursuit of traffickers.

An example of a typical case was the raid on two local distributors, Daniel and Frank Gonzales of Alpine. Hill received information that the two brothers were dealing in heroin. Hill arranged for an informant to contact the two men and attempt to purchase heroin. The informant went to the dealers' home and arranged to pick up his purchase there later that day.

With fronted money, the informer arrived ready to make payment and accept delivery. Hill, Skinner, and three U.S. Customs agents hid, surrounding the house and waiting for the exchange. Hill waited behind a car on blocks in front of the house. He could not see the transaction take place, but waited to hear the prearranged signal.

The officers rushed the home with weapons drawn. Hill entered the front door, the transition to the darkness of the home from the bright sunlight and caliche drive temporarily blinding him. With the customs agents entering from the back door, officers boxed the dealers in the kitchen. Officers arrested Daniel and Frank Gonzales, confiscating 480 grams of heroin.[9]

Frequently, as the DEA chief noted, familial ties played an integral role in the region's drug trafficking and dealing. Border dealers in the early 1960s typically sold only to other Hispanics whom they knew personally. Pushers padded their pockets by introducing others in their own communities to drug use. This practice made infiltration and information gathering difficult, because Hispanics were woefully underrepresented within law enforcement ranks.

Interoffice communication often netted information. In one of several similar notifications Hill received, Captain Frank Probst passed on information from Upton County Sheriff Gene Eckols. Under interrogation a prisoner revealed that he purchased marijuana from Joe Cano in Alpine. The prisoner added that he buys it in "a Prince Albert can or rolled in cigarettes."

These circumstances helped link to Cano several arrests for small-scale possession, in which the "stash" was stored in a

Prince Albert can. The informant revealed that Cano usually drove to the border where he met with his contact. He loaded the marijuana in his pickup truck's toolbox and returned to Alpine, where he stashed it "somewhere around town." The informant added that Cano would not sell to a "total" stranger, but only to one who was brought to him by someone he had already sold to.[10] Cano certainly had familial ties in Mexico, being directly related to the famous Chico Cano, Mexican revolutionary and folk hero.

By the late 1960s, young Anglos became more common as smugglers and as dealers in the region, particularly as the radical influences affecting the nation's universities slowly established a beachhead on the Sul Ross University campus. Campus police at Sul Ross frequently provided information to Hill regarding suspected activities of students, based on tips and observations. Information on one suspect netted positive results.

Hill, U.S. Customs agents, and local sheriff's department deputies had watched a particular student for a month on suspicion of possessing, selling, and transporting marijuana. The suspect, pulled over for a traffic violation by a sheriff's deputy, was subsequently arrested on a misdemeanor charge after marijuana was found in his car. This provided Hill with enough evidence to obtain a warrant to search his residence.

Hill, along with a U.S. Customs agent and campus police officer, entered the suspect's home in student housing on the Sul Ross campus. Hill found a pound of marijuana in a plastic wrapper beside "small baggies and a quantity of bread ties."

He questioned the suspect, who revealed the details of his latest run to the border. On January 12, 1968, the young man left Alpine and traveled south to Chihuahua City, Chihuahua. He claimed to have purchased a pound of marijuana for which he paid twenty dollars cash and gave his watch, valued at approximately five dollars. He stayed in Chihuahua City two nights and returned to Alpine through Ojinaga with the marijuana hidden under the front seat of his car.[11] The student, son of a prominent family, had been snared by the drug culture and by the lure of "easy" money.

During Hill's tenure in the Big Bend country, the drug problem continued to worsen, reaching its peak after his retirement. The drug trade affected the region in terms of available money, increased presence of federal agents along the borders, and a level of violence unknown since the Mexican Revolution. Another effect of drug trafficking was growing tension in border relations and in racial/ethnic relations in the area, which had been relatively calm prior to this time, despite obvious inequities.

Perhaps the saddest casualties of the drug trade were the overshadowing of hard-working, honest border families whom Hill knew and counted as friends, and the loss of the preexisting border culture.[12] Mexican officials often expressed the sentiment that the drug problem was America's problem, not Mexico's, inferring that Americans' demand for drugs drove the market and Mexico reaped the benefits. Along *la frontera,* neither side of the river would emerge unscathed.

Despite rising crime, the law and judicial process were liberalized in the 1960s. The Civil Rights Act of 1964, the *Miranda* decision (1966), and changes in laws of arraignment and habeas corpus writs all affected the way in which Rangers, and other officers, performed their duties. Many changes were long overdue. Others seemed designed to afford criminals more rights at the expense of victims. Regardless of positive or negative impacts, landmark cases restricted the latitude officers had in the fulfillment of their duties.

The 1966 Supreme Court decision that required the "Miranda warning" initiated a trend that many officers believed favored the criminal. "There have been drastic changes in the rulings of the courts in restricting officers from interrogations, searches and seizures, and so forth," Hill said. "When I first started, we were trained in interrogation and I worked out many cases through the information gained in interrogations. Now we are required to give the Miranda Warning. . . . [W]ith a lawyer sitting beside a subject, there is no way on earth he is going to tell what he has done, tell about the crime he has committed."[13]

Like all Rangers of the time, Hill received a small card printed with the Miranda warning to read to a suspect upon arrest. He did not like the changes nor agree with them, but as long as he wore a badge he would enforce them and abide by them.

This and other laws came about largely because of law enforcement abuses. Hill believed that officers should conduct themselves beyond reproach, with the utmost integrity and fairness in the execution of their duties. Verbal interrogation utilizing psychological advantage and a steely gaze was effective, and legal, in his time. Yet, some officers physically abused suspects during interrogation. This method was illegal before *Miranda*.

These abuses resulted in increased legislative and judicial control. Hill believed that the new legislation did little to address the central issue of preventing officers from using inhumane and illegal methods to carry out their duties. Instead, he asserted, the controls placed constraints on all law enforcement officers and limited the victim's rights, and therefore, the ability of society to carry out justice.[14]

Hill expressed, in characteristic straightforward fashion, his ideas on several topics as follows: "I believe in the death penalty. I believe in not so many restrictions on the handling of the criminal. I don't believe that gun control would help one bit in law enforcement. The criminal doesn't care whether he has violated the law or not, therefore, he wouldn't care if he was violating the law by having a gun."[15]

In 1972, the Supreme Court struck down capital punishment. The decision was modified in 1976, after Hill's retirement.[16] The judicial imposition of restrictions on the death penalty was another blow to officers who believed that the ultimate deterrent to premeditated murder was no longer in place.[17]

Colonel Wilson Spier, director of the DPS, shared Hill's sentiments and summarized his beliefs in a statement made to the Sheriffs' Association of Texas in 1970. "I, for one, don't believe that anyone has a right to violate the law and engage in criminal behavior. I don't believe that persons who commit crimes while free on bail have the right to remain free. And, I don't believe that those who kill in cold blood deserve to get off but with a few years behind bars."

Spier continued, "Some will say that my attitude on the subject of crime is repressive. Some will say that punishment does not serve to deter criminal behavior. But then some haven't had the experiences we have had. Some haven't had to witness the results of horrible crimes. Some haven't had to break the news to the victims' families. And some haven't had to get down into the slime of the underworld and try to bring the perpetrators to justice."

Spier concluded, "Criminal behavior flourishes in an environment in which detection is uncertain and in which an appropriate, yet certain, punishment fails to materialize. We must not have that environment in America."[18]

By the end of the decade, the drug trade was beating a path through Hill's backyard, leaving violence and victims in its wake. Simultaneously, legal restrictions inhibited his ability to perform his duty in the manner in which he was accustomed.

Hill's America and his Big Bend had changed irrevocably. For an old Ranger who saw black and white, right and wrong, the changes were hard to take.

14

The Last Roundup

"To an Old Ranger Friend"

There are businesses of all sorts
In this world of ours,
But there never was a bond, old friend, like this,
We have drunk from the same canteen.
We have shared our blankets and tents
And have scouted and fought in all kinds of weather
And hungry and full have been
Had days of riding and days of rest,
But the memory I cling to and love the best
We have drunk from the same canteen.

———

**Ranger Lon Oden (Alpine, Texas, 1893),
from Karen Holliday Tanner and John D. Tanner,
"The Rhymin' Ranger," *Old West* 34 (Summer 1998),
eulogizing Captain Frank Jones**

THE GROWTH of the drug trade continued into the 1970s and beyond, as did the social and cultural changes that affected Texas and the Big Bend. By the time of Hill's retirement in 1974, before the largest influx of additional federal and state agents, approximately one-third of his time was dedicated to investigating the possession and smuggling of narcotics and other drugs.[1]

In 1973, the Nixon administration took steps to combat the drug epidemic. The Drug Enforcement Administration (DEA) was formed and the Bureau of Narcotics and Dangerous Drugs (BNDD) eliminated. This established a single unified federal command for the so-called war on drugs.[2] The transition, however, was not a smooth one, as conflicts over authority and jurisdiction arose with existing U.S. Customs operations.

Hill continued to work primarily with local authorities, the U.S. Customs Service, and occasionally the FBI to get the job done. Considering the scale of the increased trade, law enforcement along the border remained severely understaffed.

A 1960 Oldsmobile was parked behind a church at the edge of a small cemetery. Trinidad Fuentes and Alfredo Ramirez had driven to Presidio from Odessa that afternoon to await their contact. Responding to the flash of Ramirez's headlights, a man stepped out from behind a tombstone and into the darkness. He carried two large brown-paper grocery bags filled with small plastic baggies of marijuana.

With the successful transfer, the pair began their return trip to Odessa. Five miles south of Marfa, they approached a U.S. Border Patrol checkpoint. When a Border Patrol agent came to the window, a nervous Ramirez gunned the vehicle through the checkpoint back onto the highway. Border Patrol agents quickly initiated pursuit and radioed local authorities for assistance.

When Ramirez turned off toward Alpine at Marfa, Border Patrol agents contacted Hill. Hill radioed Skinner to set up a roadblock at U.S. Highway 90 at the city limits and then headed out the highway to meet the suspect. He encountered the Oldsmobile on the flat, near the Paisano Baptist Encampment.

Hill managed to fall in between Ramirez and the Border Patrol unit. He quickly accelerated and pulled up close behind Ramirez. Topping the hill at Twin Peaks, Ramirez and Fuentes could see the roadblock looming ahead, with Sheriff Skinner's lights flashing. Fuentes opened the window and shook out the contents of the paper bag. The deluge of marijuana baggies, many bursting on contact, hit Hill's windshield.

At the roadblock, Ramirez took a corner at high speed, attempting to turn onto a small dirt side street. He hit a parked pickup and slid into an electricity pole, breaking it in half. The high-voltage line hit the ground and shorted out, sending sparks skittering around the scene. As Hill pulled up, he could see Fuentes and Ramirez moving, illuminated by the sparks, but could not reach them due to the wreckage and electrical blockade.

Hill, Skinner, Deputy Stutz, and the Border Patrol agents quickly began to pursue the two men on foot, leaving a deputy behind to secure the dangerous scene. The search continued throughout the night. Hill returned to the wrecked vehicle and examined it, finding the remaining paper bag. At dawn, he drove out the Marfa highway, near the gate of the Baptist encampment, to begin the search for wayward marijuana baggies.

In the daylight, Hill and Skinner were able to track one of the men (it turned out to be Ramirez) from the wreck site to the Santa Fe Railway, where they determined he caught a freight train headed for Ojinaga. Later that day, Brewster County deputies discovered Fuentes in the attic of a local resident.

Hill contacted officers in Ojinaga, who apprehended Ramirez. Fuentes was sentenced to eight years in the state penitentiary.[3]

In the late 1960s and early 1970s as Hill approached retirement, he sadly watched the loss of life to drug overdose escalate. Young people in his communities, as well as across the nation, became more involved in the use of illegal narcotics. In 1971, Hill took proactive steps to educate high school students and teachers about the dangerous effects of drugs.

Hill invited Elmer Terrell, chief of the DPS Narcotics Division, to speak with students and teachers of the Alpine, Marathon, and Marfa public schools. Long before the Drug Abuse Resistance Education (DARE) program and similar organized efforts, Hill saw positive interaction with law enforcement and educated young people as a means of combating the growing problem.

Hill wrote to Terrell in a letter of thanks, "Your lecture and display of narcotics was most informative. I commend you and your department." Unfortunately, the preventive route did not deter everyone from involvement with illegal drugs. Increasingly popular on college campuses around the country, the so-called counterculture started to gain influence at Sul Ross State University in Alpine.[4]

The 1970s saw a drastic increase in the number of cases Hill handled on the college campus. Arrests of college students for possession of marijuana, heroin, and peyote were much more prevalent than in the sixties.

The president of Sul Ross University, Dr. Normand McNeal, contacted Hill with concerns over suspected "un-American activities related to drug and narcotics use, sale and transport." McNeal described the students under suspicion, including one who "attended Tulane University last year and was active in organizing demonstrations by the Tulane Liberation Front that marched on Washington D.C."

Concerned with the mounting violence on college campuses across the nation, McNeal requested that Hill arrange an undercover agent to "cope with this type of student." McNeal stated that he could confidentially enroll this agent in classes. He emphasized his concern, adding that he hoped "something could be done before any violence erupts at Sul Ross State University."[5] Hill then contacted Captain Riddles, who directed his request to the DPS Narcotics Division.

In 1971, four students stole large quantities of gunpowder, dynamite, and ammunition from an area business. The students used the materials to create homemade bombs. They experimented with their creations, blowing up small devices outside dorm windows, in a pasture outside of town, and under a highway bridge. However, when the students placed a bomb under a water fountain on the first floor of the Health and P.E. Building, they captured the attention of the university president.

Dr. McNeal was determined to find out whether this was just a college prank or part of a larger scheme. Hill again received a call from the president.[6] He investigated and arrested the students for theft, with other charges pending.

Drug trafficking continued in Big Bend National Park in the early 1970s, negatively affecting tourism. Steve Frye, a park ranger, noted, "The drug trade was significant and the NPS [National Park Service] did not solve the problem of drug trafficking. . . . There was a hell of a lot of drugs coming across the border." Stationed at the Castolon Ranger District, Frye saw the process firsthand: "Dealers leaked information to [NPS] Rangers about mule trains coming across the river and then they would cross at another site."[7]

Adding to the bad press for the park, in the mid-1970s a drug dealer turned informant appeared on *The Tonight Show.* When asked by the show's host, Johnny Carson, where along the border is the easiest to cross, the informant responded, "Big Bend National Park."

At the time of Hill's retirement in 1974, the circumstances in which he worked as a Texas Ranger in the Big Bend had changed drastically since 1947. The types of cases he dealt with, the increased number of federal officers involved, the strained interaction with law officers south of the border, and the position of power held by smugglers—all these factors combined to create a climate far removed from the horseback scout duty of his early days.

Technological advances, an urbanizing society, and improved communications affected the Big Bend to some degree. But the underlying factor that forever altered the character of the Big Bend was the illegal drug trade. Initially, the enterprise was ethnically and socioeconomically polarizing. As it grew in size and influence, it affected all residents, directly or indirectly, and created a poisoned atmosphere of distrust and fear on both sides of the border. The Last Frontier had certainly lost its innocence.

Issues of rising crime spawned from the drug trade were not limited to the Big Bend country. Soon public sentiment in Texas drove state legislators to combat the growing problem. Benefiting from this legislative emphasis on crime, the Ranger force increased from sixty-two to eighty as of September 1, 1970.

On the same date, the department's organizational structure was altered, with the addition of the position of senior Ranger captain to coordinate Ranger activities. The first DPS senior Ranger captain, Clint Peoples, received the promotion from his position as captain of Company F.

In 1973, a year before Hill's retirement, the Ranger Service celebrated its 150th anniversary. The role of the Ranger as citizen soldier, protecting the frontier, had certainly changed since its inception.

Residential and small-business robberies escalated nationally in the late 1960s and into the 1970s, fueled by increased drug usage. Burglars even targeted the U.S. customhouse at Presidio in 1973. Property was taken primarily from the "seizure room" and was made up almost entirely of narcotics.[8]

A specific type of theft was unique to the region, however. The mining of cinnabar ore began in Terlingua in 1903. The ore, after processing, produces quicksilver, also known as liquid mercury. The mining of quicksilver in the Terlingua–Study Butte area continued into the early 1970s.

In May 1970, Hill investigated the theft of mercury from the Study Butte Diamond Alkali Mine. A division of Diamond Shamrock, the mine had ceased operations two months earlier. One employee, George Robert Miller, remained on the job to process previously mined cinnabar ore to extract the liquid mercury. Miller also served as security, protecting the essentially abandoned mine property.

Miller reported to the company approximately one-half flask of mercury mined per day (forty pounds). His instructions were to store the mercury in the mine warehouse for sale later. The sale of mercury required a license, which Miller did not possess.

Miller made the mistake of attempting to sell some of the company's product to a licensed seller, Glen Pepper, offering a 25 percent cut. Pepper reported Miller's offer to Hill, who arranged for Pepper to accept Miller's offer and capture Miller in the act.

Hill arrived in Study Butte at a local store, in view of Miller's mobile home residence. He watched from a pay phone while Pepper conducted the exchange. In view of the road, Miller moved several bricks from around the bottom of his trailer, revealing the flasks that held the mercury.

Hill waited for Miller to load five flasks into Pepper's car, receive payment, and allow Pepper to drive away from the scene. Then he approached the trailer. Miller answered the door and submitted to search and arrest without resistance.

After moving countless bricks, Hill recovered fifteen more flasks from under the trailer, totaling 1,140 pounds. Hill placed Miller in the Brewster County Jail, charged with felony embezzlement and possession of liquid mercury without a bill of sale.[9]

Increases in crime, locally and nationally, translated to higher risk for officers. In 1973, a total of 260 federal, state, and local law enforcement officers were killed when performing job-related duties. The following year, that number climbed to a record high 271. Only in 2001, because of the number of officers killed in the World Trade Center Towers on September 11, have more officers died in the line of duty. The 1970s remain the deadliest decade in U.S. law enforcement history.[10]

On April 27, 1973, Presidio County Sheriff Ernest D. "Hank" Hamilton's name was added to the list of fallen officers. Shortly before 3:30 p.m., the Presidio County sheriff's office at Marfa received a call about a parked car two miles off U.S. Highway 90 on the Ralston Ranch. A Ralston Ranch worker called to complain that the man had parked on private property. Marfa Border Patrol officers also spotted the vehicle from their aerial surveillance and called in to report. Sheriff Hamilton, along with twenty-two-year-old deputy William Massey, took the call.

The officers arrived at the parked car, which bore out-of-date California license plates. Sheriff Hamilton approached the 1965 Olds sedan to question the lone occupant. The man, George Sylvester Duckworth, claimed to have permission from a ranch worker to park there. Hamilton explained that the same worker had called to complain about his parking on private property.

After arguing briefly, Duckworth took a .22 Beretta pistol from under the front seat and shot Sheriff Hamilton four times in the chest. He then turned and directed his fire at Deputy Massey, shooting him in the upper left arm. Duckworth fled on foot.

While Duckworth ran into the nearby pasture, the injured Massey flagged down a vehicle and went into town to notify officers. Border Patrol agents found Duckworth, having returned to

Presidio County Sheriff Ernest
D. "Hank" Hamilton upon taking
office (January 1973). Hamilton
was killed in the line of duty on
April 27, 1973.

his car, sitting quietly in the driver's seat next to the slain sheriff. The officers arrested Duckworth without incident. Justice of the Peace Narciso Sanchez, Jr., pronounced Hamilton dead at the scene.[11]

When Hill arrived, the coroner had already removed Hamilton's body. Hill's attention was drawn immediately to the disheveled man sitting in the back of the patrol car—handcuffed hands in his lap, a vacant expression on his face.

Hill met Border Patrol officers who started toward his vehicle upon seeing him approach. Border Patrolmen Brenner, O'Donnell, Bonner, Tidwell, Sloss, Wall, and Worrell, along with Marfa city police officer Danny Luna had effectively secured the scene of the crime. Officers began photographing the crime scene and collecting, identifying, and marking evidence for laboratory and court use.

O'Donnell told Hill that he had given the suspect the statutory warnings and advised him of his rights. He added that he had yet to get a coherent statement out of the prisoner. He turned custody of Duckworth over to Hill.

Hill moved through the group of officers and approached the Border Patrol vehicle where Duckworth sat. Meeting the killer's gaze, Hill sensed Duckworth's instability. He began his questioning in a calm, calculated way. Duckworth, wary, revealed a rough version of the incident, although he was not forthcoming with details. With sunset approaching, Hill directed his attention to the activities around him.

Meanwhile, District Attorney Aubry Edwards arrived. He attempted to get a statement from Duckworth. Duckworth became angry with Edwards, drawing Hill's attention away from evidence collection. He moved over to the vehicle with Duckworth and Edwards. The prisoner heatedly advised Edwards that he did not wish to talk anymore as he was tired.[12]

Duckworth turned his fractious gaze to Hill. He announced

that he had tape-recorded the entire interaction with Hamilton and that the tape could tell what happened better than he could.

Hill took the tagged tape recorder from the evidence collected. He carried it back over to the patrol car and slid in the seat beside Duckworth, placing the tape recorder between them. He rewound the tape and pressed play.

Sitting beside the killer, just hours after the murder, Hill listened to Hamilton's last words. He described the horrific contents of the damning tape, "I could hear the gunshots when he killed Sheriff Hamilton. . . . I heard Sheriff Hamilton breathe his last breath as he fell on the mike in the seat of the car."[13]

Hill transported Duckworth to the Ector County Jail, where he was incarcerated, awaiting trial. After carefully making a copy of the tape, Hill drove to Austin to hand deliver the tape to the DPS lab. There he sat for hours meticulously listening to the disturbing communication, to ensure transcription of the exact words.

The Morrow and Cooksey cases remained burned in his memory. Hill was not about to lose Hamilton's murderer to the courts. He would ensure that every possible bit of evidence was available. Duckworth would pay for his crime to the full extent of the law, which at the time would not allow for the death penalty.[14] The audiotape was later admitted as incriminating evidence at the trial that convicted Duckworth, who was sentenced to life imprisonment.[15]

Hill initiated a thorough investigation of Duckworth. He began in Odessa where he and Captain Riddles questioned their prisoner. A retired air force major, Duckworth lived at Norton Air Force Base in California.

Duckworth had become angered when the State of California refused the registration of his 1965 Olds sedan until he added the required pollution equipment to meet California emissions standards. Duckworth decided to drive the vehicle to San Antonio, where he could establish residency and register the vehicle in Texas without having to purchase the pollution equipment.[16]

Hill discovered other tapes in Duckworth's vehicle and a key to an airport locker in Las Vegas, Nevada. Hill contacted authorities in Nevada, who soon procured additional audiotapes from the locker and forwarded them to Hill.

It became evident that Duckworth had set out to fulfill a vendetta against officers whom he considered oppressive. The contents of the tapes revealed hours of paranoid tirades about officers following him and putting him under surveillance. "I am fed up with being pushed around," Duckworth recorded.[17]

A taped telephone conversation records Duckworth's convoluted interaction with a lawyer named Hunt. "I need to talk to someone about the surveillance that is going on and the threatening action by police. I have reached a point I can't take any more of it. I have tried to get out and challenge the police, including an F.B.I. agent, to ask what the hell they want from me and no one will answer."[18]

Another tape in Duckworth's possession chronicled a conversation with an Arizona State Police trooper who pulled Duckworth over for expired tags. The Arizona trooper asked, "Why the tape recorder?" Duckworth replied, "Well I have been harassed enough by you people. The last thirty months I have been stopped over three hundred times." After contacting the Arizona State Police, Hill realized Duckworth made the tape the day before Hamilton was killed.[19]

Duckworth was a powder keg ready to explode. Hamilton became the object of his furious paranoid outburst. Hill recalled, "Hank was a good friend of mine. He had only been in the Sheriff's office from January to April when he was killed."[20]

Owing to improvements in body armor and, arguably, to the return of the death penalty in some states beginning in 1976, the succeeding decades saw the on-duty mortality rate for officers decline. Slowly, legislation and judiciary practices struck a balance between the civil rights of the accused and those of society.

Despite the numerous socioeconomic and political changes affecting the Big Bend, livestock smuggling and theft cases remained a constant. Whether the theft involved two Hereford heifers or two hundred head of goats, Hill was called in to investigate. Up until his retirement, he worked pastures on horseback for brand inspection, tracking, and "close work." In the saddle, Hill was in his element, and the world still made sense.

In January 1971, in response to a request from Lester Housinger of the U.S. Department of Agriculture and Elmo Miller of the U.S. Customs Service, Hill began an investigation of cattle smuggling on the McCutchin Ranch, near Presidio. Hill, along with Rangers McKinney, Hodges, Sessums, and Allee, rounded up cattle in four pastures holding four hundred head. Rangers discovered nine head of smuggled Mexican stock, which they seized and trailered to the U.S. Customs facility at Presidio.[21] The U.S. Customs Service filed criminal charges against McCutchin at the federal courthouse in El Paso.

Hill continued to use horses frequently in his work. By the 1970s, with improved road conditions, he was usually able to trailer his horse closer to the site of an investigation or manhunt.[22] Most of the ranches that were at one time accessible only by horse or jeep now could be accessed via a county road. Helicopters were available for air support, and more of the borderland had two-way communications, although not all. The region had changed and with it the way of doing business for those chosen to protect it.

Hill, however, would have one last roundup in the Big Bend of his memory where telephone lines did not venture and roads did not encroach. For three days, he would ride the border country with his Company E Rangers, chasing Mexican cattle across the cactus-filled, fenceless terrain of Big Bend National Park.

Texas Rangers Company E (1974). *Left to right:* **Captain Jim Riddles, Arthur Hill, Sid Merchant, H. R. Block, Tol Dawson, Clayton McKinney, Arthur Sikes, Charley Hodges, Alfred Allee Jr., Gene Graves, Bud Newberry, Grady Sessums, Sergeant J. P. Lynch.**

In 1973, Lester Housinger again requested Hill's assistance in the removal of "trespass" stock that had wandered from Mexico, across the narrow river, into Big Bend National Park.

The roundup of trespass stock in the Big Bend had a long-standing tradition. Park personnel likened the sale of unclaimed trespass stock to that of the sale of bat guano in Carlsbad National Park—small payoff for an annoying problem.

Hill and other Rangers had previously assisted with the roundup of trespass stock in the park. Housinger wrote in his request to Hill, "As you will recall, this same type of operation was accomplished on the Middleton Ranch, approximately four miles above Candelaria, Texas, in 1971. The operation proved very successful because of the excellent cooperation between several state and federal agencies, especially that of the Texas Rangers."

Hill, Housinger, Riddles, U.S. Customs agent Bill Broman, and park representatives met at Big Bend National Park headquarters several days before the roundup to finalize plans. Housinger outlined his instructions, "All Rangers are requested to be responsible for their own food, water, bedding, etc." Housinger continued,

"It is likely that it will be necessary to camp out two nights." That was nothing for an old Ranger who began his career in scout duty for months at a time.

Hill passed on the supply advice to Rangers participating in the roundup. He informed his Company E Rangers that the National Park Service agreed to make horses and saddles available. Hill added his own amendment to the supply list, "I'm sure all Rangers will have their rifles."[23]

At a neighboring ranch, the Rangers assembled to begin their trek along the river and adjoining land to gather wayward livestock. The Ranger camp consisted of Sergeant J. P. Lynch (Midland), Alfred Allee, Jr. (Ozona), Ken Blanchard (Midland), Tol Dawson (Pecos), Charlie Hodges (Midland), Clayton McKinney (Sierra Blanca), and Grady Sessums (Del Rio).

Park rangers, U.S. Customs agents, and a U.S. Customs helicopter met Rangers at the ranch. The helicopter and radios took a lot of the guesswork out of locating stray stock.

Hill and his Company E compadres spent three days in the Big Bend among the greasewood, sotol, cactus, and mesquite chasing cattle. As the old saying goes, "A Ranger is not a Ranger unless he is in the mesquite." For those three days, they were Rangers in the old tradition.

Hill stopped his horse at the Rio Grande border, a strange divider in a desert landscape. The river flowed by, as it had twenty-six years before on his first scout duty—camping with Captain Cowsert. Hill felt fortunate to have served in the era he had.

In 1947, he had foreseen the end of scout duty. Now he saw a new era approaching that belonged to the younger men who now rode with him. While his horse drank, his gaze followed the changeless river, searching the canyons that rose farther upstream. He smiled.

The roundup of April 1973 was a success. Rangers loaded confiscated livestock into U.S. Customs trailers and delivered

**Texas Rangers involved in roundup of trespass stock in Big Bend National Park
(April 1973). Ranger Hill at far left. Note helicopter in background.**

them to holding pens in Presidio. Animals remained there until claimed by their owner, who paid a fine to secure the release.

In a letter of thanks to DPS director Wilson Spier, the veterinarian in charge of the region, Frank Hamilton, formally quantified the success of the operation stating, "A total of 46 bovine and 12 equine were apprehended."

Hamilton added, "We are most grateful for the help extended by all of your people, but most especially for the assistance of Ranger Hill in organizing the roundup."[24]

At the time of his retirement, Hill had the distinction of having the most time in service as an active Ranger, along with DPS classmate Lewis Rigler. Both men received their trooper certifications and Ranger appointments on the same dates.[25]

The brotherhood was changing along with the times. But for those three days in 1973, the older generation and the next shared the camaraderie of Ranger camp. Together they rode mountain trails along the timeless river in the hoof prints of their predecessors. The torch had passed.

15

"A Beautiful Challenge"

The Rangers found the land a beautiful challenge. Here, one had to ride and trail as efficiently as the Indian. Here, reinforcements were too far away to be of consequence. Here many Rangers left their hearts.

John L. Davis, *The Texas Rangers: Images and Incidents,* 129

THE TEXAS RANGER post in the Big Bend has been continuously manned since the Rangers' association with the DPS, first at Marfa and then at Alpine. Border problems and sparse local law enforcement have necessitated the Ranger presence.

Pete Crawford, Leo Bishop, and Joe Bridge preceded Hill, beginning in 1935. After Hill's retirement, his post was filled by Alfred Allee, Jr. (1975–1977), Clayton McKinney (1977–1985), Joaquin Jackson (1986–1993), Ronald Stewart (1994–1995), and then by Sergeant David Duncan since 1995. The tradition continues, and Hill's twenty-seven-year tenure set a standard.[1]

Hill began his service with those who started their careers on horseback and made the transition to automobiles, and with those who received appointment from the Adjutant General's Office and saw the Rangers move under DPS control. Rangers such as Gully Cowsert, Charlie Miller, Houston White, Frank Mills, and M. T. Gonzaullas were his mentors. His contemporaries included

Rangers Riddles, Rigler, Arnold, Ray, Nance, Klevenhagen, Crowder, and Allee, Sr. By 1974, a new generation was in place.

Alfred Allee, Jr., summed it up: "Coming up, I knew that old bunch. They were just different; had a sense of honor; knew how to get the job done. That old bunch, they were Rangers all the time."[2] In a time before mandatory work hours, when the Rangers were a living symbol of the law in the rural communities where many spent most of their lives, the assessment was accurate.

The older generation of Rangers, most born before World War I, had different life experiences, views, and perceptions compared to their successors. In turn, the life experiences of the last of the horseback Rangers still in the Service when Hill and his contemporaries began their Ranger careers were also different. Like the cycles of family, the generations are different, but the bond is the same.

The Ranger tradition continues to evolve. In 2003, the Texas Rangers celebrated their 180th anniversary with a force comprising 116 members. Rangers continue to investigate major crimes, including "cyber-crime" and identity theft. Meanwhile, Rangers still pursue and apprehend smuggled livestock along the Rio Grande.[3]

Walter Prescott Webb addressed this idea more than seventy years ago when he wrote, "The Rangers are what they are because their enemies have been what they were. The Rangers had to be superior to survive. Their enemies were good. . . . The Rangers had to be better."[4]

In 1974, Arthur Hill, at sixty-five, had reached the age of mandatory retirement from the Department of Public Safety. He "hung up his gun belt" on July 31, 1974.

Hill had always carried his Texas Ranger Weekly Activity Notebook in his jacket or back pants pocket. In the notebook, he listed his activities for each day, number of hours worked, and the number of miles accumulated on his state vehicle in the process. These notes he used toward the end of the month to complete required paperwork.

As he pulled up to his house at the end of the workday, his habit was to complete the record for that day. On July 31, he filled in the pertinent information as he always did, "Worked in and around Alpine on theft and burglary investigation with local officers: 12 duty hours, 40 miles in [state car]." Hill thoughtfully added, to no one but himself, "This completes my career as a Texas Ranger with twenty-seven years in the Rangers and six years in Texas Highway Patrol, totaling thirty-three years with the Texas Department of Public Safety, lacking one month."[5]

Earlier in the summer, Captain Jim Riddles and Sergeant J. P. Lynch of Company E and DPS representatives organized a retirement party for Hill at the Alpine Country Club. Guests included DPS administrators, Rangers, and others with whom Hill had worked, plus friends and family.

Riddles decided that the menu had to include fish. Every summer the Hills invited all Company E Rangers to their home for a fish fry following their annual fishing trip to Vallecito Lake in southwestern Colorado. Riddles had fond memories of the fellowship and good food on the Hills' rock patio behind their Alpine home.

Like many retirement parties, speakers told of their memories of Hill and of shared experiences. Perhaps Captain Riddles paid Hill the biggest compliment when he, following other speakers, took the podium. "The thing that really impresses me most about Arthur, [which] none of them [previous speakers] mentioned, but all of them knew. I had the privilege on three or four occasions to work in the same area that Arthur had. I don't know whether all of you will understand, but I'll just sum it up this way. When I got there and Arthur had been there, all of them 'old sorries' [habitual criminals] was gentle." Hill had done his job well.[6]

Sergeant Lynch followed Captain Riddles and summarized Hill's most important achievements in two sentences: "You've got a good family. You've got the respect of the people where you live and where you work. Partner, it's been a pleasure."[7]

With that, Hill uncomfortably took the podium to address his family, friends, and co-workers. He quickly got to the point that he had practiced and wanted to communicate. "To me, it is the fulfillment of a fascinating journey in my life. I am most grateful for the privilege of serving Texas and my community these many years as [a] Texas Ranger. It has been a long, interesting, and exciting career. I have been privileged to work for and with the finest officers on Earth. For this long and eventful journey, I am most appreciative."[8]

After retirement, Hill maintained a law enforcement commission as a Special Ranger. Until 1980, he worked on a contract basis, investigating cases in the region for private interests. He assisted area law enforcement occasionally as their numbers and budgets were small.

As a Special Ranger, Hill was required to maintain firearms proficiency and recertify every two years. In a 1983 letter to assistant DPS director Colonel Leo Gossett, Hill wrote, "I appreciate very much my Special Ranger Commission. I will fulfill my firearms qualification soon. I haven't put on a pistol since qualifying last year, but can think of at least three or four good reasons for doing so. Fortunately, those reasons are still in the penitentiary. It's the three or four that I can't think of that concern me." Hill carried a Special Ranger commission until his death. And in the top of his boot, he carried a snub-nosed Smith and Wesson .38 pistol—just in case.[9]

Throughout his retirement, Hill received calls from parole boards notifying him of the release of certain prisoners. Sometimes a parole board requested his recommendation on the parole of a prisoner he had arrested. Hill worried about what would hap-

Hill's last badge as an active Ranger, and his Special Ranger badge
that he carried until his death in 1987.

pen when he was no longer available to remind parole boards of
the details surrounding the human tragedy of a given crime. He
worried about the continuity of good relations that he fostered
within the community, between branches of law enforcement,
and with Mexican authorities.[10] Sadly, he saw these elements of
harmony slipping away.

At retirement, Hill had served as a Ranger twenty-four hours a
day for close to half of his life. If not for the stability and support
of his wife, Hill attested, he would never have made it. Ruby
completed her education degree at Sul Ross and taught three generations of Alpine first graders to read and write. She maintained
the home and had a warm plate waiting for him whenever he returned. More often than not, she had no idea when that would be.

In retirement, the Hills finally had the opportunity to make up
for lost time—fishing, traveling, and enjoying family. These activities slowed in 1983 when Hill suffered a major stroke that severely affected his right side. With the same tenacity he brought

to everything he did, Hill set about rehabilitation. Through great effort, he eventually was able to walk and use his right arm.

Arthur and Ruby planned one last big vacation to Alaska. Hill wanted to see the unspoiled wilderness of the Far North.

In early May 1987, Hill's daughter, Martha, her husband, George, and their youngest son, Stanley, came to spend the weekend in Alpine. They worked all day Saturday preparing the travel trailer for the upcoming trip to Alaska.

On Sunday afternoon, the family climbed into Hill's 1982 Grand Marquis to "make the loop" as he called it—to drive around the area. They rode up around the college and out the Marfa Highway.

They drove out toward Marfa as far as the old air base and made their way back toward town. Despite his stroke and partial loss of peripheral vision, Arthur was always the first to spot pronghorn antelope grazing on the high plains. As they neared the Twin Peaks, they pulled to the side of the road to see their old house and reminisce before continuing.

As they arrived at the outskirts of Alpine, a horse caught Arthur's eye. They slowed the car, pulled off the road, and circled around a small pen. Ribs showed along the horse's side. The soil in the makeshift pen was concrete hard. No bucket or sign of water was evident.

Arthur and his grandson stood at the pen. Both could not believe the state of the horse. Arthur grew angry as he and the others searched for a bucket to water the horse. They finally came across a small container and provided the horse enough water to last until Hill could make inquiries as to the owner's name and report the neglect to authorities. He promised his grandson that he would return with feed and hay when the feed store opened.[11]

The family returned home to an early evening meal. After supper, Arthur relaxed on the front porch swing, as was his custom. The BB gun, propped against the side of the house, saw much use scaring birds away from his fruit trees. Martha and family collected their things and prepared to drive home. They all gathered on the porch to say their good-byes.

The sun had begun to set, casting pink hues and streaks of purple across the West Texas sky. He sat with his hands in his lap, fingers interlaced, and thumbs slowly circling one another. They conversed about the pecan trees and the grapevines, questioned if the peaches would make after a late frost. Arthur reassured his grandson that he would see to the horse, almost getting himself worked up again.

He stopped the motion of his thumbs and smiled, surveying his family's faces. "You know," he began, "I have enjoyed my life and my profession. If I had it to do over again, I wouldn't change a thing."[12]

At dawn, Arthur and his friend Harry Carpenter went to the feed store and then drove out to feed the neglected horse. Harry knew the name of the horse's owner, and Hill reported the abuse before breakfast. He immediately called Martha. It was important that his grandson know that he had fed and watered the horse and everything would be all right.[13]

That night, May 5, 1987, Hill suffered a fatal heart attack while he slept. He was buried in the Alpine Cemetery, looking out across the rugged Glass Mountains, and carried to his final rest by Rangers past and present of his beloved Company E.[14]

Many DPS administrators, local and federal officers, and the governor honored Hill. The greatest tribute, however, to his life of service and his legacy to the community was the attendance of a broad cross-section of Big Bend residents who paid their respects, including ranchers, executives, cowboys, professors, laborers, miners, wax choppers, and educators, both Anglo and Hispanic.[15]

Hill had a special attachment, forged from years of ranging on horseback and by automobile, to the land and to the people of the Big Bend. In his last interview, Hill said, "I am really proud of, when I look back over my career, that most of it was spent right here in the Big Bend country. I think the law abiding citizens respect me for what I have done, and I think I have made it a little easier for the man who comes in to take my place." The region was home, and Hill was one tile in the continuously evolving mosaic of the Big Bend.[16]

Historian John L. Davis noted the affection of Frontier Rangers for the character and wildness of the Big Bend. "The Rangers found the land a beautiful challenge. Here, one had to ride and trail as efficiently as the Indian. Here, reinforcements were too far away to be of consequence. Here many Rangers left their hearts."[17]

In his years of service, Ranger Hill did not seek the spotlight or recognition for his accomplishments. He was satisfied to do "right because it was right," and to make a difference in the lives of the people whom he served and protected.

In a career that began on horseback patrol and scout duty in Ranger camps along the Rio Grande, Hill was one of the few who had the privilege of experiencing the work of a Ranger as it had been and as it had become, leaving behind a legacy of integrity and commitment.

It was here, in the Big Bend, that Texas Ranger Arthur Hill left his heart as well, with the people and the land that make up Texas's Last Frontier.

Notes

Abbreviations

ABB Archives of the Big Bend, Sul Ross State University, Alpine, Texas

CAH Center for American History, University of Texas at Austin

DPS Texas Department of Public Safety, Austin

HFC Hill Family Collection, Texas Ranger Hall of Fame Research Center, Waco; Archives of the Big Bend; Sul Ross State University, Alpine, Texas

JHC Junior Historians Collection, Marfa Public Library, Marfa, Texas

TRHF Texas Ranger Hall of Fame and Museum, Waco

TSHA Texas State Historical Association, Handbook of Texas Online, http://www.tsha.utexas.edu/handbook/online

UTPB University of Texas Permian Basin Library, Odessa

Introduction

1. Cox, *Silver Stars and Six Guns;* Texas State Archives Online, "Rangers and Outlaws," http://www.tsl.state.tx.us/treasures/law/index.html; TSHA, s.v. "Texas Rangers," http://www.tsha.utexas.edu/handbook/online/articles/view/TT/met4.html. The point is debated as to the original date of organization for the Ranger Service with many arguing that the actual title of "Ranger" does not appear in legislation until 1835. In deed and function, if not in name, the group can trace their organizational beginnings to the earlier date.

2. Department of Public Safety (DPS), *50th Anniversary Celebration,* 6.

3. Ibid.

4. Utley, "Tales of the Texas Rangers," 41.

5. DPS, *50th Anniversary Celebration,* 6.

6. Ibid.

7. Wilkins, *Law Comes to Texas,* 2–24.

8. TSHA, s.v. "Texas Rangers," 3–4; Davis, *The Texas Rangers,*
49–56.

9. Cox, "From Horses to Helicopters."

10. Wilkins, *Law Comes to Texas,* 216–222.

11. There are well-documented accounts, throughout the history of
the Rangers, of incidents of mistreatment of Texans of Hispanic heritage,
as well as other minority Texans, by individual and small groups of
Rangers. Charles H. Harris III and Louis R. Sadler delineate some events
during the Mexican Revolution in *The Texas Rangers and the Mexican
Revolution: The Bloodiest Decade, 1910–1920.* The introduction serves
only to give a general overview of the purpose and achievements of the
Ranger Service as a whole in their early history for readers unfamiliar
with the background of the organization. Also not outlined in detail in
the brief introduction is the fact that the ranks of Rangers during the
early years included Texans of Mexican heritage as well as Native Americans. This was unusual in law enforcement and citizen militias in the
United States at this time. All Rangers made contributions to the Texas
that emerged. For a comprehensive list of Republic of Texas–era Rangers
of Hispanic and American Indian heritage, see TRHF (online):
http://www.texasranger.org/ReCenter/Hispanic_Indian_Rangers.htm.

12. TSHA, s.v. "Mexican Revolution," http://www.tsha.utexas.edu/
handbook/online/articles/MM/pqmhe.html.

13. Texas State Library and Archives Commission: Texas Treasures:
"Rangers and Outlaws," http://www.tsl.state.tx.us/treasures/law/
index.html.

14. TSHA, s.v. "Texas Rangers."

15. Ibid.

16. DPS, *Golden Anniversary Pictorial and History Book,* 52, 55; Cox, *Silver Stars and Six Guns,* 16.

17. Jenkins, *I'm Frank Hamer,* 179–208.

18. DPS, *Golden Anniversary Pictorial and History Book,* 31–33.

19. Ibid., 43.

20. Lewis Rigler to Arthur Hill, personal communication, Gainesville, Texas, June 1974, audiotape, HFC. (Unless otherwise indicated, all citations of "Hill" in chapter notes are to "Arthur Hill.")

1 In the Shadow of Santa Anna Mountain

1. TSHA, s.v. "Santa Anna," http://www.tsha.utexas.edu/ handbook/online/articles/SS/hjs8.html.

2. Ibid.

3. TSHA, s.v. "Camp Colorado," http://www.tsha.utexas.edu/ handbook/online/articles/CC/qbc8.html.

4. Cox, *Texas Ranger Tales II,* 242.

5. TSHA, s.v. "Robert M. Coleman," http://www.tsha.utexas.edu/ handbook/online/articles/CC/fco18.html.

6. Bell County Historical Commission, *Story of Bell County, Texas,* 179; Hill, interview by Theresa Whittington, Alpine, Texas, April 28, 1976, transcript, ABB.

7. Martha Hill Spinks, interview by author, Eldorado, Texas, 2004.

8. TSHA, s.v. "Coleman County," http://www.tsha.utexas.edu/ handbook/online/articles/CC/hcc15.html.

9. A. Hill, interview by Whittington, Alpine, April 28, 1976, ABB; Hill, interview by Debbie Elolf, Texas Ranger Headquarters, Company F, Waco, Texas, May 19, 1979, transcript, TRHF.

10. M. H. Spinks, interview by author, Eldorado, Texas, 2004.

11. Ibid.

12. Marjorie Hill King, interview by author, Eldorado, Texas, 2004.

13. Ibid.

14. The Senior Class, 1930, Santa Anna High School, *The Mountaineer, 1930,* HFC.

15. M. H. King, interview by author, Eldorado, Texas, 2004.

16. Hill, interview by Elolf, Waco, Texas, May 19, 1979, TRHF.

17. Coleman County Historical Commission, *History of Coleman County and Its People,* 111.

18. Hill, interview by Elolf, Waco, Texas, May 19, 1979, TRHF.

19. Hill, personal résumé, HFC; Senior Class, 1930, Santa Anna High School, *The Mountaineer, 1930,* HFC.

20. National Park Service, "Carlsbad Caverns," http://www.nps.gov/cave/history.htm.

21. Hill, discussion with Spinks family, Alpine, Texas, December 1985, audiotape, HFC.

22. Hill, personal résumé, HFC; M. H. Spinks, interview by author, Eldorado, Texas, 2004.

23. Hill, personal résumé, HFC.

24. Ruby Kerby Hill, personal communication with author.

25. Ibid.

26. Arthur Hill, Western Union telegram correspondence to Frank Hill, April 20, 1933, HFC.

27. R. K. Hill, personal communication with author.

28. Hill, personal résumé, HFC.

29. Hill, National Guard honorable discharge, January 21, 1936, HFC.

30. R. K. Hill, personal communication with author.

31. Hill, Deputation record, State of Texas, Coleman County, February 12, 1941, HFC.

32. R. K. Hill, personal communication with author.

33. Homer Garrison and Hill Foreman to Hill, undated, HFC.

34. The Apollo Program, "Apollo 11 (AS-506): Lunar Landing Mission," http://www.nasm.si.edu/collections/imagery/apollo/AS11/a11.htm (accessed May 12, 2007).

2 "Five Hundred Dollars Is Too Damned Much . . ."

1. "State Highway Patrol Examinations," *Santa Anna News,* July 20, 1941, HFC.

2. Ibid.

3. Garrison and Foreman to Hill, undated, HFC.

4. Ibid.

5. DPS, *50th Anniversary Celebration, 7.*

6. DPS, *Golden Anniversary Pictorial and History Book,* 61–62, 58, 144.

7. Bill Harris, quote listed on display, Texas Highway Patrol Museum, San Antonio, Texas.

8. DPS, *50th Anniversary Celebration,* 8–10; TSHA, s.v. "Department of Public Safety," http://www.tsha.utexas.edu/handbook/online/articles/TT/mctrp.html.

9. DPS, *50th Anniversary Celebration,* 7; DPS, *Golden Anniversary Pictorial and History Book,* 31–34.

10. DPS, *50th Anniversary Celebration,* 7.

11. Ibid., 7–10.

12. Ibid., 8; Col. Wilson Spier, speech to 1941 DPS Highway Patrol School Reunion, Austin, Texas, 1985, audiotape, HFC.

13. TSHA, s.v. "Homer Garrison, Jr.," http://www.tsha.utexas.edu/handbook/online/articles/GG/fga34.html.

14. DPS, *50th Anniversary Celebration,* 8.

15. Spier, speech to 1941 DPS School Reunion, Austin, Texas, 1985, HFC.

16. "Camp Mabry," *Texas Police Journal,* September 1960, 1–2, 20–21; "West Point of Texas Police," *Dallas Morning News,* October 26, 1941, HFC.

17. Exhibit Information, Texas Military Forces Museum, Camp Mabry, Austin, Texas; TSHA, s.v. "Camp Mabry," http://www.tsha.utexas.edu/handbook/online/articles/view/CC/qbc18.html.

18. Albers, *Life and Reflections of a Texas Ranger,* 18; Hill, interview by author, Alpine, Texas, December 1986, audiotape, HFC; Bob Arnold, "A Legend in His Own Time: R. M. 'Red' Arnold," *Texas Ranger Dispatch,* Winter 2002, http://www.texasranger.org/dispatch/9/Arnold2.htm.

19. Capt. Royal C. Phillips, Commanding Military Division, Texas Highway Patrol School, *Military General Order No. 3,* Roster of the Military Company, September 5, 1941, p. 3, HFC.

20. Ibid., *Military General Order No. 2,* Roster of the Military Division, September 5, 1941, HFC; Hill, interview by author, Alpine, Texas, December 1986, HFC.

21. "West Point of Texas Police"; Seventh DPS Highway Patrol School, classwork and handouts, HFC; Hill, personal communication with author.

22. R. K. Hill, personal communication with author.

23. Hill, interview by author, Alpine, Texas, December 1986, HFC.

24. Ibid.

25. Hill, personal communication with author.

26. State of Texas, DPS, Highway Patrol Identification, October 1, 1941, HFC.

27. Hill, interview by author, Alpine, Texas, December 1986, HFC.

28. Hill, Highway Patrol graduation photograph with patrol number, HFC.

29. Exhibit Information, Texas Highway Patrol Museum, San Antonio, Texas; confirmation with photographs from HFC.

30. Homer Garrison and Hill Foreman to Arthur Hill, October 22, 1941, HFC.

31. TSHA, s.v. "Seymour, TX," http://www.tsha.utexas.edu/handbook/online/articles/view/SS/hgs7.html.

32. Hill, personal communication with author; M. H. Spinks, interview by author, Eldorado, Texas, 2004.

33. Hill, discussion with Spinks family, "Seymour Stories," Alpine, Texas, December 1985, audiotape, HFC.

34. M. H. Spinks, interview by author, Eldorado, Texas, 2004.

35. Hill, interview by Elolf, Waco, Texas, May 19, 1979, TRHF.

36. Ibid.

37. DPS, *50th Anniversary Celebration,* 10.

38. Hill, Criminal Case Report, September 20, 1944, HFC.

39. M. H. King, interview by author, Eldorado, Texas, 2004.

40. Hill, Criminal Case Report, November 17, 1942, HFC.

41. TSHA, s.v. "Crowell, TX," http://www.tsha.utexas.edu/handbook/online/articles/view/CC/hjc22.html.

42. M. H. Spinks, interview by author, Eldorado, Texas, 2004.

43. Hill, discussion with Spinks family, "Seymour Stories," Alpine, Texas, December 1985, HFC.

44. Ibid.

45. M. H. Spinks, interview by author, Eldorado, Texas, 2004.

46. Hill, discussion with Spinks family, "Seymour Stories," Alpine, Texas, December 1985, HFC.

47. Ibid.

48. Ibid.

49. Ibid.

50. Ibid.

51. Homer Garrison and Hill Foreman to Arthur Hill, October 26, 1945, HFC.

52. Hill, discussion with Spinks family, "Seymour Stories," Alpine, Texas, December 1985, HFC.

53. Ibid.

54. Hill to Homer Garrison, August 14, 1947, HFC.

55. Homer Garrison and W. J. Elliot to Hill, February 4, 1947, HFC.

56. Gully Cowsert to Hill, August 20, 1947, HFC.

57. Hill to W. J. Elliot, August 19, 1947, HFC.

3 The Last Frontier

1. Thompson, *History of Marfa and Presidio County,* 2:395–397.

2. Schreiner, *Pictorial History of the Texas Rangers,* 150–151; "Ranger Joe Bridge Dies on Tuesday," unknown news source, TRHF, Bridge vertical file.

3. Hill, interview by Dr. Avillar, Alpine, Texas, December 1985, audiotape, HFC; DPS, *Texas Ranger,* 3; DPS, *Golden Anniversary Pictorial and History Book,* 52.

4. Martha Hill Spinks, interview by author, Kerrville, Texas, 2006.

5. Grady Hill, "Gully Takes New Aim at Fishing," *San Angelo Standard Times,* January 6, 1958, TRHF; Schreiner, *Pictorial History of the Texas Rangers,* 172–173.

6. M. H. Spinks, interview by author, Eldorado, Texas, 2004.

7. Smithers, *Chronicles of the Big Bend,* 83–90.

8. Company E at Ranger Camp on Alamito Creek, 1949, photograph, HFC.

9. "Texas Ranger Company 'E,'" *DPS Chaparral* 2, no 2 (March–April 1949): 48, HFC.

10. Ibid.

11. TSHA, s.v. "Big Bend National Park," http://www.tsha.utexas.edu/handbook/online/articles/view/BB/gkb2.html.

12. Welsh, *Landscape of Ghosts, River of Dreams,* http://www.nps.gov/archive/bibe/adhi/adhi4.htm.

13. Barry Caver, "Welcome from Texas Rangers Company 'E,'" http://www.texasranger.org/today/companyE.htm.

14. DPS, Roster of Texas Ranger Force, October 14, 1947, HFC; DPS, Roster of Texas Ranger Force, February 11, 1948, HFC.

15. DPS, *DPS News* 4, no. 4 (1948): 8, printed excerpt from *Texas Sheep and Goat Raisers' Magazine,* July 1948, TRHF.

16. Hill, interview by author, Alpine, Texas, December 1986, HFC.

17. Ibid.

18. "Houston White, Sheriff and Texas Ranger, Dies," *Hamilton Herald-News,* July 3, 1969, TRHF; account of Ranger Homer White's death, *Hamilton Herald-News,* unknown date, TRHF.

19. DPS, *Texas Ranger,* 3.

20. Hill, interview by Whittington, Alpine, Texas, April 28, 1976, ABB.

21. DPS, *Texas Ranger,* 1; DPS, *Golden Anniversary Pictorial and History Book,* 52.

22. TSHA, s.v. "Texas Rangers."

23. DPS, *50th Anniversary Celebration,* 10.

24. Utley, "Cattle Industry in the Big Bend," 419–441; Casey, *Alpine, Texas,* 15–16.

25. Casey, *Alpine, Texas,* 23.

26. Hill, interview by Elolf, Waco, Texas, May 19, 1979, TRHF.

27. TSHA, s.v. "Brewster County," "Pecos County," "Terrell County," "Jeff Davis County," and "Presidio County." The square mileage of each county was used to determine an approximation of the total area covered.

28. National Park Service, "The Original Settlers of Big Bend," http://www.nps.gov/bibe/historyculture/original_settlers.htm (accessed May 12, 2007).

29. "Law Officers Find Challenge in Vast Country," *Austin American Statesman,* June 5, 1986, TRHF.

30. Schreiner, *Pictorial History of the Texas Rangers,* 200–201; Clara Landers, "Texas Ranger Jim Nance," *El Paso Times,* January 29, 1967, TRHF.

31. Landers, "Texas Ranger Jim Nance."

32. Ibid.

33. M. H. Spinks, interview by author, Eldorado, Texas, 2004.

34. Hill, personal communication with author.

4 Rio Grande Rendezvous

1. Hill, Case Reports 1947–1957, HFC (a review of cases shows overall trends in frequency of specific types of crime).

2. Webb, *Texas Rangers,* 475.

3. Smithers, *Chronicles of the Big Bend,* 56–65.

4. University of Texas at Austin, College of Liberal Arts, "Wax, Men, and Money: Candelilla Wax Camps along the Rio Grande," http://www.texasbeyondhistory.net/waxcamps/index.html.

5. Casey, *Mirages, Mysteries, and Reality,* 181–184.

6. Ibid.

7. Hill, Criminal Case Report, August 20, 1952, HFC.

8. Ibid.

9. Louis Ortega, Voluntary Statement to DPS, Presidio County, Texas, July 25, 1952, HFC.

10. Hill, Criminal Case Report, August 20, 1952, HFC; Francisco Martinez, statement to Miguel Velarde Delgado, Chief of Department of Preliminary Investigation, Chihuahua, Chihuahua, Mexico, August 4, 1952, HFC.

11. Hill, Criminal Case Report, August 20, 1952, HFC.

12. Hill, personal communication with author.

13. Jim Heim, U.S. State Department special agent, Juárez, Chihuahua, Mexico, telephone conversations with author, June–July 2004; Joe Thompson, U.S. Customs special agent (ret.), Presidio, Texas, telephone conversation with author, October 10, 2004. Our discussions pertained to the process of extradition and Mexican law.

14. Jim Heim, telephone conversations with author, June–July 2004; Joe Thompson, telephone conversation with author, October 10, 2004; David Duncan, telephone conversation with author, June 2004.

15. Hill, Criminal Case Reports 1947–57, HFC.

5 Brush Country Ranger

1. Edwin Bowers, director of Field Operations, USDA Cattle Fever Tick Eradication Program, Laredo, Texas, telephone conversation with author, June 2004; Bruce Lawhorne, "Texas, U.S. Have Faced Foot-and-Mouth Disease Threat Before," AgNews, April 2001.

2. TRHF, "Texas Rangers Paperwork 1875," http://www.texasranger. org/history/rangerHistory.htm.

3. Hill, Criminal Case Report, January 20, 1952, HFC.

4. Casey, Alpine, Texas, 362.

5. Hill, interview by author, Alpine, Texas, December 1986, HFC.

6. Hill, Criminal Case Report, February 13, 1949, HFC.

7. Hill, Criminal Case Report, December 28, 1954, HFC.

8. Hill to Gully Cowsert, February 6, 1955, HFC.

9. John J. Givens, U.S. Customs, assistant supervising agent, El Paso, Texas, to Homer Garrison, October 6, 1955, HFC.

10. Homer Garrison to John J. Givens, October 10, 1955, HFC.

11. Hill to Gully Cowsert, April 2, 1948, HFC.

12. Christina Stopka, "Partial List of Texas Ranger Company and Unit Commanders," http://www.texasranger.org/ReCenter/commanders.htm.

13. Hill to Gully Cowsert, November 15, 1949, HFC.

14. Hill, interview by Avillar, Alpine, Texas, December 1985, HFC.

15. Hill, interview by author, Alpine, Texas, December 1986, HFC.

16. M. T. Gonzaullas to Gully Cowsert, May 18, 1949, HFC; M. T. Gonzaullas to Homer Garrison, June 8, 1949, HFC; Gully Cowsert to M. T. Gonzaullas, May 18, 1949, HFC; Homer Garrison to Hill, June 7, 1949, HFC. The preceding comprises all communication relative to Hill's back injury.

6 "They Rode for the Brand"

1. Hill, Criminal Case Report, August 31, 1950, HFC.

2. Ibid.

3. "Sheriff Nabs Convict," *Alpine Avalanche,* September 6, 1950, ABB.

4. Hill, Criminal Case Report, October 2, 1956, HFC.

5. M. H. Spinks, interview by author, Eldorado, Texas, 2004.

6. Voluntary Statement of Juan Rodriguez-Velasquez, Alpine, Texas, September 26, 1956, HFC.

7. Hill, Criminal Case Report, March 17, 1955, HFC.

8. Ibid.

9. Hill, Criminal Case Report, December 18, 1948, HFC.

10. TSHA, s.v. "Fort D. A. Russell," http://www.tsha.utexas.edu/handbook/online/articles/FF/qbf14.html.

11. Hill, Criminal Case Report, December 18, 1948, HFC.

12. Andrew A. Spinks, interview by author, New Braunfels, Texas, March 2006.

13. Hill, interview by author, Alpine, December 1986, HFC.

14. Crumpton, Travers to Hill, June 24, 1950, HFC; "Rangers Confiscate Slot Machines after Country Club Raid," *Fort Stockton Pioneer,* June 1950, HFC.

15. Hill to Cowsert, July 5, 1948, HFC.

16. "Texas Ranger Company 'E,'" *DPS Chaparral* 2, no. 2 (March–April 1949), HFC.

7 The Borderland

1. Hill, interview by author, December 1986, Alpine, Texas, HFC.

2. Casey, *Alpine, Texas,* 269.

3. M. H. Spinks, interview by author, Eldorado, Texas, 2004, HFC.

4. Caver, "Welcome from Texas Rangers Company 'E.'"

5. Hill, Criminal Case Report, August 19, 1948, HFC.

6. Stillwell, *I'll Gather My Geese.*

7. Hallie Crawford Stillwell, interview by Jim Cullen, Alpine, Texas, August 7, 1985, transcript, ABB.

8. Hill to Gully Cowsert, June 7, 1954, HFC.

9. Frank Hamer, Jr., interview by Randy Lish, San Marcos, Texas, October 26, 2001, referenced by Lish, http://members.aol.com/earpmorgan.

10. Hill to Cowsert, June 7, 1954, regarding Hill's explanation for the events of the Fulcher arrest, which was under investigation, HFC.

11. Peter J. Pitchess, sheriff, Los Angeles County, to R. A. Miles, chief of police, Austin, Texas, December 23, 1964, HFC.

12. Hill, Criminal Case Report, March 14, 1951, HFC.

13. Hill, Criminal Case Reports 1947–1957; review reveals overall trends in crime in the region.

14. Hill, Criminal Case Report, September 11, 1950, HFC.

15. Hill, Texas Rangers Weekly Activity Notebook, June 3–5, 1957, HFC.

16. Hill, Criminal Case Report, March 6, 1959, HFC.

17. M. H. King, interview by author, Eldorado, 2004, HFC.

8 "El Corrido de José Villalobos"

1. Judy Dodson, "O. W. 'Blackie' Morrow: Sheriff of Presidio County, 1946–1950," 1963.05, JHC; Cathy Vann, "Ottis Whitfield Morrow," 1963.05, JHC; telephone interview on Thanksgiving, November 25,

2004, with Richard Morrow; "Tribute Paid by Friends to the Memory of Ottis Morrow," *Big Bend Sentinel,* March 17, 1950, CAH.

2. Hill, Criminal Case Report, April 1, 1950, HFC.

3. "Youth Admits Shooting Officer Who Gave Life Transporting Prisoner," *Big Bend Sentinel,* March 17, 1950, CAH.

4. Vann, "Ottis Whitfield Morrow," JHC; Patty McKenzie, "Three Suspects in Mysterious Shooting Sought," *El Paso Times,* March 13, 1950, UTPB.

5. Hill, Criminal Case Report, April 1, 1950, HFC.

6. Ibid.

7. George Dolan, "2nd Charged in Murder of Morrow," *Fort Worth Star-Telegram,* March 19, 1950, CAH-TUA; "Youth Admits"; "Mexican Taken in Slaying of Texas Sheriff," *Odessa American,* March 16, 1950, UTPB.

8. Hill, Criminal Case Report, April 1, 1950, HFC.

9. "Presidio Sheriff Shot to Death," *El Paso Times,* March 13, 1950, CAH.

10. Hill, Criminal Case Report, April 1, 1950, HFC; "Presidio Sheriff Is Slain on Road: Fingerprint Expert Sent from Austin," *Fort Worth Star-Telegram,* March 13, 1950, CAH.

11. Hill, Criminal Case Report, April 1, 1950, HFC.

12. Ibid.

13. Ibid.

14. TSHA, s.v. "Fort Leaton," http://www.tsha.utexas.edu/handbook/online/articles/view/FF/uef10.html; TSHA, s.v. "Ochoa, Texas," http://www.tsha.utexas.edu/handbook/online/articles/view/OO/hto3.html.

15. Arturo Ochoa, telephone conversation with author, August 2004; "Juan Ochoa, Presidio County Native, Devotes Life to Law Enforcement," *El Paso Times,* unknown date, Ochoa family private collection.

16. Thompson, *History of Marfa and Presidio County,* 192, 375; "Juan Ochoa, Presidio County Native."

17. Wiletta McKenzie, "Border Sleuth Ochoa Takes Big Role in Trail-

ing Killer," *El Paso Times,* March 19, 1950, Ochoa family private collection.

18. Hill, Criminal Case Report, April 1, 1950, HFC.

19. "Youth Admits"; "Hunt Is Still on for Slayer of Texas Sheriff," *Odessa American,* March 14, 1950, UTPB; "Ranger Believes Man Sought Is Handcuffed," *El Paso Times,* March 14, 1950, UTPB.

20. "Presidio Sheriff Shot to Death"; "Posse Tracks Sheriff's Murderer," *El Paso Times,* March 14, 1950, UTPB.

21. "Posse Tracks Sheriff's Murderer."

22. Patty McKenzie, "Slayer of Sheriff Fled to Mexico on Day of Killing, Officers Learn," *El Paso Times,* March 15, 1950, UTPB; "Mexican Police Hunt for Slayer of Texas Sheriff," *Odessa American,* March 15, 1950, UTPB.

23. Hill, Criminal Case Report, April 1, 1950, HFC.

24. Ibid.

25. Prof. Saúl Armendáriz, interview by author, Ojinaga, Chihuahua, Mexico, June 19, 2004, hand-drawn map and notes in Spanish, translation by Delia Herrera and Charles Lacy, HFC.

26. Ibid.

27. Ojinaga Web site, "Peguis Canyon," http://ojinaga.com/Peguis/peguis.html.

28. "Youth Admits"; Mary K. Earney, "The Killing of Presidio County Sheriff Ottis 'Blackie' Morrow," *Further than Nearer, Mas lejos que cerca: Judges, Lawyers, and Cases of the 83rd State Judicial District of Texas, 1917–1983,* Ochoa family private collection.

29. "Youth Admits."

30. Hill, Criminal Case Report, April 1, 1950, HFC.

31. "Mexican Taken in Slaying of Sheriff."

32. George Dolan, "Border Town President Lacking Authority," *Fort Worth Star-Telegram,* March 17, 1950, CAH.

33. Wiletta McKenzie, "Border Sleuth Ochoa Takes Big Role in Trailing Killer," *El Paso Times,* March 20, 1950, UTPB.

34. Hill, Criminal Case Report, April 1, 1950, HFC; "Officers Face

Extradition Problem with Man Held in Sheriff's Death," *Odessa American,* March 17, 1950, UTPB.

35. Edmundo Nieto, interview by author, Presidio, Texas, June 19, 2004; Earney, "Killing of Ottis 'Blackie' Morrow."

36. Hill, Criminal Case Report, April 1, 1950, HFC; George Dolan, "Mexico to Move Killer: Examination Is Barred," *Fort Worth Star-Telegram,* March 17, 1950, CAH.

37. Patty McKenzie, "Captured Man Admits Killing," *El Paso Times,* March 17, 1950, UTPB.

38. "Extradition Work Begins in Hearing," *El Paso Times,* March 18, 1950, UTPB.

39. Dolan, "2nd Charged in Murder."

40. "Youth Admits."

41. Dolan, "Mexico to Move Killer."

42. "Injunction Will Block Removal," *El Paso Times,* March 19, 1950, UTPB.

43. George Dolan, "Texans Unable to Quiz Suspect," *Fort Worth Star-Telegram,* March 17, 1950, CAH.

44. Hill, interview by Avillar, Alpine, Texas, December 1985, HFC.

45. Patty McKenzie, "Prisoner Claims 'Self-Defense,'" *El Paso Times,* March 19, 1950, UTPB.

46. Hill, discussion with Ranger Sergeant Robert Favor, Alpine, Texas, December 1986, HFC.

47. Ibid.

48. Nieto, interview by author, Presidio, June 19, 2004; Armendáriz, interview by author, Ojinaga, Chihuahua, June 19, 2004, HFC; M. H. Spinks, interview by author, Eldorado, Texas, 2004.

49. Hill, discussion with Favor, Alpine, Texas, December 1986, HFC.

50. Ibid.

51. "Efforts Continue to Obtain Custody of Officer's Killer," *Big Bend Sentinel,* March 24, 1950, CAH.

52. Hill, discussion with Favor, Alpine, Texas, December 1986, HFC.

53. Armendáriz, interview by author, Ojinaga, Chihuahua, June 19,

2004, HFC; Hill, discussion with Favor, Alpine, Texas, December 1986, HFC.

54. Hill, discussion with Favor, Alpine, Texas, December 1986, HFC.

55. Armendáriz, interview by author, Ojinaga, Chihuahua, June 19, 2004, HFC.

56. Hill, interview by Whittington, Alpine, Texas, April 28, 1976, ABB.

57. Armendáriz, interview by author, Ojinaga, Chihuahua, June 19, 2004, hand-drawn map and notes in Spanish, trans. Herrera and Lacy, HFC.

58. Christina Stopka and Rebekkah Lohr, "In the Ranging Tradition: Texas Rangers in Worldwide Popular Culture," http://www.texasranger.org/ReCenter/popular.htm.

59. Ibid.

60. Radio Memories, "Tales of the Texas Rangers," http://www.radiomemories.com/radiomemories/talesofthetexasrangers.html; Bill O'Neal, "Tales of the Texas Rangers," *Texas Ranger Dispatch,* no. 5 (Fall 2001), http://www.texasranger.org/dispatch/5/ReelRangers.htm.

61. Malsch, *"Lone Wolf" Gonzaullas, Texas Ranger,* 189–198.

62. Hill, personal communication; photographs, HFC.

9 Doin' Time in Big D

1. DPS, *50th Anniversary Celebration,* 10–13. DPS, *Agency Strategic Plan, 2007–2011,* 24.

2. DPS, *50th Anniversary Celebration,* 10–13.

3. Ibid., 11.

4. Day, *Captain Clint Peoples, Texas Ranger;* Hill, Texas Rangers Weekly Activity Notebook, October–November 1957, with references to command decisions and orders from DPS Major Guy Smith; Puckett, *Cast a Long Shadow,* 102. The consolidation of all DPS commands under a regional major was in the original legislation passed as per the recommendation of the Texas Research League's study. By December

1957, it became evident that the system of a DPS regional commander over the Ranger captain would not work, and the new reorganization structure was altered to allow for Ranger captains to report directly to the Ranger chief (Homer Garrison) once again. Most references date the revision to September 1, the effective date of original reorganization.

5. DPS, *50th Anniversary Celebration,* 12.

6. TRHF, "Texas Ranger Robert A. 'Bob' Crowder: 1901–1972," http://www.texasranger.org/halloffame/Crowder_Bob.htm; Rigler and Rigler, *In the Line of Duty,* 165–166.

7. Hill, Texas Rangers Weekly Activity Notebook, April 1957, HFC.

8. "E. J. 'Jay' Banks," *Texas Lawman* 29, no. 1 (April 1969): 10, TRHF; Mills, *Legend in Bronze,* 181.

9. TRHF, "Texas Ranger Timeline: 1936," http://www.texasranger.org/history/Timespecial.htm; pictures of Dallas Company B Headquarters office, HFC.

10. Joe Davis, telephone conversation with author.

11. Hill, Texas Rangers Weekly Activity Notebook, April 1957, HFC.

12. Hill, interview by author, Alpine, December 1986, HFC.

13. "Gun Battle Forestalls Big Hold Up," *Dallas Morning News,* April 30, 1957, CAH; Puckett, *Cast a Long Shadow,* 111–112.

14. Hill, interview by author, Alpine, December 1986, HFC; Phil Record, "Practice Run Proved Undoing of Well-Laid Robbery Scheme," *Fort Worth Star-Telegram,* April 30, 1957, CAH.

15. Hill, interview by author, Alpine, Texas, December 1986, HFC.

16. Record, "Practice Run Proved Undoing."

17. Meed, *Texas Ranger Johnny Klevenhagen,* 173–183.

18. Ann Jones, "Hard to Keep Silence about the Plot," *Fort Worth Star-Telegram,* May 1, 1950, CAH; Record, "Practice Run Proved Undoing."

19. Hill, interview by author, Alpine, Texas, December 1986, HFC; Hill, Texas Rangers Weekly Activity Notebook, April 1957, HFC.

20. Hill, Texas Rangers Weekly Activity Notebook, April 1957, HFC; Bill Hitch, "Badman Gene Paul Norris, Friend, Mowed Down by Police,"

Fort Worth Star-Telegram, April 30, 1950, CAH; Puckett, *Cast a Long Shadow,* 163.

21. Record, "Practice Run Proved Undoing"; Redding, "Top Gun of the Texas Rangers," 72; Hitch, "Badman Gene Paul Norris."

22. Hill, interview by author, Alpine, Texas, December 1986, HFC.

23. TRHF, "Shining Stars: Three Centuries of Texas Rangers: Jim Ray," http://www.texasranger.org/Journal/PapersIssue2.htm/Articles/Shining_Stars_Ray.htm.

24. Hill, interview by author, Alpine, Texas, December 1986, HFC.

25. Ibid.

26. Ibid.; Hill, Texas Rangers Weekly Activity Notebook, April 1957, HFC.

27. River Oaks Area Historical Society, "Guest Speakers' Stories: Ann Arnold, July 12, 1999," http://www.riveroakshistory.com/new_page_2.htm.

10 The Lone Star Steel Strike

1. Gene Lantz and Elaine Lantz, "Some Texas Labor History up to 1995," http://victorian.fortunecity.com/palace/400/hist1995.htm; Hill, Texas Rangers Weekly Activity Notebook, September–October 1957, HFC.

2. Franklin, "Daingerfield Iron and Steel Project," 54–65; Morris County Scrapbook, Barker Texas History Center, University of Texas at Austin.

3. Rigler and Rigler, *In the Line of Duty,* 68–70.

4. Hill, Texas Rangers Weekly Activity Notebook, September–October 1957, HFC.

5. Rigler and Rigler, *In the Line of Duty,* 68–70; Hill, Case Reports, Interviews, and Investigation Notes, HFC; "2 Daingerfield Steel Plant Workers Severely Beaten in Brawl over Strike," *Dallas Times Herald,* October 30, 1957, HFC.

6. Mills, *Legend in Bronze,* 181.

7. Puckett, *Cast a Long Shadow,* 102–103.

8. Hill, Texas Rangers Weekly Activity Notebook, October 1957, HFC.

9. Ibid.; "Rangers, Patrolmen Sent to East Texas," *Dallas Morning News,* November 1, 1957, CAH.

10. "Rangers, Patrolmen Sent to East Texas."

11. Hill, Case Reports, Interviews, and Investigation Notes, HFC.

12. Arnold, "Legend in His Own Time."

13. Hill, Case Reports, Interviews, and Investigation Notes, HFC; "Rangers, Patrolmen Sent to East Texas."

14. "Blasts Belt 13 Towns: 'Definitely Sabotage,' Says Ranger," *El Paso Times,* October 28, 1957, HFC; Hill, Case Reports, Interviews, and Investigation Notes, HFC.

15. "Daingerfield Steel Plant Workers Severely Beaten."

16. Hill, Case Reports, Interviews, and Investigation Notes, HFC; "Rangers, Patrolmen Sent to East Texas."

17. Carl Estes, "Capt. Banks Takes Over," in Puckett, *Cast a Long Shadow,* 105.

18. Hill, Case Reports, Interviews, and Investigation Notes, HFC; Rigler and Rigler, *In the Line of Duty,* 69–70; Hill, Rangers Weekly Activity Notebook, October–November 1957, HFC; "Rangers Arrest Trio in Beatings," *Dallas Morning News,* November 1, 1957, CAH.

19. "Rangers, Patrolmen Sent to East Texas."

20. Puckett, *Cast a Long Shadow,* 103–104.

21. Rigler and Rigler, *In the Line of Duty,* 70–73.

22. Hill, Rangers Weekly Activity Notebook, October–November 1957, HFC; Arnold, "Legend in His Own Time."

23. Lewis Rigler to Hill, personal communication, audiotape, HFC.

24. TRHF, "Texas Ranger Timeline," http://www.texasranger.org/history/Timespecial.htm.

25. Hill, Rangers Weekly Activity Notebook, Correspondences, Case Reports, Investigation Notes, Company B Records, HFC.

26. Hill, Rangers Weekly Activity Notebook, December 1957, HFC; George Robey and Fred Pestage, Theft Investigation Report, Texas Mid-Continent Oil & Gas Association, undated, HFC.

27. Hill, Rangers Weekly Activity Notebook, Correspondences, Case Reports, Investigation Notes, Company B Records, HFC.

28. DPS, Job Evaluation Program, Instructional Manual, HFC; Hill, Texas DPS Performance Evaluation Report, Texas Ranger Company B, July 8, 1957, HFC.

29. Hill, Ranger Weekly Activity Notebook, September 1957, HFC.

30. Jim Wilson, "Charlie Miller: A Unique Ranger," *Shooting Times,* August 2002.

31. Hill, Ranger Weekly Activity Notebook, June 1957, HFC.

32. Ibid.

33. Major Guy Smith to Joe Fletcher, December 6, 1957, HFC.

34. Hill, Ranger Weekly Activity Notebook, June 1957, HFC.

35. Hill, interview by Elolf, Waco, Texas, May 19, 1979, TRHF.

36. M. H. Spinks, interview by author, Eldorado, Texas, 2004, HFC.

37. "Former Ranger Captain Jay Banks Makes Statement to Newspaper Concerning His Resignation," *Dallas Times Herald,* May 31, 1961, CAH; "Ranger Jay Banks Resigns," *Texas Lawman,* April 1960, TRHF.

38. Texas Instruments, "About Jack," http://www.ti.com/corp/docs/kilbyctr/jackstclair.shtml.

11 Times Are a-Changin'

1. Hill to individual Rangers of Company B, July 25, 1958, HFC.

2. DPS, *50th Anniversary Celebration,* 13–15.

3. Hill to Captain Frank Probst, Memorandum, Subject: State Inventory, April 3, 1959, HFC; Texas Rangers Commemorative Commission, *Texas Rangers Sesquicentennial Anniversary,* 102–105.

4. TRHF, "Historic Badges of the Texas Rangers," http://www.texasranger.org/history/HistoricBadges.htm; Schreiner, *Pictorial History of the Texas Rangers,* 220–223.

5. Glenn Elliott, "Now You Know: The Cinco Peso Badge," TRHF.

6. TRHF, "Historic Badges of the Texas Rangers"; Schreiner, *Pictorial History of the Texas Rangers,* 220–223.

7. DPS, *50th Anniversary Celebration,* 13–15.

8. Ibid.

9. Sheffield, "Joaquin Jackson."

10. Texas Rangers Commemorative Commission, *Texas Rangers Sesquicentennial Anniversary,* 112.

11. Ibid., 114; Hill, interview by Whittington, Alpine, Texas, April 28, 1976, ABB; TRHF, "James E. 'Jim' Riddles: 1910–1975," http://www.texasranger.org/halloffame/Riddles_James.htm; Hill, personal communication with author.

12. Hill, Criminal Case Reports 1959–69, HFC (a review of reports shows trends in casework during this time period).

13. Hill, Criminal Offense Report, May 4, 1966, HFC.

14. Hill, Criminal Offense Report, October 20, 1965, HFC.

15. Commander Rutillo Martinez, Chihuahua State Police, statements by suspects, Chihuahua, Chihuahua, Mexico, August 7, 1961, HFC.

16. Octavio Ramos Carrasco to Jim Nance, August 9, 1961, HFC.

17. Hill, Criminal Offense Report, July 27, 1965, HFC.

18. Hill, Criminal Case Reports 1959–1969, HFC.

19. Hill, Criminal Offense Report, November 3, 1964, HFC.

20. Hill, Criminal Case Report, March 19, 1963, HFC; J. P. Parker, Justice of the Peace, sworn statements of witnesses, Alpine, Texas, March 5, 1963.

21. James C. Henderson, voluntary statement, HFC; DPS, Transcript of Criminal Record: Paul Knapp, HFC.

22. Hill, Criminal Offense Report, September 3, 1963, HFC; Crawford C. Martin, Texas secretary of state, to Pennsylvania Governor William W. Scranton, March 19, 1963, HFC; Commonwealth of Pennsylvania, receipt for warrant fees, March 27, 1963, HFC.

12 A Harsh Land

1. Hill, Criminal Offense Report, July 31, 1965, HFC.

2. Hill to DPS laboratory, May 27, 1965; J. D. Chastain, DPS laboratory manager, to Ernest Barnett, Presidio County sheriff, June 17, 1965, HFC; Ibid.

3. "Woman in Chartreuse: Remote Village May Hold Key," *San Angelo Standard Times,* unknown date, HFC.

4. W. E. Lockhart, MD, to Hallie Stillwell, July 29, 1965; J. D. Chastain to Hill, August 9, 1965, containing results from DPS laboratory, HFC; "Identification Desired," *DPS Bulletin,* August 12, 1965, HFC.

5. Hill, Criminal Offense Report, May 5, 1960, HFC.

6. Poppa, *Drug Lord,* 129.

7. Hill to Frank Probst, December 23, 1959, HFC.

8. Lewis Cash to J. S. Nance and Hill, transcribed oral statement, Dryden, Texas, November 11, 1965, HFC.

9. Dalton Hogg to J. S. Nance, transcribed oral statement, Dryden, Texas, November 4, 1965, HFC.

10. "It Would Take a Thousand Men a Hundred Years. . . ," *San Angelo Standard Times,* November 19, 1965, HFC; "Rangers, SW Lawmen, Conduct Big Search," *El Paso Times,* November 19, 1965, HFC.

11. Isidro Blanco to J. S. Nance, transcribed oral statement, Billings Ranch, Texas, November 8, 1965, HFC.

12. Graczyk, "Texas' Longest Unsolved Mass Killing."

13. Hill, Investigation or Progress Report, September 17, 1968, HFC; Hill, Rangers Weekly Activity Notebook, September 1968, HFC.

14. Hill, interview by Whittington, Alpine, Texas, April 28, 1976, ABB.

15. M. H. Spinks, interview by author, Eldorado, Texas, 2004.

16. Ibid.

17. Hill, Criminal Case Report, February 14, 1959, HFC; Hill, interview by Avillar, Alpine, Texas, December 1985, HFC; Hill, interview by Alpine Elementary student, Alpine, Texas, unknown date, audiotape, HFC; "Alpine Guns Spit at Fleeing Auto," *El Paso Times,* February 14, 1959, HFC; Helen Burgess, "Trio Nabbed after Wild Alpine Chase," *El Paso Times,* February 14, 1959, HFC.

18. Orval Edmiston, Criminal Offense Report, January 10, 1969, HFC; Mike Cox, "Area Texas Rangers on Job at Schleicher County Strike Scene," *San Angelo Standard Times,* unknown date, HFC.

13 "Plumo o Oro"

1. Hill, Criminal Case/Offense Reports 1959–1969, HFC (a review of case files shows trends in crimes involving drugs and drug use); Luís Astorga, Discussion Paper No. 36, "Drug Trafficking in Mexico: A First General Assessment," United Nations Education, Scientific, and Cultural Organization, http://www.unesco.org/most/astorga.htm.

2. Smithers, *Chronicles of the Big Bend,* 56–62 (demonstrates early smuggling organization); Ragsdale, *Big Bend Country,* 86; Poppa, *Drug Lord,* 6v7.

3. Poppa, *Drug Lord,* 5–11, 19–33.

4. Joe Thompson, U.S. Customs special agent (ret.), telephone interview by author, October 10, 2004.

5. Thomas A. Constantine, DEA administrator, to Senate Foreign Relations Committee, Subcommittee on the Western Hemisphere, Peace Corps, Narcotics, and Terrorism, February 26, 1998, http://www.globalsecurity.org/security/library/congress/1998_h/ct980226.htm.

6. National Park Service, "From Good Neighbors to Armed Camps."

7. Ibid.

8. Kate Doyle, "Operation Intercept: The Perils of Unilateralism," National Security Archive, http://www.gwu.edu/~nsarchiv/NSAEBB/NSAEBB86

9. Hill, Criminal Case Report, January 23, 1963, HFC.

10. Frank Probst to Hill, July 17, 1961, HFC.

11. Hill, Criminal Case Report, February 28, 1968, HFC.

12. Thomas A. Constantine to Senate Foreign Relations Committee, February 26, 1998, http://www.globalsecurity.org/security/library/congress/1998_h/ct980226.htm.

13. Hill, interview by Whittington, Alpine, Texas, April 28, 1976, ABB; Hill, interview by Elolf, Waco, Texas, May 19, 1979, TRHF.

14. Hill, interview by Elolf, Waco, Texas, May 19, 1979, TRHF.

15. Parsons, review of *Ed Gooding: Soldier, Texas Ranger;* Hill, interview by Whittington, Alpine, Texas, April 28, 1976, ABB; Hill, interview by Elolf, Waco, Texas, May 19, 1979, TRHF.

16. In 1972, the U.S. Supreme Court ruled capital punishment un-
constitutional in the case of *Furman v. Georgia.* The court found that
capital punishment sentencing was applied disproportionately to certain classes of defendants, notably those who were black or poor. This
ruling imposed a de facto death penalty moratorium. In response, many
state legislatures revised procedures used in imposing the death penalty
to conform to the *Furman* decision. In *Gregg v. Georgia* (1976) and other
cases the same year, the Court articulated the two principal features that
capital sentencing procedures must employ in order to comport with the
Eighth Amendment. First, an appellate review oversees the application
of objective criteria in the direction and limitation of sentencing discretion. Second, the sentencing process must take into account the character and record of individual defendants.

17. Bedau, *Death Penalty in America,* 16; Colonel Wilson Spier to
Sheriff's Association of Texas, Beaumont, Texas, July 24, 1972, transcribed speech, Texas State Archives.

18. Colonel Wilson Spier, to Sheriff's Association of Texas, Beaumont, Texas, July 24, 1972, transcribed speech, Texas State Archives.

14 The Last Roundup

1. Hill, Criminal Case Report, February 25, 1970, HFC.

2. U.S. Department of Justice, DEA, "The History of the DEA from
1973–1998," http://www.usdoj.gov/dea/pubs/history/index.html.

3. Hill, Criminal Case Reports 1970–74, HFC.

4. Hill to Elmer Terrell, Chief DPS Narcotics Division, April 22,
1971, HFC.

5. Hill, Criminal Case Report, April 16, 1971, HFC; Hill to Jim Riddles, September 18, 1970, HFC.

6. Ibid.

7. Welsh, *Landscape of Ghosts, River of Dreams;* National Park Service, "From Good Neighbors to Armed Camps."

8. Hill, Criminal Offense Report, November 15, 1973, HFC.

9. Hill, Criminal Case Report, April 25, 1971, HFC.

10. National Law Enforcement Officers Memorial Fund, "Police

Facts," http://www.nleomf.com/TheMemorial/Facts/history.htm.

11. "Gunshots Fatal to Presidio County Sheriff," *Big Bend Sentinel,* unknown date, HFC; Clara Landers, "Man Kills Sheriff in Presidio County," *El Paso Times,* April 28, 1973, HFC. Hill, Criminal Offense Report, May 5, 1973, HFC; Daniel W. Luna, Criminal Offense Report, April 27, 1973, HFC.

12. Hill, Criminal Offense Report, May 5, 1973, HFC.

13. Hill, interview by Whittington, Alpine, April 28, 1976, ABB; Hill, interview by author, Alpine, December 1986, HFC.

14. M. H. Spinks, interview by author, Eldorado, Texas, 2004.

15. Hill, Criminal Offense Report, May 5, 1973, HFC.

16. Ibid.

17. George Duckworth, tape recording, evidence, HFC.

18. George Duckworth, telephone conversation with Mr. Hunt, unknown date, transcript, HFC.

19. Officer Cox, Arizona Highway Patrol, telephone interview by Charles Martin, District Attorney's Office, Texas 83rd Judicial District, May 17, 1973, transcript, HFC.

20. Hill, interview by author, Alpine, Texas, December 1986, HFC; "E. D. Hamilton, Presidio County Sheriff, January 1973 to April 1973," Presidio County Sheriff's Collection, Marfa Public Library, Marfa, Texas.

21. Hill, Criminal Case Report, October 7, 1973, HFC.

22. Hill, interview by Alpine Elementary student, Alpine, Texas, unknown date, HFC.

23. Lester Housinger to Jim Riddles, April 2, 1973, Texas State Archives; Hill to Jim Riddles, December 9, 1970, HFC.

24. Frank G. Hamilton, veterinarian in charge, to Colonel Wilson Spier, July 20, 1971.

25. Rigler to Hill, personal communication, Gainesville, Texas, June 1974, HFC.

15 "A Beautiful Challenge"

1. Pete Crawford to M. T. Gonzaullas, October 31, 1939, HFC; Hill, discussion with Sgt. Robert Favor, Alpine, Texas, December 1986,

audiotape, HFC; TRHF, "Memorials: Clayton McKinney, 1940–2004,"
http://www.texasranger.org/memorials/McKinney_Clayton.htm; David
Duncan, interview by author, Presidio County Sheriff's Office, Marfa,
Texas, June 6, 2004.

2. Draper, "Twilight of the Texas Rangers," 76.

3. Mike Cox, with updates by the Texas Ranger Hall of Fame and
Museum Staff, "A Brief History of the Texas Rangers," pt. 2,
http://www.texasranger.org/history/SilverStars2.htm (accessed May 13,
2007).

4. Ibid.

5. Hill, Rangers Weekly Activity Notebook, June–July, 1973, HFC.

6. Hill, Retirement Party Speakers, Alpine, Texas, May 1973, audiotape, HFC.

7. Ibid.

8. Ibid.

9. Hill to Leo Gossett, assistant DPS director, October 27, 1983, HFC.

10. Hill, discussion with Favor, Alpine, Texas, December 1986, HFC.

11. M. H. Spinks, interview by author, Eldorado, Texas, 2004.

12. Ibid.

13. Ibid.

14. Hill Obituary, *Alpine Avalanche,* May 7, 1987, HFC.

15. M. H. Spinks, interview by author, Eldorado, Texas, 2004; personal knowledge of author.

16. Hill, interview by Whittington, Alpine, Texas, April 28, 1976,
ABB.

17. Davis, *Texas Rangers,* 129.

Bibliography

This work relies heavily on the holdings of the Hill Family Collection comprising Texas Ranger Arthur Hill's records during his tenure with the DPS (1941–1974). References to specific documents or audiotapes within the collection are cited in the notes. A copy of the Hill Family Collection is deposited at the Texas Ranger Hall of Fame Archives in Waco, Texas. The original documents are available at the Archives of the Big Bend, Sul Ross State University, Alpine, Texas. Interviews on audiotape are available only at the Archives of the Big Bend.

Interviews, discussions, and oral histories make up an integral portion of the primary sources for this work. Among those referenced (in citations and as background information) are personal accounts of Arthur Hill, Ruby Kerby Hill, Clint Peoples, Leona Banister Bruce, Hallie Stillwell, E. A. "Dogie" Wright, and Frank Hamer, Jr.

The archival collections of the Texas State Archives, Southwest Collection (Texas Tech University), Archives of the Big Bend (Sul Ross State University), The Center for American History (University of Texas), and the vertical files of the Texas Ranger Hall of Fame provided invaluable resources. Among the newspapers consulted, the most frequently referenced are the *Big Bend Sentinel* (Marfa, Texas), *Alpine Avalanche, Fort Worth Star-Telegram, El Paso Times, Dallas Morning News, Odessa American, San Angelo Standard Times,* and *Austin American Statesman.* The bibliography includes some works that are not cited in the notes but that provided valuable background information and deeper understanding of the people, places, and events discussed.

Online resources that proved helpful include the Web sites of the Texas State Historical Association (The Handbook of Texas Online),

Texas State Archives, Texas Almanac, Texas Ranger Hall of Fame, Texas State Library and Archives Commission, and the U.S. Department of the Interior, National Park Service.

Albers, E. G., Jr. *The Life and Reflections of a Texas Ranger.* 2nd ed. Waco: Texian Press, 1998.

Arnold, Ann. *Gangsters and Gamblers: Fort Worth's Jacksboro Highway in the 1940s and 1950s.* Austin: Eakin Press, 1998.

Atkinson, Bertha. "The History of Bell County, Texas." Master's thesis, University of Texas, 1929.

Baylor County Historical Society. *Salt Pork to Sirloin: The History of Baylor County, Texas, from 1879 to 1930.* Vol. 1. Quanah, Tex.: Nortex, 1972.

Bedau, Hugo Adam. *The Death Penalty in America.* New York: Oxford University Press, 1982.

Bell County Historical Commission. *The Story of Bell County, Texas.* 2 vols. Austin: Eakin Press, 1988.

Benner, Judith Ann. *Sul Ross: Soldier, Statesman, Educator.* College Station: Texas A&M University Press, 1983.

Bluthardt, Valerie. "Urban West Texas: Alpine," *Fort Concho Report* 18 (Winter 1986–87): 96–99.

Casey, Clifford. *Alpine, Texas: Then and Now.* Seagraves, Tex.: Pioneer Book Publishers, 1981.

———. *Mirages, Mysteries, and Reality: Brewster County, Texas: The Big Bend of the Rio Grande.* Seagraves, Tex.: Pioneer Book Publishers, 1972.

———. *The Trans-Pecos in Texas History.* West Texas Historical and Scientific Society Publication 5, 1933.

Coleman County Historical Commission. *History of Coleman County and Its People.* 2 vols. San Angelo, Tex.: Anchor, 1985.

Cox, Mike. "From Horses to Helicopters." *Texas Almanac,* http://www.texasalmanac.com/history/highlights/rangers.

———. *Silver Stars and Six Guns: The Texas Rangers.* Austin: Department of Public Safety, 1987.

———. *Texas Ranger Tales: Stories That Need Telling.* Plano: Republic of Texas Press, 1997.

———. *Texas Ranger Tales II.* Plano: Republic of Texas Press, 1999.

Dallas Morning News. *Texas Almanac 2004–2005.* Dallas: Dallas Morning News, 2004.

Davis, John L. *The Texas Rangers: Images and Incidents.* San Antonio: The University of Texas Institute of Texan Cultures, 1991.

Day, James. *Captain Clint Peoples, Texas Ranger: Fifty Years a Lawman.* Waco: Texian Press, 1980.

Department of Public Safety. *Department of Public Safety Golden Anniversary Pictorial and History Book: 1935–1985.* Marceline, Mo.: Walsworth Publishing Company, 1985.

———. *Fifty Years for Texas: 50th Anniversary Celebration of the Department of Public Safety.* Austin: Texas Department of Public Safety, 1985.

———. *Texas Department of Public Safety: Agency Strategic Plan (Including Polygraph Examiners Board), Fiscal Years 2007–2011.* July 7, 2006. http://www.txdps.state.tx.us/oai/2007-2011/agstratplan 0711a.pdf.

———. *The Texas Ranger.* Austin: Texas Department of Public Safety, 1961.

Draper, Robert. "Twilight of the Texas Rangers." *Texas Monthly* 22, no. 2 (February 1994).

Franklin, John. "The Daingerfield Iron and Steel Project." *Texas Geographic Magazine,* Fall 1948.

Gillett, James B. *Six Years with the Texas Rangers, 1875 to 1881.* Lincoln: University of Nebraska Press, 1987.

Gomez, Arthur R. *A Most Singular Country: A History of Occupation in the Big Bend*. Santa Fe, N.M.: National Park Service, U.S. Department of the Interior; [Provo, Utah]: Brigham Young University, Charles Redd Center for Western Studies; Salt Lake City, Utah: Distributed by Signature Books, 1990.

Gooding, Ed, and Robert Nieman. *Ed Gooding: Soldier, Texas Ranger*. Waco: Ranger Publishing, 2001.

Graczyk, Michael. "Family's Slaying Remains Texas' Longest Unsolved Mass Killing." CBC News: World, 12:52:22 EST Mar 5, 2006. http://www.cbc.ca/cp/world/060305/w030516.html.

Gregg, John E. "The History of Presidio County." Master's thesis, University of Texas, 1933.

Hardin, Stephen. *The Texas Rangers*. London: Osprey Publishing Ltd., 1991.

Harris, Charles H., III, and Louis R. Sadler. *The Texas Rangers and the Mexican Revolution: The Bloodiest Decade, 1910–1920*. Albuquerque: University of New Mexico Press, 2004.

Hickerson, Nancy P. *The Jumanos: Hunters and Traders of the South Plains*. Austin: University of Texas Press, 1994.

Jackson, Joaquin H., and David Marion Wilkinson. *One Ranger: A Memoir*. Austin: University of Texas Press, 2005.

Jenkins, Frost. *I'm Frank Hamer*. Austin: Pemberton Press, 1980.

Jennings, N. A. *A Texas Ranger*. Norman: University of Oklahoma Press, 1997.

Kilgore, D. E. *A Ranger Legacy: 150 Years of Service to Texas*. Austin: Medrona Press, 1973.

Knowles, Thomas W. *They Rode for the Lone Star: The Saga of the Texas Rangers*. Dallas: Taylor Publishing Company, 1999.

Madison, Virginia, and Hallie Stillwell. *How Come It's Called That? Place Names in the Big Bend Country*. Marathon: Iron Mountain Press, 1997.

Malsch, Brownson. *"Lone Wolf" Gonzaullas: Texas Ranger.* Norman: University of Oklahoma Press, 1998.

Martinez, Ramiro. *They Call Me Ranger Ray.* New Braunfels, Tex.: Rio Bravo Publishing, 2005.

Maxwell, Ross A. *Big Bend Country: A History of Big Bend National Park.* Big Bend National Park, Tex.: Big Bend Natural History Association, 1985.

Meed, Douglas V. *Texas Ranger Johnny Klevenhagen.* Plano: Republic of Texas Press, 2000.

Mills, Susie. *Legend in Bronze: The Biography of Jay Banks.* Dallas: Ussery, 1982.

National Park Service. "Big Bend Administrative History: From Good Neighbors to Armed Camps: Mexico, the United States, and Big Bend National Park, 1944–1980." http://www.nps.gov/bibe/adhi/adhi17.htm.

———. "Carlsbad Caverns." http://www.nps.gov/cave/history.htm.

Parsons, Chuck. Review of *Ed Gooding: Soldier, Texas Ranger,* by Ed Gooding and Robert Nieman. *Texas Ranger Dispatch,* no. 7 (Summer 2002). http://www.texasranger.org/dispatch/7/Gooding.htm.

Paul, Lee. *Jim Peters: Texas Ranger.* Bedford, Ind.: Jona Books, 1997.

Poppa, Terrence E. *Drug Lord: The Life and Death of a Mexican Kingpin.* 2nd ed. Seattle, Wash.: Demand Publications, 1998.

Proctor, Ben. *Just One Riot: Episodes of Texas Rangers in the 20th Century.* Austin: Eakin Press, 1991.

———. "The Texas Rangers: An Overview." In *The Texas Heritage,* edited by Ben Procter and Archie P. McDonald. St. Louis: Forum, 1980.

Puckett, Linda Jay. *Cast a Long Shadow: Biographical Sketch and Career Casebook of Legendary Texas Ranger Captain E. J. (Jay) Banks.* Dallas: Ussery, 1984.

Ragsdale, Kenneth B. *Big Bend Country: Land of the Unexpected.* College Station: Texas A&M University Press, 1998.

Redding, Stan. "Top Gun of the Texas Rangers." *True Detective* (February 1963): 15–17.

Rigler, Lewis C., and Judyth Wagner Rigler. *In the Line of Duty: Reflections of a Texas Ranger Private.* Houston: Larksdale, 1984.

Schreiner, Charles, Audrey Schreiner, Robert Berryman, and Hal F. Matheny. *A Pictorial History of the Texas Rangers: That Special Breed of Man.* Mountain Home, Tex.: Y-O Press, 1969.

Shannon, Elaine. *Desperados, Latin Drug Lords, U.S.A. Lawmen, and the War America Can't Win.* New York: Viking, 1998.

Sheffield, Dick. "Joaquin Jackson." *Texas Monthly* 30, no. 7 (July 2002).

Smithers, W. D. *Chronicles of the Big Bend: A Photographic Memoir of Life on the Border.* Austin: Texas State Historical Association, 1999.

Sterling, William Warren. *Trails and Trials of a Texas Ranger.* Norman: University of Oklahoma Press, 1968.

Stillwell, Hallie Crawford. *I'll Gather My Geese.* College Station: Texas A&M University Press, 1991.

Stroud, David. "Guns of the Texas Rangers." *Texas Ranger Dispatch Magazine* 15 (Winter 2004).

Texas State Historical Association. *The New Handbook of Texas.* 6 vols. Austin: Texas State Historical Association, 1995.

Texas Rangers Commemorative Commission. *Texas Rangers Sesquicentennial Anniversary, 1823–1973.* Fort Worth: Heritage Publications, 1973.

"Texas Ranger Company 'E.'" *DPS Chaparral* 2, no. 2 (March–April 1949): 21.

Thompson, Cecilia. *History of Marfa and Presidio County, 1535–1946.* 2 vols. Austin: Nortex, 1985.

Tyler, George. *History of Bell County.* San Antonio: Naylor, 1936.

Tyler, Ron C. *The Big Bend: A History of the Last Texas Frontier.* College Station: Texas A&M University Press, 2003.

Utley, Robert M. *Lone Star Justice: The First Century of the Texas Rangers*. New York: Oxford University Press, 2002.

———. "The Range Cattle Industry in the Big Bend of Texas." *Southwestern Historical Quarterly* 69 (April 1966): 419–431.

———. "Tales of the Texas Rangers." *American Heritage* 53, no. 3 (June–July 2002): 40–47.

———. "The Texas Ranger Tradition Established." *Montana: The Magazine of Western History* 52 (Spring 2002): 2–11.

Webb, Walter Prescott. *The Texas Rangers: A Century of Frontier Defense*. Austin: University of Texas Press, 1985.

Wedin, AnneJo P. *The Magnificent Marathon Basin: A History of Marathon, Texas, Its People and Events*. Austin: Nortex, 1989.

Welsh, Michael. *Landscape of Ghosts, River of Dreams: A History of Big Bend National Park*. Washington, D.C.: National Park Service, U.S. Department of the Interior, 2002. http://www.nps.gov/archive/bibe/adhi/adhi4.htm.

West, Raymond. *Bennie C. Krueger: Texas Ranger . . . Texas Gentleman*. Jacksonville, Tex.: Kiely Printing Company, 1984.

Wilkins, Frederick. *The Law Comes to Texas: The Texas Rangers, 1870–1901*. Austin: State House Press, 1999.

———. *The Legend Begins: The Texas Rangers, 1823–1845*. Austin: State House Press, 1996.

Wood, John M., and Betty W. Cox. *Texas Ranger in the Oil Patch*. San Antonio: Woodburner Press, 1994.

Index

Page numbers in italics refer to photographs